Workshop on Sentiment Analysis Where AI Meets Psychology 2011

(SAAIP 2011)

AA005585

Held at the 5th International Joint Conference on Natural Language Processing 2011 (IJCNLP 2011)

Chiang Mai, Thailand
13 November 2011

ISBN: 978-1-62276-458-7

Printed from e-media with permission by:

Curran Associates, Inc.
57 Morehouse Lane
Red Hook, NY 12571

Some format issues inherent in the e-media version may also appear in this print version.

Printed by Curran Associates, Inc. (2012)

Association for Computational Linguistics
209 N. Eighth Street
Stroudsburg, Pennsylvania 18360

Phone: 1-570-476-8006
Fax: 1-570-476-0860

acl@aclweb.org

Additional copies of this publication are available from:

Curran Associates, Inc.
57 Morehouse Lane
Red Hook, NY 12571 USA
Phone: 845-758-0400
Fax: 845-758-2634
Email: curran@proceedings.com
Web: www.proceedings.com

Table of Contents

Preface

In recent times, research activities in the areas of Opinion, Sentiment and/or Emotion in natural language texts and other media are gaining ground under the umbrella of affect computing. Huge amount of text data are available in the Social Web in the form of news, reviews, blogs, chats and even twitter. Sentiment analysis from natural language text is a multifaceted and multidisciplinary problem. The existing reported solutions or available systems are still far from perfect or fail to meet the satisfaction level of the end users. There are many conceptual rules that govern sentiment and there are even more clues (possibly unlimited) that can map these concepts from realization to verbalization of a human being. Human psychology that relates to social, cultural, behavioral and environmental aspects of civilization may provide the unrevealed clues and govern the sentiment realization. In the present scenario we need constant research endeavors to reveal and incorporate the human psychological knowledge into machines in the best possible ways. The important issues that need attention include how various psychological phenomena can be explained in computational terms and the various artificial intelligence (AI) concepts and computer modeling methodologies that are most useful from the psychologist's point of view.

In addition to Question Answering or Information Retrieval systems, Topic-sentiment analysis can be applied as a new research method for mass opinion estimation (e.g., reliability, validity, sample bias), psychiatric treatment, corporate reputation measurement, political orientation categorization, stock market prediction, customer preference study, public opinion study and so on. Regular research papers continue to be published in reputed conferences like ACL, EMNLP or COLING. There have been an increasing number of efforts in shared tasks such as SemEval 2007 Task#14: Affective Text, TAC 2008 Opinion Summarization task, TREC-BLOG tracks since 2006 and relevant NTCIR tracks since 6th NTCIR that aim to focus on different issues of opinion and emotion analysis. Several communities from sentiment analysis have engaged themselves to conduct relevant conferences, e.g., Affective Computing and Intelligent Interfaces (ACII) in 2009 and 2011 and workshops such as "Sentiment and Subjectivity in Text" in COLING-ACL 2006, "Sentiment Analysis – Emotion, Metaphor, Ontology and Terminology (EMOT)" in LREC 2008, Opinion Mining and Sentiment Analysis (WOMSA) 2009, "Topic-Sentiment Analysis for Mass Opinion Measurement (TSA)" in CIKM 2009, "Computational Approaches to Analysis and Generation of Emotion in Text" in NAACL 2010, Workshop on Computational Approaches to Subjectivity and Sentiment Analysis (WASSA) in ECAI 2010 and in ACL 2011, FLAIRS 2011 special track on "Affect Computing" and so on.

This workshop aims to bring together the researchers in multiple disciplines such as computer science, psychology, cognitive science, social science and many more who are interested in developing next generation machines that can recognize and respond to the sentimental states of the human users and serve the society.

The workshop starts with an invited keynote talk titled "What are Subjectivity, Sentiment, and Affect?" by Prof. Eduard Hovy. The talk outlines a model of sentiment/opinion and affect, and show that they appear in text in a fairly structured way, with various components. The proper understanding of a text in terms of sentiments, opinions, and affects requires the reader as well as the system to build some kind of person profile of the author. The talk concludes by opening the door to a whole new line of research with many fascinating and practical aspects.

Bermingham and Smeaton argue that a diverse range of political insight and commentary in Twitter can model political sentiment effectively enough to capture the voting intentions of a nation during an election campaign. The Plurk micro-blogging platform is used by Tang and Chen to model emotion generation from writer and reader perspectives based on the combination of linguistic, social, behavioral and textual features in Support Vector Machine (SVM)-based classifiers. Munezero et al. introduce the antisocial behavior detection (ASBD) model for portraying the emotions pertaining to antisocial behavior.

Amgoud et al. concentrate on pairing opinion analysis with argument extraction in order to identify why opinions about a certain feature are positive or negative and also analyze the preferences of customers if the customer recommendations are given. Cambria et. al. have proposed the Sentic Corner, an intelligent user interface that dynamically collects audio, video, images and text related to the user's current feelings and activities as an interconnected knowledge base.

From the perspectives of multilingualism, Banea et al. explore the ability of senses aligned across languages to carry coherent subjectivity information. They have worked with two methods that are able to incorporate subjectivity information originating from different languages, namely co-training and multilingual vector spaces. Inui and Yamamoto describe a method for multilingual review classification by employing machine translation techniques to remove language gaps in the dataset. The sentiment-oriented sentence filtering module reduces translation errors that occur as a side-effect.

Das and Bandyopadhyay reports different interesting statistics of emotions based on individual as well as combinational roles of the general variables (intensity, timing and longevity) and physiological variables (psycho-physiological arousals) from the situational statements of the ISEAR (International Survey on Emotion Antecedents and Reactions) dataset. Chandra et al. seek to enhance the chat experience using an intelligent adaptive user interface exploiting semantics and leveraging Sentic Computing. Roshchina et al. have proposed a personality-based recommender system, TWIN ("Tell me What I Need"), that focuses on User Profile construction in the travelling domain. Ahmad et al. show that a diachronic study of the coverage of the named-entity dictionary crafted from electoral lists with key financial and economic terms added, supplemented by an affect dictionary from the General Inquirer system, helps to distinguish the winner from the losers in an election.

Lee and Renganathan present the use of Maximum Entropy technique for Chinese sentiment analysis to estimate the polarity of given comments on electronic products. Fang and Chen incorporate sentiment lexicons as prior knowledge with SVM technique and describe a method to automatically generate domain specific sentiment lexicons to improve the accuracy of sentiment analysis. The basic NLP techniques like NGram, POS-Tagged NGram along with several machine learning algorithms are used by Bakliwal et al. to identify the polarity of the movie and product reviews.

We thank Prof. Eduard Hovy for the keynote talk, all the members of the Program Committee for their excellent and insightful reviews, the authors who submitted contributions for the workshop and the participants for making the workshop a success. We also express our thanks to the IJCNLP 2011 Organizing Committee and Local Organizing Committee for their support and cooperation in organizing the workshop.

Organizing Committee
The Workshop on Sentiment Analysis where AI meets Psychology (SAAIP)
IJCNLP 2011
November 13, 2011.

Organizing Committee:

Sivaji Bandyopadhyay, Jadavpur University, Kolkata (India) (Workshop Chair)
Manabu Okumurra, Tokyo Institute of Technology, Tokyo (Japan) (Workshop Chair)
Amitava Das, Jadavpur University, Kolkata (India)
Dipankar Das, Jadavpur University, Kolkata (India)
Hiroya Takamura, Tokyo Institute of Technology (Japan)
Kritsada Sriphaew, Thammasat University (Thailand)

Program Committee:

Khurshid Ahmad, Trinity College Dublin (Ireland)
Alexandra Balahur, DLSI, University of Alicante, (Spain)
Michael Gamon, Microsoft Research (USA)
Choochart Haruechaiyasak, National Electronics and Computer Technology Center (Thailand)
Diana Inkpen, University of Ottawa (Canada)
Noriko Kando, National Institute of Informatics (Japan)
Alisa Kongthon, National Electronics and Computer Technology Center(Thailand)
Rada Mihalcea, University of North Texas (USA)
Alena Neviarouskaya, University of Tokyo (Japan)
Vincent Ng, University of Texas at Dallas, (USA)
Fuji Ren, University of Tokushima (Japan)
Paolo Rosso, Universidad Politécnica de Valencia (Spain)
Patrick Saint-Dizier, IRIT-CNRS (France)
Yohei Seki, Tsukuba University (Japan)
Swapna Somasundaran, Siemens Corporate Research (SCR), (USA)
Veselin Stoyanov, Cornell University (USA)
Carlo Strapparava, Fondazione Bruno Kessler (FBK), (Italy)
Stan Szpakowicz, University of Ottawa (Canada)
Theresa Wilson, University of Edinburgh, (UK)
Michael Zock, LIF-CNRS, Marseille (France)

Keynote Speaker:

Prof. Eduard Hovy, Information Sciences Institute of the University of Southern California

Conference Program

Sunday, November 13, 2011

8:45–9:00 Opening Remarks

9:00–10:00 *Keynote: What are Subjectivity, Sentiment, and Affect?*
Eduard Hovy

Session 1:

10:30–10:50 *On Using Twitter to Monitor Political Sentiment and Predict Election Results*
Adam Bermingham and Alan Smeaton

10:50–11:10 *Taking Refuge in Your Personal Sentic Corner*
Erik Cambria, Amir Hussain and Chris Eckl

11:10–11:30 *Towards automatic detection of antisocial behavior from texts*
Myriam Munezero, Tuomo Kakkonen and Calkin Montero

11:30–11:45 *User Profile Construction in the TWIN Personality-based Recommender System*
Alexandra Roshchina, John Cardiff and Paolo Rosso

11:45–12:00 *Enriching Social Communication through Semantics and Sentics*
Praphul Chandra, Erik Cambria and Alvin Pradeep

Lunch: 12:00–14:00

Session 2:

14:00–14:20 *Emotion Modeling from Writer/Reader Perspectives Using a Microblog Dataset*
Yi-jie Tang and Hsin-Hsi Chen

14:20–14:35 *Introducing Argumention in Opinion Analysis: Language and Reasoning Challenges*
Leila Amgoud, Florence Bannay, Charlotte Costedoat, Patrick Saint-Dizier and Camille Albert

14:35–14:55 *Sense-level Subjectivity in a Multilingual Setting*
Carmen Banea, Rada Mihalcea and Janyce Wiebe

14:55–15:15 *Applying Sentiment-oriented Sentence Filtering to Multilingual Review Classification*
Takashi Inui and Mikio Yamamoto

15:15–15:30 *Chinese Sentiment Analysis Using Maximum Entropy*
Huey Yee Lee and Hemnaath Renganathan

Coffee/Tea Break: 15:30–16:00

Sunday, November 13, 2011 (continued)

Session 3:

16:00–16:20	*Analyzing Emotional Statements – Roles of General and Physiological Variables* Dipankar Das and Sivaji Bandyopadhyay
16:20–16:35	*Incorporating Lexicon Knowledge into SVM Learning to Improve Sentiment Classification* Ji Fang and Bi Chen
16:35–16:55	*What is new? News media, General Elections, Sentiment, and Named Entities* Khurshid Ahmad, Nicholas Daly and Vanessa Liston
16:55–17:15	*Towards Enhanced Opinion Classification using NLP Techniques.* Akshat Bakliwal, Piyush Arora, Ankit Patil and Vasudeva Varma

We wish to thank our sponsors

Gold Sponsors

www.google.com

www.baidu.com

The Office of Naval Research (ONR)

The Asian Office of Aerospace Research and Development (AOARD)

Department of Systems Engineering and Engineering Managment, The Chinese University of Hong Kong

Silver Sponsors

Microsoft Corporation

Bronze Sponsors

Chinese and Oriental Languages Information Processing Society (COLIPS)

Supporter

Thailand Convention and Exhibition Bureau (TCEB)

We wish to thank our sponsors

Organizers

Asian Federation of Natural Language Processing (AFNLP)

National Electronics and Computer Technology Center (NECTEC), Thailand

Sirindhorn International Institute of Technology (SIIT), Thailand

Rajamangala University of Technology Lanna (RMUTL), Thailand

Maejo University, Thailand

Chiang Mai University (CMU), Thailand

What are Subjectivity, Sentiment, and Affect?

Eduard Hovy
USC Information Sciences Institute (ISI)
Marina del Rey, CA, USA
http://www.isi.edu/~hovy
hovy@isi.edu

Abstract

Pragmatics —the aspects of text that signal interpersonal and situational information, complementing semantics— has been almost totally ignored in Natural Language Processing. But in the past five to eight years there has been a surge of research on the general topic of 'opinion', also called 'sentiment'. Generally, research focuses on the determining the author's opinion/sentiment about some topic within a given fragment of text. Since opinions may differ, it is granted that the author's opinion is 'subjective', and the effectiveness of an opinion-determination system is measured by comparing against a gold-standard set of human annotations.

But what does 'subjectivity' actually mean? What are 'opinion' and 'sentiment'? Lately, researchers are also starting to talk about 'affect', and even 'emotion'. What are these notions, and how do they differ from one another?

Unfortunately, a survey of the research done to date shows a disturbing lack of clarity on these questions. Very few papers bother to define their terms, but simply take a set of valences such as Good–Neutral–Bad to be sufficient. More recent work acknowledges the need to specify what the opinion actually applies to, and attempts also to determine the theme. Lately, several identify the holder of the opinion. Some even try to estimate the strength of the expressed opinion.

The trouble is, the same aspect of the same object can be considered Good by one person and Bad by another, and we can often understand both their points of view. There is much more to opinion/sentiment than simply matching words and phrases that attach to the theme, and computing a polarity score. People give reasons why they like or dislike something, and these reasons pertain to their goals and plans in the case of opinions) or their deeper emotional states (in the case of affect).

In this talk I outline a model of sentiment/opinion and of affect, and show that they appear in text in a fairly structured way, with various components. I show how proper understanding requires the reader to build some kind of person profile of the author, and claim that for systems to do adequate understanding of sentiments, opinions, and affects, they will need to do so as well. This is not a trivial challenge, and it opens the door to a whole new line of research with many fascinating and practical aspects.

About The Speaker

Dr. Hovy currently holds several positions:

- Director of the Natural Language Group at Information Sciences Institute (ISI) of the University of Southern California.
- Deputy Director of the Intelligent Systems Division of ISI.
- Research Associate Professor of Computer Science at USC.
- Director of the Center for Knowledge Integration and Discovery (CKID).
- Director of Research for the Digital Government Research Center (DGRC).
- Regular High-Level Visiting Scientist, International Guest Academic Talents (IGAT) Program for the Development of University Disciplines in China (111 Program), Jan 2008–Dec 2012.
- Advisory Professor at the Beijing University of Posts and Telecommunications, Beijing, China.
- Concurrent Professor at the University of Shenyang, China, Oct 2008–Sep 2011.

Proceedings of the Workshop on Sentiment Analysis where AI meets Psychology (SAAIP), IJCNLP 2011, page 1,
Chiang Mai, Thailand, November 13, 2011.

On Using Twitter to Monitor Political Sentiment and Predict Election Results

Adam Bermingham and Alan F. Smeaton
CLARITY: Centre for Sensor Web Technologies
School of Computing
Dublin City University
{abermingham,asmeaton}@computing.dcu.ie

Abstract

The body of content available on Twitter undoubtedly contains a diverse range of political insight and commentary. But, to what extent is this representative of an electorate? Can we model political sentiment effectively enough to capture the voting intentions of a nation during an election capaign? We use the recent Irish General Election as a case study for investigating the potential to model political sentiment through mining of social media. Our approach combines sentiment analysis using supervised learning and volume-based measures. We evaluate against the conventional election polls and the final election result. We find that social analytics using both volume-based measures and sentiment analysis are predictive and we make a number of observations related to the task of monitoring public sentiment during an election campaign, including examining a variety of sample sizes, time periods as well as methods for qualitatively exploring the underlying content.

1 Introduction

For years, standard methodologies such as polls have been used by market researchers to measure the beliefs and intentions of populations of individuals. These have a number of disadvantages including the human effort involved and they can be costly and time-consuming. With the advent of social media, there is now an abundance of online information wherein people express their sentiment with respect to wide variety of topics. An open research question is how might we analyse this data to produce results that approximate what can be achieved through traditional market research. An automated solution would mean that we could "poll" a population on demand, and at low cost.

This is a challenging task however. How can we ensure that our sample has a representative distribution? How much confidence do we put in noisy signals such as sentiment analysis? The wisdom of crowds teaches us that sufficient scale should at least somewhat mitigate these problems. In this paper we review a live system we developed for the Irish General Election, 2011. Our system used a variety of techniques to provide a live real-time interface into Twitter during the election. Using the volume and sentiment data from this system we review a number of sampling approaches and methods of modelling political sentiment, replicating work of others as well as introducing novel measures. We evaluate the error with respect to polls, as well as with respect to the election result itself.

In the next section we review related research. This is followed in Section 3 by a description of our methodology. We present our results in Section 4, followed by discussion in Section 5, and we conclude in Section 6.

2 Related Work

There appears to be three research areas emerging in terms of using online sentiment to monitor real world political sentiment. First is event monitoring, where the aim is to monitor reactionary content in social media during a specified event. In the political area this would typically be a speech, or a TV debate. An example is work by Diakopoulos and Shamma who characterised the 2008 US presidential debate in terms of Twitter sentiment (Diakopoulos and Shamma, 2010). Previously Shamma et al. examined a variety of aspects of debate modelling using Twitter, beyond individual politician performance (Shamma et al., 2009). In these studies, Twitter proved to be an effective source of data for identifying important topics and associated public reaction.

A second area which has received attention is

Proceedings of the Workshop on Sentiment Analysis where AI meets Psychology (SAAIP), IJCNLP 2011, pages 2–10,
Chiang Mai, Thailand, November 13, 2011.

modelling continuous sentiment functions for predicting other real-world continuous values, for example to predict stock market values. Bollen et al. have focused on modeling public mood on a variety of axes to correlate with socio-economic factors (Bollen et al., 2009) and to predict the Dow Jones Industrial Average (Bollen et al., 2010). They report a number of interesting observations such as changes in tension and anxiety around important events and find a significant improvement in predicting the Dow Jones Industrial Average when incorporating sentiment. This work is echoed by preliminary work from Zhang et al. who also focus on emotive concepts, in this case "hope" and "fear", and correlate with a number of market indicators (Zhang et al., 2010). It is noteworthy that the emphasis in these studies is on emotive sentiment (mood states, emotions), rather than polar sentiment (positivity, negativity) which is popular in other applications. O'Connor et al. also observe leading signals in Twitter sentiment, but with respect to political opinion polls (O'Connor et al., 2010). They offer the caveat, "text sentiment is volatile ... it is best used to detect long-term trends".

A third, related area, is result forecasting. A classic example of this is predicting election results, the focus of this paper. In result forecasting, it is the final result which is used to judge the accuracy of a particular forecasting measure, rather than a continuous series. Asur and Huberman (Asur and Huberman, 2010) used Twitter volume and sentiment to predict box office takings for movies, bettering other market indicators. They find volume to be a strong predictor and sentiment to be a useful, yet weaker predictor. They also propose a general model for linear regression social media prediction which serves as a basis for our model.

More directly, related to elections is Tumasjan et al.'s work on the German federal election in 2009 (Tumasjan et al., 2010). They found that that the share of volume on Twitter accurately reflected the distribution of votes in the election between the six main parties. It is difficult to draw general conclusions from this single result however. A focus of our study is to replicate and extend these experiments with respect to the Irish General Election. Noteworthy also is an earlier study which mined content from a political prediction website and in identifying author-party valence, trained classifiers with lexical features to identify "predictive sentiment" with promising results for predicting Canadian district elections (Kim and Hovy, 2007).

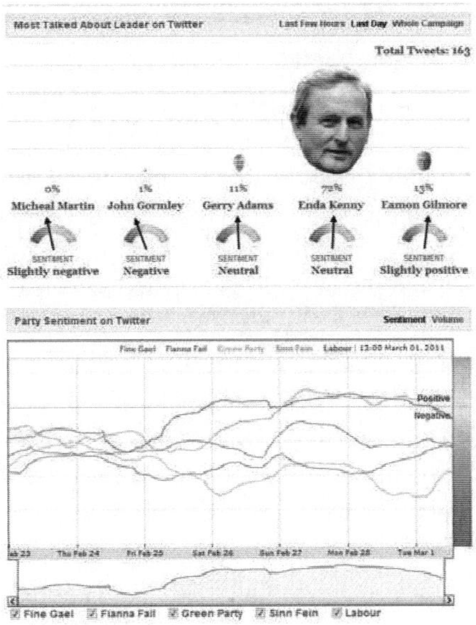

Figure 1: A screen shot of the sentiment portion of the #GE11 Real-time Twitter Tracker

The concerns around using Twitter as the basis for a prediction mechanism have been voiced by Gayo-Avello et al. who state, "we argue that one should not be accepting predictions about events using social media data as a black box." (Gayo-Avello et al., 2011) They cite the two primary caveats with using social media to inform predictive models as selection bias (inability to determine a representative sample) and potential for deliberate influence of results (through gaming and spamming for example). This is echoed by (Jungherr et al., 2011) who argue that methods of prediction using social media analytics are frequently contingent on somewhat arbitrary experimental variables.

Thus we see that predictive systems which utilise social media are both promising and challenging. The contention of our research is that the development of techniques for political public sentiment monitoring and election prediction is a promising direction requires more research work before we fully understand the limitations and capabilities of such an approach.

3 Methodology

The system we developed to evaluate our research idea was completed in collaboration with an industrial partner, an online news company[1]. The purpose of the "#GE11 Twitter Tracker" was to allow users, and our partner's journalists, to tap into the content on Twitter pertaining to the election, through an accessible dashboard-style interface. To that end, the "Twitter Tracker" featured a number of abstractive and extractive summarization approaches as well as a visualisation of volume and sentiment over time (see Figure 1).

The Irish General Election took place on 25th February, 2011. Between the 8th of February and the 25th we collected 32,578 tweets relevant to the five main parties: Fianna Fáil (FF), the Green Party, Labour, Fine Gael (FG) and Sinn Féin (SF). We identified relevant tweets by searching for the party names and their abbreviations, along with the election hashtag, `#ge11`. For the purposes of the analysis presented here, we do not consider the independent candidates or the minority parties[2]. Tweets reporting poll results were also filtered out.

3.1 Election Polls

The standard measure of error in predictive forecasting is Mean Absolute Error (MAE), defined as the average of the errors in each forecast:

$$MAE = \frac{1}{n}\sum_{i=1}^{n}|e_i| \tag{1}$$

where n is the number of forecasts (in our case 5) and e_i is the difference in actual result and predicted result for the ith forecast. MAE measures the degree to which a set of predicted values deviate from the actual values. We use MAE to compare Twitter-based predictions with polls as well as with the results of the election. To provide a reference point for our analysis, we use nine polls which were commissioned during the election. These polls guarantee accuracy to within a margin of 3% and in comparison to the final election results, had an average MAE of 1.61% with respect to the five main parties. There have been varying reports for Twitter-based predictions in the literature where the observed error can vary from very low (1.65%) (Tumasjan et al., 2010) to much higher (17.1% using volume, 7.6% using sentiment) (Gayo-Avello et al., 2011).

[1] `http://www.thejournal.ie`

[2] There is a difficulty with the minority parties and independent candidates for this election in that many of the official parties were more commonly referred to by their party alliance. This made relevance difficult to determine and such an exercise is outside the scope of this work

3.2 Predictive Measures

It is reasonable to assume that the percentage of votes that a party receives is related to the volume of related content in social media. Larger parties will have more members, more candidates and will attract more attention during the election campaign. Smaller parties likewise will have a much smaller presence. However, is this enough to reflect a popularity at a particular point in time, or in a given campaign? Is measuring volume susceptible to disproportionate influence from say a few prominent news stories or deliberate gaming or spamming? We define our volume-based measure as the proportional share of party mentions in a set of tweets for a given time period:

$$SoV(x) = \frac{|Rel(x)|}{\sum_{i=1}^{n}|Rel(i)|} \tag{2}$$

where $SoV(x)$ is the share of volume for a given party x in a system of n parties and $|Rel(i)|$ is the number of tweets relevant to party i. This formula has the advantage that the score for the parties are proportions summing to 1 and are easily compared with poll percentages. The sets of documents we use are:

- *Time-based*: Most recent 24 hours, 3 days, 7 days
- *Sample size-based*: Most recent 1000, 2000, 5000 or 10000 tweets
- *Cumulative*: All of the tweets from 8th February 2011 to relevant time
- *Manual*: Manually labelled tweets from pre-8th February 2011

When we draw comparison with a poll from a given date, we assume that tweets up until midnight the night before the date of the poll may be used. The volume of party mentions was approximately consistent in the approach to the election, meaning the *cumulative* volume function over time is linear and monotonically increasing.

3.3 Sentiment Analysis

Our previous research has shown that supervised learning provides more accurate sentiment analysis than can be provided by unsupervised methods such as using sentiment lexicons (Bermingham and Smeaton, 2010). We therefore decided to use classifiers specifically trained on data for this

	Positive	Negative	Neutral	Mixed	Total
Week 1	255	1,248	1,218	47	2,768
Week 2	629	1,289	2,411	106	4,435
Total	884	2,537	3,629	153	7,203

Table 1: Annotation counts

election. On two days, a week apart before the 8th of February 2011, we trained nine annotators to annotate sentiment in tweets related to parties and candidates for the election. The tweets in each annotation session were taken from different time periods in order to develop as diverse a training corpus as possible.

We provided the annotators with detailed guidelines and examples of sentiment. Prior to commencing anntoation, annotators answered a short set of sample annotations. We then provided the gold standard for these annotations (determined by the authors) and each answer was discussed in a group session. We instructed annotators not to consider reporting of positive or negative fact as sentiment but that sentiment be one of emotion, opinion, evaluation or speculation towards the target topic. Our annotation categories consisted of three sentiment classes (positive, negative, mixed), one non-sentiment class (neutral) and the 3 other classes (unannotatable, non-relevant, unclear). This is in line with the definition of sentiment proposed in (Wilson et al., 2005).

We disregard unannotatable, non-relevant and unclear annotations. A small subset (3.5%) of the documents were doubly-annotated. The inter-annotator agreement for the four relevant classes is 0.478 according to Krippendorff's Alpha, a standard measure of inter-annotator agreement for many annotators (Hayes and Krippendorff, 2007). We then remove duplicate and contradictory annotations leaving 7,203 document-topic pairs (see Table 1). Approximately half of the annotations contained sentiment of some kind.

The low level of positive sentiment we observe is striking, representing just 12% of the document-topic pairs. During this election, Ireland was in a period of economic crisis and negative political sentiment dominated the media and public mood. This presents a difficulty for supervised learning. With few training examples, it is difficult for the learner to identify minority classes. To mitigate this effect, when choosing our machine learning algorithm we optimise for F-measure which balances precision and recall across the classes. We

		Recall			
classifier	accuracy	pos	neg	neu	F-score
trivial	50.19	0	0	1	0.335
MNB	62.94	0.007	0.561	0.832	0.584
ADA-MNB	65.09	0.334	0.689	0.7	0.645
SVM	64.82	0.201	0.634	0.768	0.631
ADA-SVM	64.28	0.362	0.623	0.726	0.638

Table 2: Accuracy for 3-class sentiment classification

disregard the mixed annotations as they are few in number and ambiguous in nature.

Our feature vector consists of unigrams which occur in two or more documents in the training set. The tokenizer we use (Laboreiro et al., 2010) is optimised for user-generated content so all sociolinguistic features such as emoticons (":-)") and unconventional punctuation ("!!!!") are preserved. These features are often used to add tone to text and thus likely to contain sentiment information. We remove all topic terms, usernames and URLs to prevent any bias being learned towards these.

Unsatisfied with the recall from either Support Vector Machines (SVM) or Multinomial Naive Bayes (MNB) classifiers, we evaluated a boosting approach which, through iterative learning, up-weights training examples from minority classes, thus improving recall for these classes. We used Freund and Schapire's Adaboost M1 method with 10 training iterations as implemented in the Weka toolkit[3] (Freund and Schapire, 1996). Following from this, we use an Adaboost MNB classifier which achieves 65.09% classification accuracy in 10-fold cross-validation for 3 classes (see Table 2).

3.4 Incorporating Sentiment

It is difficult to say how best to incorporate sentiment. On the one hand, sentiment distribution in the tweets relevant to a single party is indicative of the sentiment towards that party. For example, if the majority of the mentions of a party contain negative sentiment, it is reasonable to assume that people are in general negatively disposed towards that party. However, this only considers a party in isolation. If this negative majority holds true for *all* parties, how do we differentiate public opinion towards them? In a closed system like an election, relative sentiment between the parties perhaps has as much of an influence.

To address the above issues, we use two novel measures of sentiment in this study. For inter-

[3]http://www.cs.waikato.ac.nz/ml/weka/

party sentiment, we modify our volume-based measure, SoV, to represent the share of positive volume, SoV_p, and share of negative volume, SoV_n:

$$SoV_p(x) = \frac{|Pos(x)|}{\sum_{i=1}^{n} |Pos(i)|} \tag{3}$$

$$SoV_n(x) = \frac{|Neg(x)|}{\sum_{i=1}^{n} |Neg(i)|} \tag{4}$$

For intra-party sentiment, we use a log ratio of sentiment:

$$Sent(x) = \log_{10} \frac{|Pos(x)| + 1}{|Neg(x)| + 1} \tag{5}$$

This gives a single value for representing how positive or negative a set of documents are for a given topic. Values for $Sent(x)$ are positive when there are more positive than negative documents, and negative when there are more negative than positive for a given party. 1 is added to the positive and negative volumes to prevent a division by zero. The inter-party share of sentiment is a proportional distribution and thus prediction error can be easily measured with MAE. Also, as it is non-parametric it can be applied without any tuning.

We fit a regression to our inter-party and intra-party measures, trained on poll data. This takes the form:

$$\begin{aligned} y(x) = \; & \beta_v SoV(x) + \beta_p SoV_p(x) + \beta_n SoV_n(x) \\ & + \beta_s Sent(x) + \varepsilon \end{aligned}$$

This builds on the general model for sentiment proposed in (Asur and Huberman, 2010). The purpose of fitting this regression is threefold. Firstly, we wish to identify which measures are the most predictive and confirm our assumption that both sentiment and proportion of volume have predictive qualities. Secondly, we want to compare the predictive capabilities of our two sentiment measures. Lastly, we want to identify under optimum conditions how a Twitter-model for political sentiment could predict our election results.

For many applications there is little to be gained from measuring sentiment without being able to explain the observed values. We conclude our study with a suggestion for how such sentiment data may be used to explore Twitter data *qualitatively* during an election.

4 Results

Comparing our non-parametric inter-topic measures with the election result, our lowest error comes for when we use all available data, with volume performing marginally better (5.58%) than the share of positive volume. Interestingly, in many of the other data sets, the share of positive volume outperforms the share of volume in terms of result prediction. Unsurprisingly, share of negative volume performs worst in all cases. Also interesting is the fact that among the worst-performing is the more accurate manually labelled data. Perhaps this is due to the gap in time between when the documents were labelled and the election. See Table 3 for the MAE for result prediction for our data sets.

	MAE		
Dataset	SoV	SoV_p	SoV_n
cumulative	0.0558	0.0576	0.0658
1 day	0.0841	0.0574	0.1248
3 days	0.0920	0.0805	0.1203
7 days	0.0790	0.0718	0.0982
last 1000	0.0805	0.0857	0.1088
last 2000	0.0795	0.0663	0.1335
last 5000	0.0723	0.0701	0.1066
last 10000	0.0926	0.0808	0.1206
manually labelled	0.0968	0.1037	0.1128

Table 3: Mean absolute error for non-parametric measures compared to election result

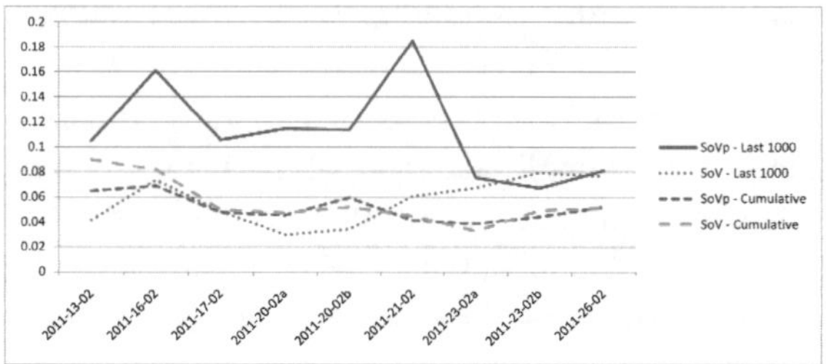

Figure 2: Mean absolute error for *cumulative* and *last 1000* sample data for SoV and SoV_p

To understand better how each of these predictive measures is performing, we look closer at two of our datasets: *cumulative* and *last 1000*. We choose *cumulative* as it performs best out of all our datasets and we choose *last 1000* as this sample size is easy to reproduce and a number frequently used in polling for sufficient sample size. This also allows us to compare a cumulative data set with a fixed volume dataset.

In Figure 2 we can see that broadly the error for the cumulative datasets improves compared to each successive poll over time. The performance of the positive share of volume and overall volume are strongly positively correlated. For the most recent 1000 document samples however, we see

Features	MAE cumulative	MAE last 1000
s	0.0996	0.1029
n	0.071	0.0661
n,s	0.0448	0.0645
p	0.0471	0.066
p,s	0.04	0.064
p,n	0.04	0.0594
p,n,s	0.0388	0.0608
v	0.0551	0.0573
v,s	0.0403	0.0547
v,n	0.0434	0.0533
v,n,s	0.0377	0.0502
v,p	0.0466	0.0538
v,p,s	0.0399	0.0542
v,p,n	0.0383	0.0486
v,p,n,s	0.0367	0.0486

Table 4: Error for regressions, trained and tested on poll data $v = SoV, p = SoV_p, n = SoV_n, s = Sent$

	MAE
Regression (cumulative)	0.0585
Regression (last 1000)	0.0804
Exit poll	0.0108

Table 6: Error for regressions, trained on poll data and official exit poll, compared to election results

the error for share of positive volume vary wildly, likely due to the low volume of tweets classified as positive. This does appear to lessen as the election draws nearer, eventually reaching the same level as the overall share of volume in the recent 1000 documents. After the initial polls however, the cumulative scores give a much lower error.

Using intra-party sentiment in Figure 3 we see that in the weeks before the election, it is difficult to discern any salient pattern. The party sentiment values all seem to be relatively close, with an average sentiment score of 0.75, approximately equal to a ratio of 1 positive document for every 6 negative documents. In the days before polling day however we observe a divergence of sentiment which continues through polling day and beyond, showing overall positive sentiment for Labour and Sinn Féin, both of whom won a record number of seats in the parliament. This trend continues for a few days after the election but by a week later has returned to values similar to those observed earlier in the campaign.

Looking at the results of the regressions which were fitted to the poll results, we see a low error, particularly for the cumulative data which has an MAE of 3.67%. In Table 5 we can see how the regression has weighted each of the factors.

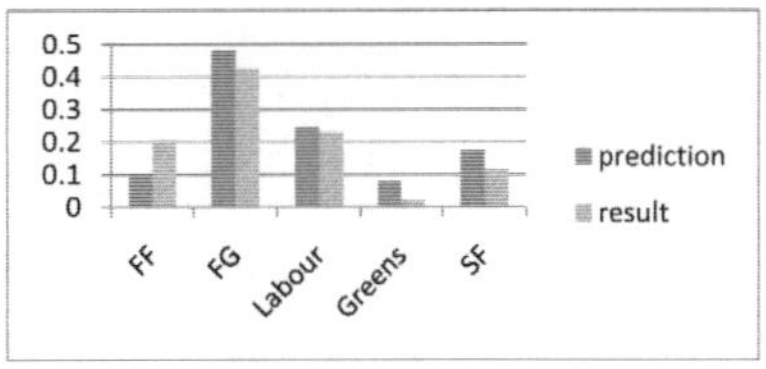

(a) Regression: Cumulative data

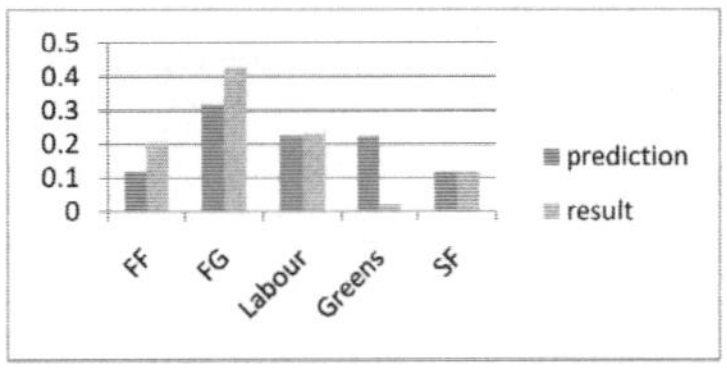

(b) Regression: Last 1000

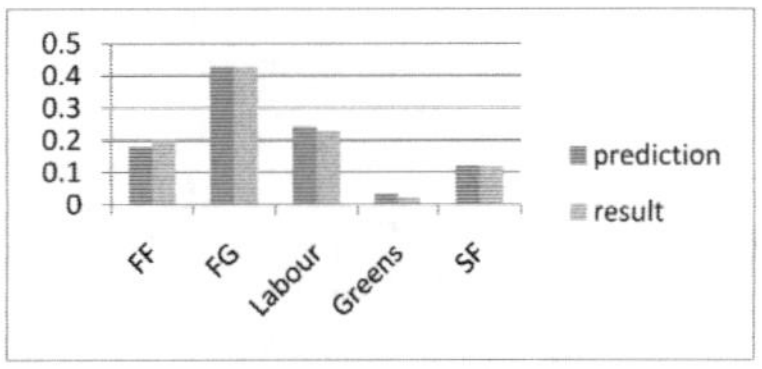

(c) Exit poll

Figure 4: Exit poll, election results and election predictions for regression trained on poll data using all features

For both datasets, the regression has placed a high weight on share of volume. Intuitively, the share of positive volume receives a positive weight and the share of negative volume receives a negative weight. Each of the sentiment scores are weighted higher for the cumulative data. In Table 4, we can see that adding in more features improves the regression accuracy but taking just two features (for example SoV_p and SoV_n) we can approach similar accuracy. In terms of the final election results, the cumulative regression outperforms the 1000 sample regression significantly with an MAE of 5.85% (see Table 6 and Figure 4).

In order to explore the content according to sentiment we define *Sentiment TF-IDF*. In this measure, we consider the entire set of documents to be the tweets relevant to a topic and thus the document frequency for a term is the number of relevant documents in which a term appears. To calculate the term frequencies for a topic-sentiment class we then concatenate all documents of that class into a single document and calculate word frequencies. Doing this for the positive and negative classes for each party provides us with the ranked terms list in Table 7. These terms may be thought of as those terms that most characterise

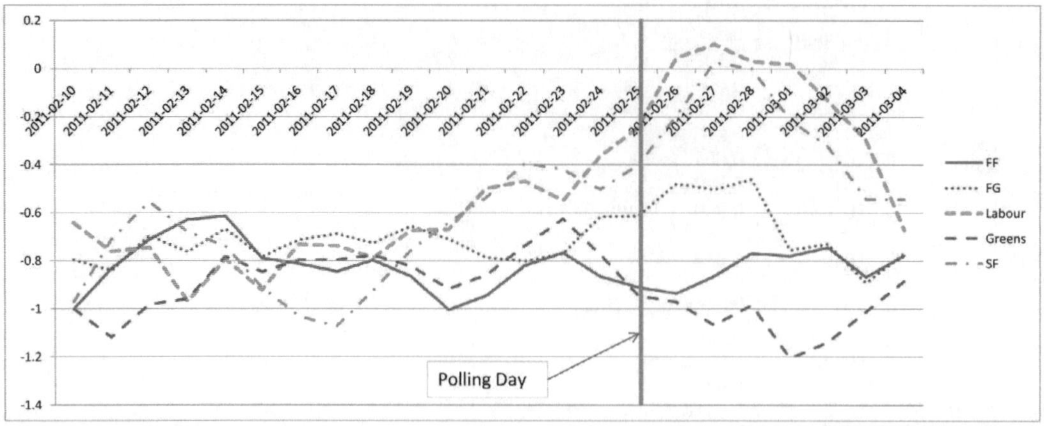

Figure 3: Daily sentiment: each data point is average of the daily $Sent$ score for a party over the previous three days

	SoV	SoV_p	SoV_n	$Sent$	ε	MAE	Correlation Coefficient
Cumulative	1.3444	0.6516	-1.0019	0.2193	0.1801	0.0367	0.9524
Last 1000	1.3339	0.2125	-0.6708	-0.0075	0.0196	0.0486	0.896

Table 5: Linear regression coefficients, error and correlation coefficient for regression fitted to poll data

the sentiment-bearing documents for that party.

5 Discussion

Overall, the best non-parametric method for predicting the result of the first preference votes in the election is the share of volume of tweets that a given party received in total over the time period we study. This is followed closely by the share of positive volume for the same time period which, despite considering only a fraction of the documents considered by share of volume, approaches the same error. Either overall share of volume or share of positive volume performs best for each dataset. As expected, negative share of voice consistently performs worst, though in some cases rivals the other measures. This is likely due to a correlation with the overall share of volume.

The error compared with the individual polls is telling as we see a downward trend for the cumulative data as more data is available. This pattern does not appear in the *last 1000* sample volume data so this is likely linked to quantity of data rather than temporal proximity to election day. The share of positive volume for the *last 1000* sample is much more erratic than we observe for the cumulative data suggesting that 1000 is perhaps too small to rely on metrics derived from subsets of the data.

Perhaps the most intriguing results is the sentiment pattern over the course of the election. In Figure 3 we see that there is a dramatic change in sentiment towards the parties for the days after polling day but that this sentiment shift had already begun before polling day. This period, from a few days before the election to approximately a week afterwards, is a period where public sentiment appears to have settled at a range of values for the parties. Outside of this time period it is difficult to separate the parties in terms of sentiment. Perhaps this is a case of Twitter users being more honest and considered with the vote and results imminent, rather than simply reactionary. The fact that this sentiment appears to be leading makes for an interesting avenue to pursue in future studies.

We achieved an MAE of 3.67% using our regressions compared to the poll results, although naturally this was overfitted, since the regressions had originally been fitted to the poll data. For that reason the error is much higher when we test with the actual result at 5.85%. It is noteworthy that this is in fact slightly worse that the best performing non-parametric measure. In both cases, the error is significantly higher than that achieved by the tradition polls.

Both the intra-party and inter-party sentiment measures appear to improve upon volume-based measures and the weights the regression assigns to them reflects this. However it is difficult to conclude that intra-party sentiment is important when inter-party sentiment is considered. In a closed system, the actual distribution of sentiment in content relevant to a given party may only matter relative to that for the other parties. Considering the regression results, it seems that capturing the share of positive volume and the share of negative volume is sufficient, particularly where a large amount of data is available. With all features for cumulative data, the coefficient for intra-party sentiment score is assigned a weight of just -0.0075 suggesting that this factor is effectively ignored by the regression.

Examining the errors, we see that our methods have particular trouble forecasting the result for the Green Party (too high) and Fianna Fáil (too low). In the former case, we suspect this is due to the selection bias in sampling Twitter. Green party members, and their supporters, tend to be more tech-savvy and have a disproportionately large presence in social media. In the latter case we speculate that although Fianna Fáil attracted low volume and plenty of negativity, they are however traditionally the largest Irish party and thus enjoyed a degree of brand loyalty.

In opinion measurement and social media analytics it is limiting to simply measure without providing means to explain measurements. Using *Sentiment TF-IDF* we can identify terms that provide a path to qualitatively exploring the dataset. We suggest using *Sentiment TF-IDF* to identify terms which can be used to identify important, sentiment-bearing documents. Doing this we were able to use the words in Table 7 to determine that people were discussing Fine Gael negatively with respect to *planting* a member of the *audience* in a popular current affairs television show. We also saw a negative reaction to the Green Party's proposal for a *citizens' assembly*. This shows that there may be further value in terms of qualitative analysis which Twitter may offer during an election.

6 Conclusion

Overall, we conclude that Twitter does appear to display a predictive quality which is marginally augmented by the inclusion of sentiment analysis. We derive two different methods for monitoring topic sentiment, intra-party and inter-party. Fitting our features to a regression we observe that volume is the single biggest predictive variable followed by inter-party sentiment. Given sufficient data, intra-party sentiment appears to be less valuable as a predictive measure. Our speculation is that the relative success of the inter-party sentiment is due to the closed nature of the system.

Our approach however has demonstrated an error which is not competitive with the traditional polling methods. A next step is to conduct a failure analysis to discern whether there is a further aspect of the content that we may able to model, or a bias we may be able to correct for which can reduce this error. We also observe a dramatic sentiment shift in the two days before polling day which hint at the election outcome. It is perhaps a deeper analysis of the sentiment distribution during this period which will produce the most beneficial application of sentiment analysis in the context of an election campaign.

There are perhaps two reasons that volume is an altogether stronger indicator than sentiment. The first is that volume may simply be a reasonable indicator of popularity in a population of people, and in this case, voting intention. The other is that sentiment in comparison is reactive and it is difficult to discriminate between sentiment which reflects the inner preferences of people, and that which is reflecting an immediate response to a given news story or event. We do see cases where sentiment is necessary. For example, the Green Party in this election had a relatively high volume, but a closer look at the content reveals that this was because people were commenting on low levels of support, an aspect not adequately captured by our sentiment analysis.

At this stage it is unclear whether confining ourselves to sentiment and volume data will allow us to approach levels of acceptable accuracy for reliable measurement. Improvement in sentiment analysis techniques and increased availability of data will likely increase performance, however the research community must address the issues of representativeness and potential for adversarial activity before these methods can be used in a credible way.

Acknowledgments

This work is supported by Science Foundation Ireland under grant 07/CE/I1147. The authors would like to thank the reviewers for their helpful feedback and comments.

	The Green Party		Fianna Fáil		Fine Gael		Sinn Féin		Labour	
	pos	neg	pos	neg	pos	neg	pos	neg	pos	neg
1	vote	happen	lesson	vinb	vote	vote	election	vinb	vote	tv3ld
2	mid	election	unparalleled	tv3ld	team	vinb	luck	plan	north	vinb
3	flyer	happening	failure	bad	children	ha	fought	point	cllr	tv3news
4	dublin	made	interesting	vote	bucket	voting	candidates	vote	dublin	vote
5	west	citizens	wake	tv3news	bearable	don	seat	job	central	baby
6	rx	assembly	east	country	day	gay	vote	creation	prefs	lost
7	oireachtas	proposal	record	voting	giving	tv3news	constituency	banks	donegal	bunch
8	candidate	hard	flyer	anglo	picture	twitter	hard	playing	fair	eating
9	welcomes	final	education	door	bebo	facebook	rain	blinder	running	communists
10	preference	obliterated	smacking	telling	yellow	planted	biased	disgraceful	great	opportunity
11	urban	poor	election	things	hope	audience	helping	don	good	major
12	man	week	b4	screwed	red	answering	campaign	racist	today	posters
13	guidelines	idea	seats	anarchist	plan	twolicy	poised	vincent	west	back
14	achieved	ireland	brilliant	day	roses	script	tonight	money	2nd	won
15	statutory	hoax	ad	friend	equality	priceless	today	tonight	govt	advising

Table 7: The most positive and negative terms for each party according to *Sentiment TF-IDF*

References

Sitaram Asur and Bernardo A. Huberman. 2010. Predicting the future with social media. *Computing Research Repository*.

Adam Bermingham and Alan F. Smeaton. 2010. Classifying sentiment in microblogs: is brevity an advantage? In *Proceedings of the 19th ACM international conference on Information and knowledge management*, CIKM '10, pages 1833–1836, New York, NY, USA. ACM.

Johan Bollen, Alberto Pepe, and Huina Mao. 2009. Modeling public mood and emotion: Twitter sentiment and socio-economic phenomena. *CoRR*, abs/0911.1583.

Johan Bollen, Huina Mao, and Xiao-Jun Zeng. 2010. Twitter mood predicts the stock market. *CoRR*, abs/1010.3003.

Nicholas A. Diakopoulos and David A. Shamma. 2010. Characterizing debate performance via aggregated Twitter sentiment. In *Conference on Human Factors in Computing Systems (CHI 2010)*.

Yoav Freund and Robert E. Schapire. 1996. Experiments with a New Boosting Algorithm. In *International Conference on Machine Learning*, pages 148–156.

Daniel Gayo-Avello, Panagiotis T. Metaxas, and Eni Mustafaraj. 2011. Limits of electoral predictions using twitter. In *Proceedings of the International Conference on Weblogs and Social Media (ICWSM) 2011, July 17-21, 2011*.

A. F. Hayes and K. Krippendorff. 2007. Answering the call for a standard reliability measure for coding data. In *Communication Methods and Measures*.

Andreas Jungherr, Pascal Jrgens, and Harald Schoen. 2011. Why the Pirate Party Won the German Election of 2009 or The Trouble With Predictions: A Response to Tumasjan, A., Sprenger, T. O., Sander, P. G., & Welpe, I. M. Predicting Elections With Twitter: What 140 Characters Reveal About Political Sentiment. *Social Science Computer Review*.

Soo-Min Kim and Eduard Hovy. 2007. Crystal: Analyzing Predictive Opinions on the Web. In *Proceedings of the Joint Conference on Empirical Methods in Natural Language Processing and Computational Natural Language Learning (EMNLP-CoNLL)*.

Gustavo Laboreiro, Luís Sarmento, Jorge Teixeira, and Eugénio Oliveira. 2010. Tokenizing microblogging messages using a text classification approach. In *AND '10: Proceedings of The Fourth Workshop on Analytics for Noisy Unstructured Text Data*, New York, NY, USA, October. ACM.

Brendan O'Connor, Ramnath Balasubramanyan, Bryan R. Routledge, and Noah A. Smith. 2010. From Tweets to Polls: Linking Text Sentiment to Public Opinion Time Series. In *Proceedings of the International AAAI Conference on Weblogs and Social Media*.

David A. Shamma, Lyndon Kennedy, and Elizabeth F. Churchill. 2009. Tweet the debates: understanding community annotation of uncollected sources. In *Proceedings of the first SIGMM workshop on Social media*, WSM '09, pages 3–10, New York, NY, USA. ACM.

Andranik Tumasjan, Timm Sprenger, Philipp Sandner, and Isabell Welpe. 2010. Predicting Elections with Twitter: What 140 Characters Reveal about Political Sentiment. In *International AAAI Conference on Weblogs and Social Media 2010*.

T. Wilson, J. Wiebe, and P. Hoffmann. 2005. Recognizing Contextual Polarity in Phrase-Level Sentiment Analysis. *Proceedings of the 2005 Conference on Empirical Methods in Natural Language Processing (EMNLP)*, pages 347–354.

Xue Zhang, Hauke Fuehres, and Peter A Gloor. 2010. Predicting Stock Market Indicators Through Twitter I hope it is not as bad as I fear. In *Collaborative Innovations Networks Conference (COINs)*.

Emotion Modeling from Writer/Reader Perspectives Using a Microblog Dataset

Yi-jie Tang and Hsin-Hsi Chen
Department of Computer Science and Information Engineering
National Taiwan University, Taipei, Taiwan
tangyj@nlg.csie.ntu.edu.tw; hhchen@csie.ntu.edu.tw

Abstract

Most recent studies on emotion analysis and detection focus on how writers express their emotions through textual information. In this paper, we model emotion generation on the Plurk microblogging platform from both writer and reader perspectives. Support Vector Machine (SVM)-based classifiers are used for emotion prediction. To better model emotion generation on such a social network, three types of non-linguistic features are used: social relation, user behavior, and relevance degree, along with textual features. We found that each of the non-linguistic features can be combined with linguistic features to achieve higher performance. In fact, the combination of linguistic, social, and behavioral features performs the best.

1 Introduction

Emotions express humans' feeling and experiences on some subject matters. They are typically recognized in text, speech, body gestures, and some visual information. Emotion mining is crucial for many applications, including customer care (Gupta, Gilbert, and Fabbrizio 2010), sale prediction (Liu, et al. 2007), game animation (Bernhaupt et al. 2007), and robot simulation (Becker, Kopp, and Wachsmuth 2004). Capturing people's feelings, predicting their reactions to events, and generating suitable emotions are typical tasks in emotion mining.

Emotion-tagged corpora are indispensable for emotion modeling. Recently, the social media known as weblogs, or blogs, encourage users to share their emotions through writing. For example, bloggers regularly use emoticons to express personal feelings in their written posts. To encourage increased reader interaction, some news media, e.g., Yahoo! Kimo News, provide a voting mechanism for news readers to express their feelings about news articles they've just read. The collection of blogger posts and news reader responses forms writer and reader emotion-tagged corpora, respectively, facilitating writer emotion and reader emotion mining.

Previous studies (e.g., Yang, Lin, and Chen 2007a; Yang, Lin, and Chen 2007b; Yang, Lin, and Chen 2008) have used an emotion-tagged weblog corpus to investigate the ways in which people express their emotions, trying to detect writers' affective status with textual contents they have written. While these studies aimed to perform emotion analysis and detection from the writer's perspective, a few papers have studied reader emotion generation (Lin, Yang, and Chen 2007; Lin and Chen 2008; Lin, Yang, and Chen, 2008) using an emotion-tagged news corpus, modeling how readers react to articles on news websites.

To study how writer emotion affects readers' feelings, Yang, Lin and Chen (2009) used the Yahoo! Kimo Blog and Yahoo! Kimo News to produce a dataset annotated with both writer and reader emotions. They constructed a document-level reader-emotion classifier using the Yahoo! Kimo News corpus, and applied the resulting classifier on the Yahoo! Kimo Blog corpus. In this way, a new blog corpus labeled with both writer and reader emotions was obtained.

The major problem with the above approach is that the reader emotion tagging on the writer corpus depends on classification performance. Plurk, a unique social network and microblogging platform, provides a new opportunity in which a dialogue consists of posts and corresponding replies. A poster begins by publishing a post along with an emotion, then a replier responds to the post and labels it with an emotion symbol. The replier serves as a reader, and also as a writer when the reply has been attached.

Proceedings of the Workshop on Sentiment Analysis where AI meets Psychology (SAAIP), IJCNLP 2011, pages 11–19, *Chiang Mai, Thailand, November 13, 2011.*

Therefore, the original poster has only a writer emotion, but the replier has both a writer emotion and a reader emotion.

In this paper, we model emotion mining from the writer perspective, reader perspective, and the combined writer and reader perspective. To collect data including both writers' and readers' emotional information, we extracted messages from Plurk, ending up with 50,000 conversations in the dataset.

Support Vector Machine (SVM) was chosen as classifiers to predict repliers' emotion. Like other related studies, this experiment included textual features for training and testing. Since the conversations collected present communication and interaction between social network users, some non-linguistic features were taken into account. As a result, 4 types of features are used, including linguistic features, social relation, user behavior, and relevance degree.

The rest of this paper is organized as follows. Section 2 discusses previous work related to emotion studies. Section 3 introduces the Plurk social network and describes the extraction of the dataset. Section 4 discusses how emotions from reader and writer perspectives are analyzed. Section 5 describes the SVM classifier, along with the feature set. Section 6 details the performance of the prediction tasks, and discusses and compares the usefulness of different types of features. The final section concludes the paper.

2 Related Work

Mishne (2005) adopts mood taggings in LiveJournal articles to train a mood classifier on document-level with SVM. Mishne and Rijke (2006) use a blog corpus to identify the intensity of community mood during some given time intervals. Jung, Choi, and Myaeng (2007) also focus on the mood classification problem in LiveJournal.

Yang, Lin, and Chen (2007a) use Yahoo! Kimo Blog as corpora to build emotion lexicons. A collocation model is proposed to learn emotion lexicons from weblog articles. Emotion classification at sentence level is experimented by using the mined lexicons to demonstrate their usefulness. Yang, Lin, and Chen (2008) further investigate the emotion classification of weblog corpora using SVM and conditional random field (CRF) machine learning techniques. The emotion classifiers are trained at the sentence level and applied to the document level. Their experiments show that CRF classifiers outperform SVM classifiers.

Lin, Yang and Chen (2007) pioneer reader emotion analysis with an emotion-tagged Yahoo! Kimo news corpus. They classify documents into reader emotion categories with SVM and Naïve Bayes classifiers (Lin, Yang and Chen, 2008). Besides classification, Lin and Chen (2008) propose pairwise loss minimization (PLM) and emotional distribution regression (EDR) to rank reader emotions. They show that EDR is better at predicting the most popular emotion, but PLM produces ranked lists that have higher correlation with the correct lists. Yang, Lin, and Chen (2009) further introduce the application of emotion analysis from both the writer's and reader's perspectives. The relationships between writer and reader emotions are discussed in their works.

Besides long articles, some studies also deal with emotion detection of short messages from microblogs and news headlines. Strapparava and Mihalcea (2007) focus on the emotion classification of news headlines. Go, Huang, and Bhayani (2009) use distant supervision for sentiment classification of Twitter messages. In their study, SVM outperforms Naïve Bayes and Maximum Entropy, and has the accuracy of 82.2%. Sun et al. (2010) focus on the Plurk microblogging platform, using text content and the NTU Sentiment Dictionary to build their feature set. These studies all focus on writer's emotions rather than reader's emotions.

Our contributions are different from the others. We employ the emotion tagging of both posters and repliers in Plurk and investigate reader and writer emotion analysis with both linguistic and non-linguistic features using a machine learning approach.

3 The Plurk Dataset

3.1 The Plurk Social Network

Plurk is a web-based social network that allows users to post short messages limited to 140 characters. From this viewpoint, Plurk is similar to Twitter and other microblogging platforms. Unlike Twitter, however, Plurk also acts like an instant messaging system because a user can see replies as soon as they are sent by another user. A post and its replies are grouped within a box on the screen, indicating that they are messages from the same conversation. Every post can be given an optional "qualifier," which is a one-word verb indicating the poster's action or feeling. There are 18 qualifiers, including Loves,

Likes, Shares, Gives, Hates, Wants, Wishes, Needs, Will, Hopes, Asks, Has, Was, Wonders, Feels, Thinks, Says, and Is. Figure 1 shows a typical conversation on Plurk. In this conversation, the first line was entered by a poster. He chose "loves" as the qualifier, stating that he "loves the iPod." The other messages were entered by other users as replies to the poster. Their messages are followed by graphic emoticons that express their emotions.

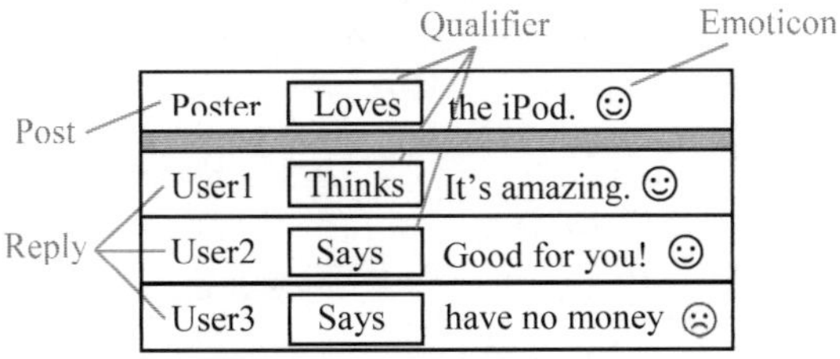

Figure 1. A conversation on Plurk

Plurk provides 78 basic graphic emoticons, and these emoticons are commonly used in users' messages. We choose 35 of the emoticons and categorize them into the positive and negative group. The other 43 are either neutral or cannot be clearly categorized, so we exclude them to minimize uncertainty. Figure 2 lists the Plurk emoticons used in this study.

Figure 2. Emoticons as positive and negative labels

Plurk is very popular in Taiwan and some other Asian countries. Figure 3 shows the number of unique daily visitors from Taiwan. As of August 2009, it has about four hundred thousand unique daily visitors, and the number keeps increasing. Thus, we can easily obtain an enough amount of data suitable for training and testing.

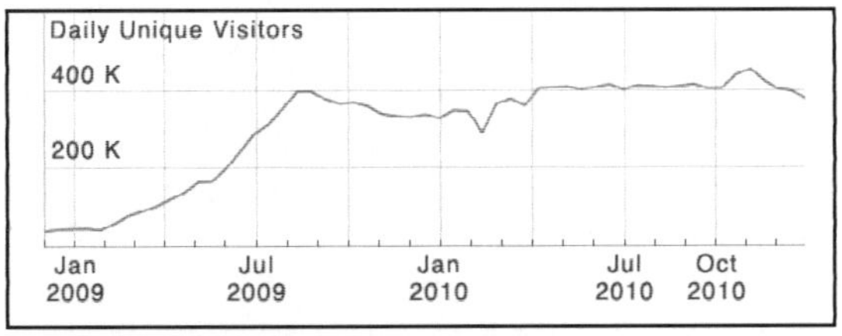

Figure 3: Number of unique daily visitors of Plurk according to Google Trends.

3.2 Dataset

We prepare our dataset from the Plurk platform. In this dataset, there are 50,000 conversations dating from Jun 21, 2008 to Nov 7, 2009, and each of them consists of a post with or without emoticon and a corresponding reply with an emoticon. All the replies have to be the first reply to a post, because this can help us make sure the reply is a response to the original post rather than to other responses. All messages are in Traditional Chinese.

We filter out some messages by their qualifiers. For example, we filter out the messages with the "share" qualifier, because most "shares" are website links or images rather than general text messages. If a message contains an emoticon that is not shown in Figure 2, it will also be filtered out. Such an emoticon does not present obvious positive or negative emotion, and will not be used in our study.

In the dataset, there are 42,115 conversations with a positive reply and 7,885 conversations with a negative reply. These conversations are obtained randomly from the Plurk website, and we think this should reflect their actual distribution on Plurk. For this reason we use this dataset without adjusting the proportion of the two emotion types. The proportion of positive conversations (84.23%) is used as baseline.

4 Reader/Writer Perspective

Most related studies focus on the analysis and detection of writer's emotion, since a writer's content has a more direct link to his emotion, and corpora containing writer's emotion are easier to find on the Web. In this paper, we try to model the generation of reader's emotion, and this kind of emotion can be related to the content written by poster, replier, or both. Depending on different perspectives, we have 3 types of models: reader model, writer model, and reader + writer model. Figure 4 shows important components in the modeling: a poster *pt* and the text *T*(*pt*) that *pt* posts; a replier *rp*, the text *T*(*rp*) used by *rp* to reply to *pt* and *rp*'s emotion *E*(*rp*); *S*(*pt*,*rp*) denotes the social relationship between *pt* and *rp*; *B*(*rp*) denotes the behavior of *rp*; and *R*(*T*(*pt*),*T*(*rp*)) denotes the relevance between post *T*(*pt*) and reply *T*(*rp*). The uses of the components will be discussed in detail in the following.

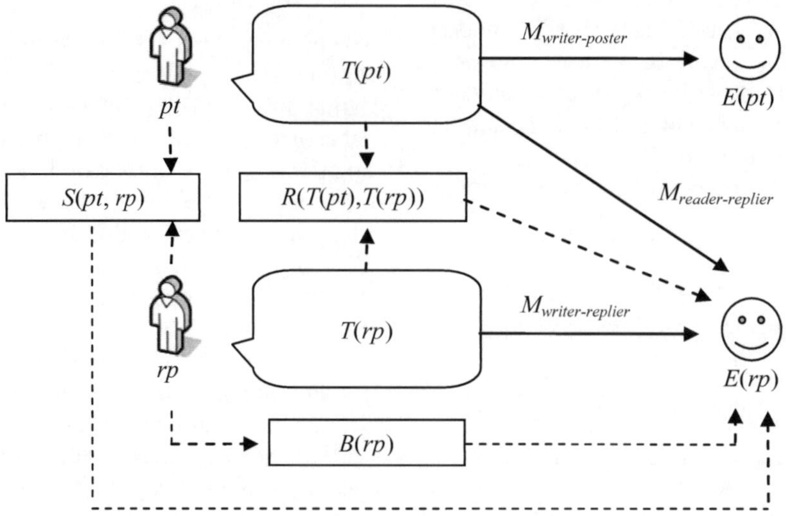

Figure 4. Different emotion generation models on Plurk

4.1 Reader Perspective

By looking at a replier's emotion from reader perspective, we can build a reader model. In this model, we assume a replier's emotion is directly generated by reading the poster's message, and then the replier expresses his emotion by using an emoticon in his reply. It is indicated by the model $M_{reader\text{-}replier}$ in Figure 4. That is, $E(rp)=M_{reader\text{-}replier}(T(pt))$, where $M_{reader\text{-}replier}$ is a function that maps $T(pt)$ into an emotion. Besides $T(pt)$, we can consider social relationship between *rp* and *pt*, and the behavior of *rp* such that $E(rp)=M_{reader\text{-}replier}(T(pt), S(pt,rp), B(rp))$.

4.2 Writer Perspective

In a conversation, both the poster and the replier produce textual contents. To model emotion generation from writer's perspective, we assume users' emotions are related to their own contents. Thus, we have two types of writer model: poster's writer model and replier's writer model. In our study, we mostly deal with replier's writer model, while poster's writer model is listed for comparison. For replier's writer model, a replier's content is used to predict his own emotion. The model $M_{writer\text{-}replier}$ in Figure 4 indicates the generation of a replier's emotion from writer's perspective. That is, $E(rp)=M_{writer\text{-}replier}(T(rp))$, where $M_{writer\text{-}replier}$ is a function that maps $T(rp)$ into an emotion. Besides $T(rp)$, we can consider social relationship between *rp* and *pt*, and the behavior of *rp* such that $E(rp)=M_{writer\text{-}replier}(T(rp), S(pt,rp), B(rp))$. For poster's writer model, a post's content is used to predict his emotion. That is, $E(pt)=M_{writer\text{-}poster}(T(pt))$.

4.3 Reader and Writer Perspective

We combine both reader and writer perspectives, and assume a replier's emotion is related to both poster's content and the replier's own content. Thus, a replier's emotion is predicted using poster's and replier's texts. In this case, $E(rp)=M_{reader\text{-}writer}(T(pt), T(rp), R(T(pt),T(rp)))$, where $M_{reader\text{-}writer}$ is a function maps $T(pt)$, $T(rp)$, $R(T(pt),T(rp))$ into an emotion. Besides textual information, we can also introduce social relationship between *rp* and *pt*, and the behavior of *rp* into this function.

5 Emotion Modeling

SVM is adopted as classifiers to predict emotion from reader and/or writer perspectives. Besides textual features, we also incorporate non-textual features such as social relation, user behavior, and relevance degree.

5.1 Text Features (*T*)

Since about 70% of Chinese words are disyllabic, and new words and slangs are commonly used in social media, we use bigrams instead of words as features. Chinese character bigrams in all poster's and/or replier's messages are extracted. We model the relationship between a bigram *w* and an emotion *e* as probability $P(w|e)$.

A training set is composed of conversations between posters and repliers. A conversation scenario between a poster and a replier is as follows. A poster *pt* writes down a post *T*(*pt*) with emotion *E*(*pt*). After a replier *rp* reads the post *T*(*pt*), *rp* writes down a reply *T*(*rp*) with emotion *E*(*rp*). Note poster *pt* writes and replier *rp* reads the same message *T*(*pt*), and express emotions *E*(*pt*) and *E*(*rp*), respectively. In contrast, replier *rp* reads and writes different messages, i.e., *T*(*pt*) and *T*(*rp*), with the same emotion *E*(*rp*).

In this way, we have three data sets $D_{writer\text{-}poster}$, $D_{reader\text{-}replier}$, and $D_{writer\text{-}replier}$. Here, $D_{writer\text{-}poster}$ is composed of all the messages of posters along with their emotions. $D_{reader\text{-}replier}$ consists of all the messages which repliers read and emotions they express. $D_{writer\text{-}replier}$ denotes a set of messages and emotions that repliers make. These three data sets are used to train $P_{writer\text{-}poster}$, $P_{reader\text{-}replier}$, and $P_{writer\text{-}replier}$, respectively.

To apply SVM in the experiments, libSVM is used as the classification tool (Chang and Lin 2001). The libSVM parameter selection tool found that C=3 and gamma=0.13 yielded the best results.

5.2 Social Relation (*S*)

The text-based emotion model does not consider the personalization issue. Intuitively, each replier has his own preference. Social relationship between a poster and a replier is the first cue. We measure the social relationship between two users with their interaction degree. The following three features are proposed.

S_1 defines an interaction degree between users u_1 and u_2 as their total number of interactions.

$$S_1(u_1, u_2) = \sum_{(u_1,u_2)\in D} 1 \tag{1}$$

where *D* is a multiset of conversations (u_1, u_2), and u_1 and u_2 are poster and replier in the conversation.

Feature S_2 considers how often user u_1 posts messages.

$$S_2(u_1, u_2) = \frac{S_1(u_1,u_2)}{(end-start)\sum_{(u_1,replier)\in D} 1} \tag{2}$$

Where *start* and *end* denote the starting day and the ending day of the interaction between user u_1 and u_2. Here S_2 equals to S_1 divided by the frequency of posts by poster u_1.

We also consider how often a replier posts a reply. S_3 defined as follows captures this idea.

$$S_3(u_1, u_2) = \frac{S_1(u_1,u_2)}{(end-start)\sum_{(poster,u_2)\in D} 1} \tag{3}$$

5.3 User Behavior (*B*)

Individual user behavior is another feature. It models the subjective tendency of a user. The history of a specific replier shows which emotions he tends to express often. B_{-int} defines the negative tendency of user *u*.

$$B_{-int}(u) = \frac{C(E(u)=0)}{C(E(u)=0)+C(E(u)=1)} \tag{4}$$

where *u* is a replier, *E*(*u*) is the replier's emotion with a value 0 (negative) or 1 (positive). *C* is the frequency of $E(u)$. This indicator does not take the interaction with posters into account.

We also consider how often he expresses his positive emotion to a specific poster. This feature is called interactive behavior (B_{+int}) and is defined as follows.

$$B_{+int}(u) = \frac{C(E(u)=1)}{\sum_{(poster,u)\in D} 1} \tag{5}$$

In some cases, replier's behavior history is not available. We use back-off smoothing to deal with this issue. Interactive user behavior after smoothing (B_s) is defined as:

$$B_s\big(E(rp) = e \big| \mathrm{T}(pt)\big) = \begin{cases} P(E(rp) = e|pt = u) & \text{if } \sum_{e\in EM,} C(E(rp) = e, pt = u) > K_1 \\ P(E(rp) = e) & \text{if } \sum_{e\in EM,} C(E(rp) = e) > K_2 \\ P(E(RP) = e) & \text{otherwise} \end{cases} \tag{6}$$

where *rp* is a replier, *pt* is a poster, and *RP* is a set of all repliers. We set K_1 and K_2 to 1 in the experiments.

5.4 Relevance Degree (*R*)

Although a post and its reply are in the same conversation, they are not necessarily on the same topic or fully related to each other. This may affect the use of emoticons, so we also deal with relevance degree. *R*(*T*(*pt*), *T*(*rp*)) is defined as follows:

$$R(T(pt), T(rp)) = \begin{cases} 1 & \text{if there exists an anaphoric element in } T(rp) \\ 0.5 + \dfrac{\text{total overlapped bigrams in } T(pt) \text{and } T(rp)}{\text{total bigrams in } T(pt)} & \text{otherwise} \end{cases} \tag{7}$$

If there exists an anaphoric element or a conjunction in replier's message, then we say the conversation is related and assign relevance degree to 1. Nine anaphoric elements and 43 conjunctions are adopted. Otherwise, we check if the post and the reply overlap. More overlapped words mean more related. We assume the post and the reply have some basic relationship, so that the default relevance degree is set to 0.5. In current design, although the relevance degree is measured based on some linguistic markers, we still call it a non-linguistic feature for comparison with Text feature.

5.5 Normalization

The size of the linguistic feature set is much larger than the three non-linguistic feature sets, so we apply the following vector normalization method to deal with the issue:

$$F = (f_1, f_2, f_3, \dots, f_n) \quad (8)$$

$$NF = (nf_1, nf_2, nf_3, \dots, nf_n) \quad (9)$$

$$nf_i = \frac{f_i}{\sqrt{f_1^2 + f_2^2 + f_3^2 + \dots + f_n^2}} \quad (10)$$

F is a vector representing a feature set with n features $f_1, f_2, f_3, \dots, f_n$. To get the normalized F, each f value is divided by the length of F. Thus, we have the normalized F, which is defined as NF above, with features $nf_1, nf_2, nf_3, \dots, nf_n$.

6 Results and Discussion

Classifiers were trained and tested with 10-fold cross-validation. In this section, the results of the models from the three perspectives are shown and discussed.

6.1 Text Features (T)

T	Reader model	80.67%
	Writer model	**88.75%**
	Reader+Writer model	88.71%
S		82.78%
B_{-int}		84.14%
B_{+int}		86.25%
B_s		86.93%
R		81.53%

Table 1. Accuracy of different feature sets

First, we use an individual feature set at a time to compare their performance. The linguistic feature set (T) is used to model replier's emotion generation from three different perspectives. When performing the prediction task with the reader model and the writer model, 3,000 bigrams from either poster's or replier's messages were used, respectively. For performing the task with the reader + writer model, all the bigrams from both the reader and writer models were used, for a total of 6,000 features.

Table 1 shows that the writer model and the reader+writer model achieved much higher performance than the reader model. The performance of the writer model is slightly higher than that of the reader+writer model, but the t-test shows that the difference is insignificant. The performance of the writer model and the reader+writer model is higher than the baseline (84.23%), while the performance of the reader model is lower than that of the baseline.

Interactive user behavior (B_{+int}) outperformed non-interactive user behavior (B_{-int}), and achieved performance (86.25%) higher than the baseline. After applying back-off smoothing, the interactive user behavior (B_s) proved to achieve even higher performance (86.93%), which is the best among all non-linguistic feature sets.

Social relation (S) and relevance degree (R) performed lower than the baseline, with relevance degree (R) performing the worst. Most replies should be related to their posts since they are in a conversation, and because participants are usually friends. However, 85.27% of conversations have a relevance degree of 0.5, the lowest value, which means there were not anaphoric elements, conjunctions, and overlaps. Relevance is not easy to be measured accurately between two short messages. In summary, when each of the non-linguistic feature sets is used individually, the following results are seen: $B_s > B_{+int} > B_{-int} > S > R$. For the behavior feature set, back-off smoothing is useful. In addition, the behavior pattern in response to a specific poster is more useful than to all posters, suggesting that the affective interaction between two given users may be based on a certain pattern.

6.2 Combination of Feature Sets

Experimentation with some combinations of different feature sets was also conducted. Table 2 shows the results of these combinations, from reader, writer, or reader and writer perspectives. Writer models still outperformed reader models, and are slightly better than reader+writer models for all feature combinations except for the SVM model with the $T + B_s + S$ combination.

When combined with textual features, the behavioral feature set was still more powerful than social relation and relevance degree. However, all these 3 feature sets are helpful since paired t-tests show that the differences between T and $T + B_s$, T and $T + S$, and T and $T + R$ to be significant ($p < 0.05$).

	Reader Models	Writer Models	Reader + Writer Models
T	80.67%	88.75%	88.71%
$T+S$	83.42%	89.60%	89.26%
$T+B_s$	88.02%	91.42%	91.16%
$T+R$	82.73%	89.14%	88.93%
$T+B_s+R$	88.14%	91.48%	91.27%
$T+B_s+S$	**88.42%**	**91.60%**	**91.61%**
$T+B_s+S+R$	88.37%	91.53%	91.30%

Table 2. Accuracy of models with different feature set combinations

Because B_s is most useful when used with textual features, $T+B_s$ with $T+B_s+S$ and $T+B_s+R$ were compared to see how S and R can improve performance. For the reader models with SVM, the difference between $T+B_s$ and $T+B_s+S$ was significant ($p < 0.05$), but the difference between $T+B_s$ and $T+B_s+R$ was insignificant. This shows that $T+B_s+S$ is a more useful combination than $T+B_s+R$. For writer and reader + writer models, $T+B_s+S$ still outperformed $T+B_s+R$.

Although each of the 3 non-linguistic features can improve performance, combining all of them ($T+B_s+S+R$) does not achieve the highest performance. The highest performance is achieved by the combination of $T+B_s+S$, regardless of which perspective is used. According to results from the paired t-test, the difference between $T+B_s+S+R$ and $T+B_s+S$ is insignificant for the reader model and the writer model. This shows that that although adding R to the combination does not decrease the performance significantly, it is also not helpful. The reasons for this may be the following: both social relation and interactive behavior are related to interaction between two specific users, so their effects may overlap; only 14.73% of conversations have a relevance value higher than 0.5.

6.3 Different Perspectives

For all feature set combinations, the writer models and the reader+writer models achieve better performance than the reader models. These differences are significant according to the paired t-tests, which suggests that for predicting a replier's emotion, the message generated by the replier him- or herself contains more useful information than the message generated by the poster and then read by the replier.

When using the textual feature set only, the reader model's SVM performance (80.67%) was much lower than the writer model's (88.75%) and that of the reader+writer model (88.71%). When T is used with B_s and S, in contrast, the SVM performance of the reader model is 88.42%, only slightly lower than the performance of the writer model (91.60%) and the reader+writer mode (91.61%). This indicates that when modeling emotion generation on a social network, non-linguistic features play more important roles.

The performance of textual feature set for the writer model with SVM is 88.75%, slightly higher than that for the reader+writer model (88.71%). According to results of the paired t-test, the difference between them is insignificant. For the $T+B_s+S$ combination, the performance of the reader+writer model (91.61%) is slightly higher than the performance of the writer model (91.60%), though the difference is also insignificant. Thus, it makes little difference in performance whether emotion generation is modeled from writer perspective or both reader and writer perspectives. In this series of experiments, 91.61% was the highest accuracy achieved.

6.4 Writer Model

As mentioned in the Section 4, another kind of writer model exists, for which the content is written by the poster, of which was also included as experiment with poster's writer model. In this case, only the linguistic feature set can be used. Results seen included an accuracy of 89.19%. Results of t-test for the posters' and repliers' writer model showed the difference as insignificant ($p<0.082$). However, it is important to note that the dataset used for the posters' writer model differs from the one used for the repliers' writer model, so this comparison is for reference only.

7 Conclusion

To better model emotion generation on a microblogging platform with social network characteristics, different models from the reader and/or writer perspectives were included in the experiment, and showed their differences. Discoveries included that predicting emotion from the reader perspective is more challenging than from the writer perspective. In addition, using non-linguistic features with linguistic features for emotion prediction resulted in discovering that each of the non-linguistic feature sets is useful.

In this study, the combination of all feature sets did not achieve the best performance. In future work, the weights and combination methods of different feature sets will need to be further studied. Additional efforts will also be needed to precisely represent the characteristics of user interaction and message contents. The relevance degree used in this study, for example, deals with only anaphoric elements, conjunctions, and overlapped bigrams in this study. Other factors and resources also will be needed to more effectively determine the relevance of two messages.

As this paper suggests, a writer model is different from a reader model. The same bigrams or words can have different effects on writers' and readers' emotional expression. For example, greetings can cause a positive reader response even if the writer uses a negative emoticon and shows some negative feelings. Thus, these findings suggest that reader emotion be further explored in future studies.

The models presented in this paper are useful for a wide range of applications, especially those related to conversation and interaction between humans and machines. They can also help improve the performance of automated customer service and writing assistance systems, in which readers' emotional responses are important. Different types of features can be used for different application domains. The behavioral feature, for example, can be used when a user's conversation history is available.

References

C. Becker; S. Kopp; and I. Wachsmuth. 2004. Simulating the Emotion Dynamics of a Multimodal Conversational Agent. In *Proceedings of Tutorial and Research Workshop on Affective Dialogue Systems,* 154-165.

R. Bernhaupt; A. Boldt; T. Mirlacher; D. Wilfinger; and M. Tscheligi. 2007. Using Emotion in Games: Emotional Flowers. In *Proceedings of the International Conference on Advances in Computer Entertainment Technology,* 41-48.

C.C. Chang and C.J. Lin. 2001. LIBSVM: a Library for Support Vector Machines. Software available at http://www.csie.ntu.edu.tw/~cjlin/libsvm.

N. Gupta; M. Gilbert; and G.D. Fabbrizio. 2010. Emotion Detection in Email Customer Care. In *Proceedings of the NAACL HLT 2010 Workshop on Computational Approaches to Analysis and Generation of Emotion in Text,* 10-16.

A. Go; L. Huang; and R. Bhayani. 2009. *Twitter Sentiment Classification Using Distant Supervision.* CS224N Project Report, Stanford University, Stanford, CA.

Y. Jung; Y. Choi; and S.H. Myaeng. 2007. Determining Mood for a Blog by Combining Multiple Sources of Evidence. In *Proceedings of International Conference on Web Intelligence.* 271-274.

H.Y. Lin and H.H. Chen. 2008. Ranking Reader Emotions Using Pairwise Loss Minimization and Emotional Distribution Regression. In *Proceedings of Conference on Empirical Methods in Natural Language Processing,* 136-144.

H.Y. Lin; C.H. Yang; and H.H. Chen. 2007. What Emotions Do News Articles Trigger in Their Readers? In *Proceedings of 30th Annual International ACM SIGIR Conference,* 733-734.

H.Y. Lin; C.H. Yang; and H.H. Chen. 2008. Emotion Classification of Online News Articles from the Reader's Perspective. In *Proceedings of International Conference on Web Intelligence,* 220-226.

Y. Liu; X. Huang; A. An; and X. Yu. 2007. ARSA: A Sentiment-Aware Model for Predicting Sales Performance Using Blogs. In *Proceedings of the 30th Annual International ACM SIGIR Conference,* 607-614.

G. Mishne. 2005. Experiments with Mood Classification in Blog Posts. In *Proceedings of the 1st Workshop on Stylistic Analysis of Text for Information Access*, Salvador, Brazil.

G. Mishne and M. De Rijke. 2006. Capturing Global Mood Levels Using Blog Posts. In *Proceedings of AAAI 2006 Spring Symposium on Computational Approaches to Analysing Weblogs,* 145-152.

Y.T. Sun; C.L. Chen; C.C. Liu; C.L. Liu; and V.W. Soo. 2010. Sentiment Classification of Short Chinese Sentences. In *Proceedings of 22nd Conference on Computational Linguistics and Speech Processing,* Nantou, Taiwan, 184-198.

C. Strapparava and R. Mihalcea. 2007. Affective Text. In *Proceedings of the 4th International Workshop on Semantic Evaluations*, 70–74.

C.H. Yang; H.Y. Lin; and H.H. Chen. 2007a. Building Emotion Lexicon from Weblog Corpora. In *Proceedings of 45th Annual Meeting of Association for Computational Linguistics*, 133-136.

C.H. Yang; H.Y. Lin; and H.H. Chen. 2007b. Emotion Classification Using Web Blog Corpora. In *Proceedings of 2007 IEEE/WIC/ACM International Conference on Web Intelligence,* 275-278.

C.H. Yang; H.Y. Lin; and H.H. Chen. 2008. Sentiment Analysis in Weblog Using Contextual Information: A Machine Learning Approach. *International Journal of Computer Processing of Languages* 21(4): 331–345.

C.H. Yang; H.Y. Lin; and H.H. Chen. 2009. Writer Meets Reader: Emotion Analysis of Social Media from both the Writer's and Reader's Perspectives. In *Proceedings of International Conference on Web Intelligence,* 287-290.

Towards automatic detection of antisocial behavior from texts

Myriam Munezero
School of Computing
University of Eastern Finland
mmunez@cs.joensuu.fi

Tuomo Kakkonen
School of Computing
University of Eastern Finland
tuomo.kakkonen@uef.fi

Calkin S. Montero
School of Computing
University of Eastern Finland
calkinm@gmail.com

Abstract

The automatic analysis of emotional content of text has become pervasive and has been applied in many fields of research. The work reported in this paper is in particular interested in modeling antisocial behavior and the emotional states that define it. We introduce the *antisocial behavior detection* (ASBD) model for portraying the emotions pertaining to antisocial behavior. In addition to describing negative affective states, our model uses the concepts of action tendencies and evidences in order to predict possible acts of antisocial behavior based on input texts. We outline a design for an antisocial behavior detection system based on the ASBD model.

1 Introduction

Emotions connect individuals to the social world and, hence, are the triggers of many social psychological phenomena, such as altruism, antisocial behavior, and aggression (Parrot, 2001). To be able to identify and classify a behavior, one has to understand the behavior itself and the emotional states (e.g. happiness, sadness and anger) that pertain to it. This paper focuses on modeling the emotional states that characterize antisocial behavior.

We define antisocial behavior as any unconsidered action against others that may cause harm or distress to society. Antisocial behavior has been linked to disruptive and impulsive behaviors, bullying, and in extreme cases, school shootings (Flory et al, 2007; Sutton et al, 1999; Borum et al, 2010).

Upon reviewing the available data about extreme antisocial behavior, O'Toole (2000) reported that often the individuals involved have disclosed in advance their plans orally or in written form. In particular, the Internet has been used as the outlet for the expression of their emotional states through the use of blogs or video sites (Crowley, 2007). In many cases these troubled people have written and publicly distributed documents over the web in the form of manifestos as a way of shouting out their intentions before engaging in their acts of violence (Web search, Dec 2010). Interestingly, little research has been done regarding the automatic analysis of the media in order to warn the pertinent authorities of the threat.

The aim of our research is the automatic analysis of texts in order to uncover emotions and possible behavioral traits related to antisocial behavior. By analyzing and identifying these specific traits in writings we seek to determine hints of antisocial behavior while the possible acts of violence that may follow are still in their planning stages.

As a cornerstone, this paper introduces our proposed model of emotions for the detection of antisocial behavior from text sources. Section 2 reviews the related previous and ongoing research on antisocial behavior and briefly introduces the circumplex model of emotions. Section 3 outlines our proposed model of emotions and its connection to antisocial behavior. Design of a system for detecting antisocial behavior based on the ASBD model is outlined in Section 4. Conclusions and directions for future work are given in Section 5.

2 Background Work

2.1 Research on antisocial behavior and associated emotions

Antisocial behavior has been substantially researched in the fields of psychology and education (Borum et al, 2010). It can manifest itself or be expressed in different ways; it can range from aggression to verbal abuse, from conduct disord-

Proceedings of the Workshop on Sentiment Analysis where AI meets Psychology (SAAIP), IJCNLP 2011, pages 20–27, *Chiang Mai, Thailand, November 13, 2011.*

er to delinquencies (Foster, 2005). In our work we are interested in the emotional traits of antisocial behavior that can be perceived linguistically in people's writings.

Notably, aggression is the behavioral state that is most directly associated with antisocial behavior (Clarke, 2003). Other types of behavioral states also associated with antisocial behavior include violence, hostility, and lack of empathy. Behavioral states in this paper are considered as a result of emotions. For example, hostile and aggressive inclinations are a result of depression and anger (Parrot, 2001).

Antisocial behavior has also been linked to several negative emotions. Some of these emotions include anger, frustration, arrogance, shame, anxiety, depression, sadness, low levels of fear, and lack of guilt (Cohen, 2005). Many of these emotions have been shown detectable in writings (Gill et al, 2008).

2.2 Previous work on automatic detection of antisocial behavior

Sentiment analysis and opinion mining are established areas of study within the NLP research community and both have received a raising amount of attention over the last decade. Although negative emotions like anger and sadness have been identified in writings, the detection of antisocial behavior from text per se is a new area of research interest. The analyses of texts written by terrorist groups and the automatic detection of criminal behavior have received some attention from the NLP community. While terrorism and crime might be regarded as extreme forms of antisocial behavior, they form a rather narrow sub-part of the whole issue we are dealing with in this work. Nonetheless, as no previous general models for detecting antisocial behavior from text exist, we provide an overview of the work done in the context of terrorism and criminal behavior since they are also a result of negative emotions.

Perhaps the most notable related work is carried out in a research project entitled "Intelligent information system supporting observation, searching and detection for security of citizens in urban environment" (INDECT) (The INDECT consortium, 2009). The project aims at "automatic detection of terroristic threats and recognition of serious criminal ("abnormal") behavior or violence" based on multi-media content. Within context of INDECT, such abnormal behavior is defined as "criminal behavior", and specifically as "behavior related to terrorist acts, serious criminal activities or criminal activities in the Internet".

The work presented in this article differs from the one done in the INDECT project in the focus of the research. While INDECT aims at using the analysis of images and video to text, our focus is on the analysis of text data.

2.3 Circumplex model

While most of the work on sentiment analysis has been done based on the theories of basic emotions, our work however starts from a different view - the circumplex model. Whereas the basic emotions based models (e.g. Ekman, 1992) divide all human emotions into a limited set of discrete and independent categories (such as fear, anger), the circumplex model, first proposed by Russell (1980), asserts that emotions can be characterized in a two-dimensional space: pleasure-displeasure and arousal-sleep. In this model, emotions are seen as a linear combination of the two dimensions rather than judged belonging or not belonging into a specific basic emotion category. This allows for a "fuzzy" characterization of emotions.

Posner et al. (2005), for example, stated that the fact that people have difficulties in assessing their own emotions implies that "individuals do not experience, or recognize, emotions as isolated, discrete entities, but that they rather recognize emotions as ambiguous and overlapping experiences". The circumplex model provides a starting point for the development of our model of emotions. For a full description of the circumplex model see (Russell, 1980; Posner et al, 2005).

3 Model for Detection of Antisocial Behavior from Texts

Based on the relevant literature on antisocial behavior (see Section 2), we developed the ASBD model (Figure 1) that takes into consideration *negative emotional states* (Section 3.1), *action tendencies* (Section 3.2) and *evidence* (Section 3.3) that may lead into those *behavioral states* that are associated with antisocial behavior.

3.1 Circumplex-based model of emotions related to antisocial behavior

The left-hand side of our model, shown in Figure 1, illustrates 14 interplaying emotions (not an exhaustive list) that may lead to antisocial behavior. These discrete emotions are seen in a two dimensional space within the unpleasantness and

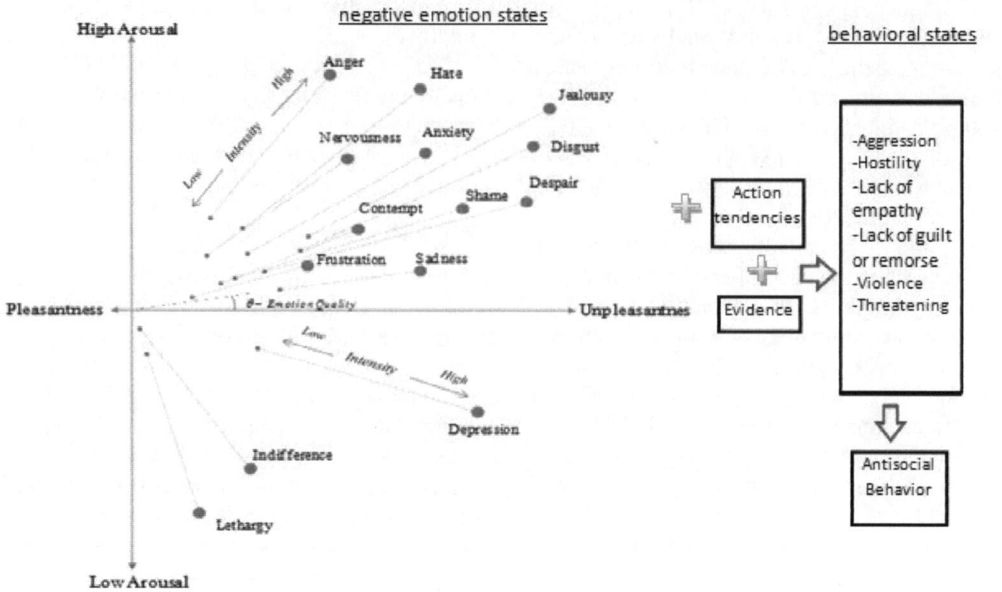

Figure 1. Model of antisocial behavior

arousal dimensions. As previously stated, this spatial representation has been adopted from Russell's 1980) circumplex model of emotions. In our proposed model, each emotion type is placed within the two dimensional space according to its subjective proportion of unpleasantness and arousal as given by Reisenzein (1994) and Russell (1980).

The proportion of unpleasantness and arousal of a specific emotion determines its *emotion quality,* which is represented by the angle between the emotion type and the unpleasantness axis. The conceptual *emotion intensities* used in our model are taken from the works of Reisenzein (1994). Reisenzein demonstrated that the intensity of an emotion can be represented by the distance from a subjective neutral point (hedonic neutrality and medium arousal level) to a point in the space symbolizing that emotion. The subjective neutral point of the space corresponds to a neutral emotional state; a state in which there is no emotion present. The minimum intensity for an emotion (denoted in Figure 1 by a small dot along the line towards the neutral point) is the neutral state for that particular emotion.

3.2 Connecting emotions to behaviors

While the way in which emotions and behaviors are connected has been heavily debated in psychological and social science literature (see, for example Green, 1970; Lyons, 1978; Baumeister et al, 2009) there does not, however, appear to be a lack of consensus that such a connection exists.

Table 1. Emotions and associated behaviors

Emotion	Associated behavior	Source
hurt feelings, shame leading to rise of anger	Aggression and conflict escalation	Maiese, 2005
anger, resentment, hatred	Give rise to cycle of violence	
feeling agitated, angry, fearful	"…cause disputes to escalate and sometimes even cause negotiations to break down."	
chronic anger	Endorsement of aggressive solutions, and identification with delinquent peers".	Granic and Butler, 1998
anger	Provides sufficient impetus for the formation of the intention to correct what is perceived as a problem.	Cho and Walton, 2009
frustration	Increased aggression	Verona and Curtin, 2006 Clarke, 2003

Regardless of the precise way in which the connection between emotion and behavior occurs in the human brain, in our model we adopt the notion of emotions as influencing or participating in shaping the mind's processes, including those which activate behavior (Russell, 2003).

What can be concluded based on Table 1 is that emotions do influence the motivational state of a person to carry out an action or behavior. We use the notions of action tendency and evidence to model this connection.

Action Tendency

In order to link the emotion to a possible action outcome, the ASBD model supplements the circumplex representation of emotions with Frijda's (1986) concept of *action tendencies* (ATs).

Frijda (1986)' emotion theory associates emotions to a small set of action tendencies (see Table 2.), which are defined as "states of readiness to execute a given kind of action [which] is defined by its end result aimed at or achieved". For example, in the case of negative emotions, reaching the corresponding end state should mitigate its experience (e.g., anger subsides once one believes the object of one's anger has been removed) Frijda (1986). Table 2, provides some examples of ATs.

Table 2, tells us that, for example, in the case of anger, a person is in a "state of readiness" to remove their obstruction. However, ATs should not be mistaken for intentions, while intensions are goal-directed, ATs are stimulus driven (Frijda, 1986). Hence, a person's intentions or manner in which they are planning to carry out the action is only revealed to us through additional information (evidence) in the text.

Emotion	Function	Action tendency	End state
desire	consume	approach	access
anxiety	caution	inhibition	absence of response
anger	control	agonistic	obstruction removed
fear	protection	avoidance	own inaccessibility
disgust	protection	rejecting	object removed

Table 2. Classification of some action tendencies. Adapted from Frijda (1986) (p.88)

Evidence

In addition to using the concept of ATs, we draw from Green's (1970) concept of *evidence* to describe indications of antisocial behavior linked to negative emotions. Green describes evidence as the actions or reactions that a person ordinarily carries out or has when they experience a particular emotion within "appropriate circumstances". Thus, instead of directly connecting antisocial behavior to specific negative emotions we describe those behaviors that a certain emotion might evoke under specific conditions: 'B is the behavior a person is likely to engage in when, among other things, they feel emotion E in C circumstances'.

While various types of circumstances leading to anti-social behavior have been suggested (see for instance the references given in Table 1), we do not believe that it is possible to reliably detect all of them based on a piece of text. Taking Maiese (2005) as an example, she suggests that being angry and fearful may cause disputes to escalate when "a person feels that their interests are threatened". It would be impossible to make judgments about such a condition without having access to detailed information about the situation the author is facing. Such background information is almost impossible to obtain based solely on analyzing few text fragments written by an author.

Thus we confine ourselves to a subset of these circumstances in which we believe we can obtain from text fragments and user profiles. The subset, though not exhaustive includes the following:

- Age: Moffitt (1993) has noted that antisocial behavior is almost ten times more common among adolescents than other age groups.
- Gender: It is commonly accepted that males are more prone to extreme forms of antisocial behavior, such as violence, delinquency and physical aggression (Björkqvist et al, 1992).
- Presence of frustration: Research has revealed a strong link between frustration and antisocial behavior, showing that frustration can lead to extreme manifestations of antisocial behavior such as aggression (Clerk, 2005).

In addition, we expand this concept of evidence to include keywords, such as 'kill', shoot', 'gun', abuse', etc, that are commonly expressed by people exhibiting violent and antisocial behavior.

4 Design of an antisocial behavior detection system based on the proposed model

The ASBD model serves as the backbone for the design of an antisocial behavior system. The system will function as follows. When it receives an input text, it first detects the emotions (quality and intensity) in the text. Next, it resolves the ATs corresponding to each detected emotion. Thirdly, the system identifies the available evidence (both in the input text and from external sources, for instance, user profiles). Finally, the system uses all the collected information to predict the behavioral state connected with the input. Figure 2 illustrates the system design.

As shown in Figure 2, the system consists of three components. The Emotor component combines the circumplex-based model for detecting emotions along with their corresponding ATs.

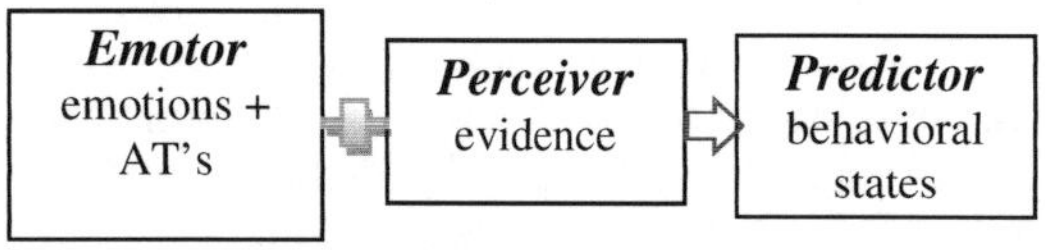

Figure 2. Architecture of an antisocial behavior detection system based on the ASBD model. Adapted from (Frijda and Moffat, 1994)

The Perceiver component collects the pieces of evidence from the input document and other sources. The Predictor component finally combines the information collected by the Emotor and Perceiver in order to predict which behavioral state associated to antisocial behavior might occur.

Figure 3 gives an example of the process of detecting potential anti-social behavior with the proposed system. As illustrated in Figure 3, the Emotor component first automatically detects and analyses the emotion qualities and intensities present in the two input sentences (*s1* and *s2*) based on the circumplex model. It makes use of a supervised classification algorithm developed through a human-annotated corpus to resolve the emotion quality and intensity. Thus s*1* is resolved to be near the emotion 'disgust' and *s2* near the emotion 'anger'. The Emotor component then identifies the ATs connected to these two emotions. s*1* is defined to have the AT 'rejecting' and *s2* 'agonistic' (see Table 2).

The Perceiver collects sets of evidence, such as the writer's gender and age if they are available in the text or the user profile. In addition, it is able to detect the keywords related to various forms of antisocial behavior such as violence, racism and crime. To that end, we are developing an ontology and an ontology-based information extraction tool. The antisocial behavior, conflict and violence (ABCV) ontology currently consists of a 19-class classification system for terms related to antisocial behavior and is capable of detecting a total of 340 terms related to these classes. The predictor finally collects the analysis results from the Emotor and Perceiver, and based on a statistical classification algorithm, it resolves that *s1* could indicate potential hostile behavior and *s2* is showing signs of threatening behavior.

4.1 Data model

A key design issue related to the implementation of the proposed system architecture was the data model. Our main aim was to come up with an extensible data model that is based on a standard. We therefore opted for the *EmotionML* (Emotion Mark-up Language) that was recently introduced by W3C as a working draft standard for representing emotions in text (Baggia et al, 2011).

EmotionML is an XML-based mark-up language that provides a standard interface between components. It defines a set of vocabularies for representing emotion-related states (Schröder and Pelachaud, 2011). EmotionML comes with the vocabulary definition for Frijda's (1986) ATs. This pre-defined set, however, does not support the circumplex-based representation of emotions. EmotionML is flexible enough to allow us to define our own vocabularies depending on the needs of our model and system.

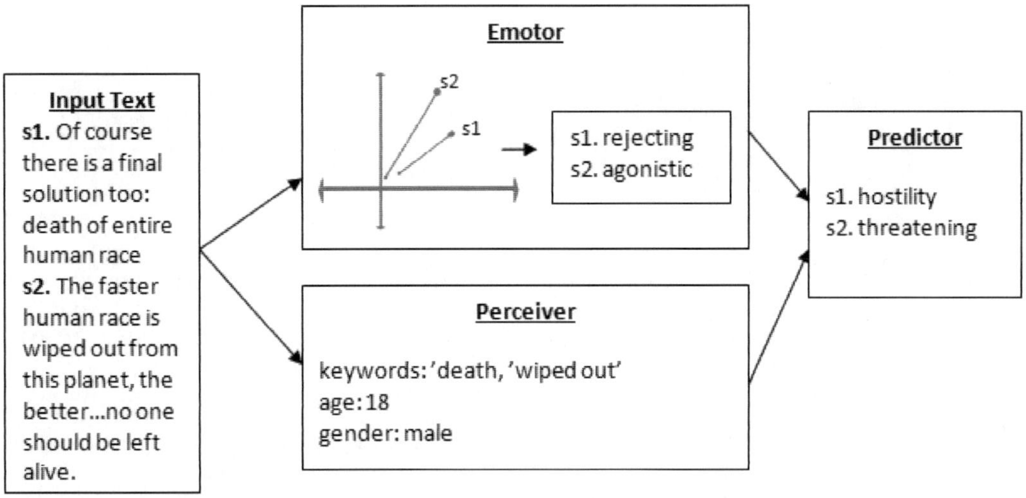

Figure 3. Example of antisocial behavior detection process. s1 and s2 are two sample input sentences. Example sentences cited from (OddCulture, 2011).

4.2 Vocabulary definition of emotions and action tendencies

As the Emotor component is representing emotions the circumplex-based model, we need to define a new vocabulary in accordance to the structure of EmotionML. As described above, our emotional model has two values for representing an emotion: quality and intensity. These can be defined in EmotionML as follows:

<vocabulary type = "dimension"
id="cplex">
<item name="quality" />
<item name="intensity" />
</vocabulary>

Let us assume that we want to describe the emotion 'anger' which has an emotion quality of 81 degrees (when taking the unpleasant axis as 0degrees) and an intensity value of 0.5. The definition for 'anger' would appear in an EmotionML document inside <emotion> tags as:

<emotion dimension-set="#cplex">
<dimension name = "quality"
val ue="81degrees"/>
<dimension name = "intensity"
value = "0.5"/>
</emotion>

In addition, the Emotor module annotates the text with the available default set of ATs. The AT for the emotion 'anger' would appear in an EmotionML document as (Ashimura et al, 2011):

<emotion dimension-set="#cplex" action-tendency-set="#frijda-subset">
<dimension name = "quality"
value="81degrees"/>
<dimension name = "intensity"
value = "0.5"/>
<action-tendency name="agonistic"
value="0.9"/>
</emotion>

Furthermore, in our XML-based document representation, the Perceptor module annotates the evidence in the text with <evidence> tags.

Vocabulary definition for behavioral states

Whenever the Predictor component receives information from the Emotor and Perceiver component, it analyses and computes the value of a behavioral state. The Predictor component also outputs in EmotionML format. The vocabulary of the behavioral states is defined as follows:

<vocabulary type="behavior-state"
id="antisocial-subset">
<item name="violence"/>
<item name="aggression"/>
<item name="hostility"/>
<item name="threats"/>
</vocabulary>

Let us consider an example:

<emotion behavior-state="#antisocial-subset ">
< behavior-state name = "violence" value="0.3"/>
< behavior-state name = aggression" value = "0.5"/>
</emotion>

In addition to the above representations, EmotionML allows us to provide reference information regarding the resolved behavior. For example, if the behavior resolved is 'hostility' we can reference the following values:

- Who expressed the behavior (experiencedBy)
- To whom the behavior is directed at (targetedAt).

The <reference> element may occur as a child of the <emotion> element (Baggia et al, 2011).

5 Conclusion and Future Work

We have reviewed the previous research work on antisocial behavior, its defining emotions and automatic detection from texts. We also proposed ASBD, a combined model of negative affect states, ATs, evidence and behavioral states that have been shown to lead to antisocial behavior.

In addition, the paper outlined the architecture of antisocial behavior detection system based on the ASBD model. The system design consists of three modules that communicate with each other using the standard EmotionML markup language. We defined new EmotionML vocabulary sets which pertain to the purpose of our system.

Our future work involves the implementation of the outlined system. The next steps in this work include collecting and annotating a corpus with the proposed annotations and running sentiment detection experiments by applying the circumplex model.

Acknowledgments

This work was supported by the "Detecting and visualizing emotions and their changes in text" project, funded by the Academy of Finland.

References

Kazuyuki Ashimura, Paolo Baggia, Felix Burkhardt, Alessandro Oltramari, Christian Peter, and Enrico Zovato. 2011. Vocabularies for EmotionML. W3C Working Draft 7 April 2011. [Cited: 01.06.2011] www.w3.org/TR/2011/WD-emotion-voc-20110407/

Paolo Baggia, Felix Burkhardt, Catherine Pelachaud, Christian Peter and Enrico Zovato. 2011. Emotion Markup Language (EmotionML) 1.0. W3C Working Draft 7 April 2011. [Cited: 01.06.2011] www.w3.org/TR/2011/WD-emotionml-20110407/

Roy F. Baumeister, Nathan C. DeWall, Kathleen D. Vohs and Jessica L. Alquist. 2009. Does Emotion Cause Behavior (Apart from Making People Do Stupid, Destructive Things)? In Christopher R. Agnew, Donald E. Carlston, William G. Graziano, and Janice R. Kelly (eds.). *Then a Miracle Occurs: Focusing on Behavior in Social Psychological Theory and Research.* 119-137. Oxford University Press, New York, USA.

Kaj Björkqvist, Kirsti M. J. Lagerspetz and Ari Kaukiainen. 1992. Do Girls Manipulate and Boys Fight? Developmental Trends in Regard to Direct and Indirect Aggression. *Aggressive Behavior*, 18(2):117-127.

Randy Borum, Dewey G. Cornell, William Modzeleski and Shane R. Jimerson. 2010. What Can Be Done About School Shooting? *A Review of the Evidence. Educational Researcher*, 39(1):27-37.

Seungho Cho and Laura R. Walton. 2009. Integrating Emotion and the Theory of Planned Behavior to Explain Consumers' Activism in the Internet. *Institute for Public Relations*, Gainesville, Florida, USA.

David Clarke. 2003. *Pro-social and Anti-social Behavior.* Routledge. New York, USA.

Lisa J. Cohen. 2005. Neurobiology of Antisociality In: C. Stough. (ed.). *Neurobiology of Exceptionality.* Kluver Academic/Plenum Publishers, New York, USA. 107-124.

Sean Crowley. 2007. Finland Shocked at Fatal Shooting. BBC News. [Cited: 10.12.2010] http://news.bbc.co.uk/1/hi/world/europe/7084045.stm

Paul Ekman. 1992. An Argument for Basic Emotions. *Cognition and Emotion*, 6:169-200.

Janine D. Flory, Jeffrey H. Newcorn, Carlin Miller, Seth Harty and Jeffrey M. Halperin. 2007. Serotonergic Function in Children with Attention-Deficit Hyperactivity Disorder: Relationship to Later Antisocial Personality Disorder. *The British Journal of Psychiatry*. 190:410-414.

Sharon L. Foster. 2005, Aggression and Antisocial Behavior in Girls. In Debora Bell, Sharon L. Foster, Eric J. Mash (eds). *Handbook of Behavioral and Emotional Problems in Girls. Issues on Clinical Child Psychology.* Springer, New York, USA. 149-180.

Nico H. Frijda. 1986. *The emotions. Studies in emotion and social interaction.* Cambridge University Press, Cambridge, UK.

Nico H. Frijda, David Moffat. 1994. Modeling emotion. *Cognitive Studies*, 1(2):5-15.

Alastair J. Gill, Robert M. French, Darren Gergle and Jon Oberlander. 2008. The Language of Emotion in Short Blog Texts. *Proceedings of the 2008 ACM Conference on Computer Supported Cooperative Work*. ACM, New York, USA. 299-302.

Isabela Granic and Stephen Butler. 1998. The Relation Between Anger And Antisocial Beliefs In Young Offenders. *Personal Individual Difference*. 24(6):759-765.

Harvey O. Green. 1970. The Expression of Emotion. *Mind*, 79(316):551-568.

William E. Lyons. 1978. Emotions and Behavior. *Philosophy and Phenomenological Research*. 38(3):410-418.

Michelle Maiese. 2005. "Emotions." Beyond Intractability. In Guy Burgess and Heidi Burgess (eds.). *Conflict Research Consortium*, University of Colorado, Boulder.

Terrie E. Moffitt. 1993. Antisocial Behavior: A Developmental Taxonomy. *Psychological Review*, 100(4): 674-701.

OddCulture. The Pekka Eric Auvinen Manifesto. [Cited: 02.06.2011] www.oddculture/weird-news-stories/the-pekka-eric-auvinen-manifesto/

Marry Ellen O'Toole. 2000. School Shooter: A Threat Assessment Perspective. National Center for the Analysis of Violent Crime, Federal Bureau of Investigation, Quantico, Virginia, USA.

Gerrot W. Parrot. 2001. *Emotions in Social Psychology*. Taylor & Francis. Philadelphia, Pennsylvania, USA.

Jonathan Posner, James A. Russell and Bradley S. Peterson. 2005. The Circumplex Model of Affect: An Integrative Approaches to Affective Neuroscience, Cognitive Development and Psychopathology. *Development and Psychopathology*. 17:715-734.

Rainer Reisenzein. 1994. Pleasure-Arousal Theory and the Intensity of Emotions. *Journal of Personality and Social Psychology*, 67(3):525-539.

James A. Russell. 1980. A Circumplex Model of Affect. *Personal and Social Psychology*. 39(6):1161-1178.

James A. Russell. 2003. Core Affect and the Psychological Construction of Emotion. *Psychological Review*. 110(1):145-172.

Jon Sutton, Peter K. Smith and John Swettenham. 1999. Social Cognition and Bullying: Social Inadequacy or Skilled Manipulation? *British Journal of Developmental Psychology*, 17: 435-450.

The INDECT Consortium. 2009. XML Data Corpus: Report on Methodology for Collection, Cleaning and Unified Representation of Large Textual Data from Various Sources: News Reports, Weblogs, Chat. [Cited: 10.12.2010] http://www.indect-project.eu/files/deliverables/public/INDECT_Deliverable_4.1_v20090630a.pdf/view.

Edelyn Verona and John J. Curtin. 2006. Gender Differences in the Negative Affective Priming of Aggressive Behavior. *Emotion*, 6:115-124.

Web Search. "school shooting manifesto". [Cited: 10.12. 2010.].

Introducing Argumention in Opinion Analysis: Language and Reasoning Challenges

Camille Albert, Leila Amgoud
Florence Dupin de Saint-Cyr, Patrick Saint-Dizier
IRIT-CNRS, 118, route de Narbonne
31062 Toulouse cedex France
amgoud,dupin,stdizier@irit.fr

Charlotte Costedoat
Prometil
42 Avenue du Gal Decroute
31100 Toulouse, France
c.costedoat@prometil.com

Abstract

This paper concentrates on pairing opinion analysis with argument extraction in order to identify why opinions about a certain feature are positive or negative. The objective is to have a better grasp at the underlying elements that support the analysis. In a second stage, given customer recommendations, the goal is to identify the preferences or priorities of customers, e.g. fares over welcome attitude. This induces customers value systems. Finally, we give elements of the implementation based on the <TextCoop> platform, dedicated to discourse analysis.

1 Introduction

Nowadays, there is an increasing need for an opinion analysis tool. While politicians may find it useful to analyze the popularity of new proposals or the overall public reaction to certain events, companies are definitely interested in consumer attitudes towards a product and the reasons and motivations of these attitudes. It is therefore essential to accurately and quickly analyze opinion intensity on a particular object. In addition to finding a quantitative and qualitative rating, it provides different information on the object like the most important features for people and the weaknesses of the object. The conjunction of efforts in language processing and artificial intelligence is a new promising way to address the problem. Argument analysis (Walton et al. 2008), (Reed, 1998) is a central challenge that has seldom been carried out in such a framework in particular paired with opinion analysis, where the semantics of evaluative expressions remains by large an open issue. The introduction of domain or common-sense knowledge (Breck et al. 2004) for the interpretation of these expressions is also an open issue.

In order to be able to analyze opinion, besides the language processing aspects and semantic interpretation challenges, we need to define efficient models for aggregating the different opinions reported on the web (Ashley et al. 2002), (Amgoud et al. 2005). We will take advantage of existing works in social choice theory, namely on judgment aggregation. The output would be a final rating of the object as well as a global rating of each feature and a list of key features. The main difficulty will be the choice of the aggregation function. Different kinds of simulations can also be made, in particular in order to know which feature(s) should be improved in order to alter the global rating of an object (Amgoud et al. 2001) (Keil, 2000) (Pollock 1974). Finally, we may help a user to get an opinion on an object. The idea is to ask the user to give her preferences on the set of features, then using an efficient multiple-criteria decision system, we could give an appropriate recommendation.

In this paper we first address the language point of view focusing on argument identification and extraction. Then, we introduce the main formal aspects of an aggregation system that allows to efficiently and accurately compute opinion values and their arguments, as found in various texts. The project is now in a development stage, implemented within the <TextCoop> platform and the Dislog language (under submission).

2 The global situation of opinion analysis

The current stage of opinion analysis is somewhat more oriented towards the analysis of short texts: blogs, in particular consumer blogs, news editorials or short news messages. This requires a more accurate linguistic analysis. A smaller amount of texts is then necessary, allowing opinions to be elaborated for a larger variety of topics. The assumption is to consider that the products or persons being evaluated can be qualified by means of a few salient predefined properties or attributes.

Proceedings of the Workshop on Sentiment Analysis where AI meets Psychology (SAAIP), IJCNLP 2011, pages 28–34, *Chiang Mai, Thailand, November 13, 2011.*

These properties may however be more or less independent from each other, salience is another important feature, which may depend on the text author. For example, for a political person: honesty, rigor, friendliness, capacity to listen to people, etc. For a hotel, welcome attitude, cleanliness, calm, fares, proximity of restaurants or attractions, quality of breakfast, etc. are salient properties from the consumer point of view. These properties may not correspond to the most salient ones from the product provider point of view: e.g., fares become profit.

In terms of argumentation, a statement in the hotel domain such as *very friendly welcome* can be interpreted as: *This hotel is good because the staff is very friendly*, or: *welcome is good because it is very friendly*. The argument is organized as follows: *this hotel is good* is the conclusion, while *because the staff is very friendly* is its support. The conclusion can also be attacked by other statements which are negatively oriented: ... *but it is really noisy because of heavy air traffic*. In fact, the conclusion summarizes the general feeling or recommendation of the customer, this conclusion being supported or attacked by various statements. The conclusion orientation w.r.t. its attacks and supports reveal the customer preferences and priorities: in our example, the hotel is good even if it is noisy: welcome has a higher priority over noise.

Product description in newspapers or technical brochures abound in product descriptions based on e.g. charts of properties with yes/no indications or marks. Using these properties in opinion analysis results, in general, in an analysis of the opinion per attribute, based on an a priori classification of adjectives or closely related evaluative expressions identified as having a positive or a negative orientation. While this obviously constitutes a major progress w.r.t. the previous stage, the results remain quite limited. In particular:
- properties are not necessarily independent from each other; dependencies may be difficult to identify, and their impact on opinion cohesion difficult to establish (Redeker 1990) (Miltasaki et al. 2004),
- a number of texts abound in evaluative expressions with very rich forms, including metaphors, which need grammatical elaborations and an accurate semantic interpretation,
- some evaluative elements are very much domain and property dependent (Potts 2007), for example *high* is either positive or negative depending on the objects it applies to and possibly the point of view: *high salary* versus *high taxes*. Accurate and contextually constrained lexical resources are necessary to avoid misinterpretations,
- we observed incorporation phenomena where the attribute and its evaluation are merged into a single term (*mal assis (uncomfortable seats), bon marché (cheap)*),
- we also observed a number of situations where the evaluation is given without any explicit mention of the evaluated property, because in general that property is easy to infer for a standard reader,
- finally, we noted that a number of discourse structures can be interpreted as evaluative forms. For example, giving a list of close-by touristic attractions for a hotel indicates that it is well-located for tourists, even though this is not explicitly said.

3 Identifying the motivations of an opinion

While the results produced by this second stage are of much interest and can produce accurate opinion analysis, e.g. taking into account temporal aspects for opinion evolution analysis, one of the main limitations is that there is no 'deep' analysis behind the satisfaction or dissatisfaction rates that would indicate *why* consumers are happy, unhappy with, approve or disapprove a certain political or economical decision. Such an analysis would also, in the long term, allow to induce some of the main priorities or preferences of consumers. This involves a deeper semantic interpretation of evaluative expressions and some discourse analysis following e.g. (Marcu 1997), (Saito et al. 2006).

A closer analysis of the expression of opinions, in e.g. consumer blogs, allow a deeper analysis of the pair property - value. The property is in general expressed by a short natural language expression (e.g. a noun or an event). This is the head of the structure: it 'subcategorizes' for an evaluative expression and, since it conveys the context, it gives the evaluative expression its interpretation in context. The evaluative expression, which can be very complex, contains itself its own head term, often an adjective, which may be modified by several types of constructions. In general, the formulation of the opinion has the following abstract form:
property - evaluative expression.
The evaluative expression is often a complex se-

mantic structure that integrates in one or a few words several aspects:

- a positive or negative orientation (Cheng et al. 2008) (Kim et al. 2007) (Takamura et al. 2005),
- the strength of that orientation, which may be elaborated via composition, from the various elements of the expression,
- an implicit qualification of the orientation, which is often very rich (for example *cheap fares* and *competitive fares* do not convey exactly the same meaning)
- various circumstances, realized e.g. by discourse structure(s), e.g. an illustration, which may also be interpreted as an argument,
- a number of arguments which are often incorporated into the main evaluative term.

We argue that interpreting arguments in opinion texts allows to identify why consumers like or dislike a product, a political decision, etc. and to determine, more generally, classes of values or preferences. Identifying arguments and value systems is therefore a major step in opinion analysis. For example, in a hotel, a result could be that fares and breakfast are more crucial than the room design.

In the remainder of this section, we develop a few prototypical cases of argument realization in consumer blogs. Our investigations have been conducted on French; English glosses are given for the sake of readability, however it must be noted that English structures may be quite different. Our corpora include opinions blogs on hotels, restaurants, hifi products and banking products.

If we consider consumer blogs from a global point of view, we note that they are in general short, well-written, with a direct style, and a clear aim of being explicit and accessible to a majority of readers. In most cases a few anecdotes illustrate the evaluation. A consumer blog ends (or begins) by a recommendation statement, that summarizes the overall feeling about the product or person at stake, in text form or by means of icons, e.g. a number of stars.

3.1 Adjectival incorporation of arguments

The theory of incorporation (Baker 1988) postulates a prelexical level, language independent, where the different 'facets' of a concept receive a kind of conceptual realization, which is not yet lexical. Then, given a language, this concept receives one or more language (lexical) realizations where some of these facets are no longer linguistically realized for various reasons. By lexical realizations we mean a single word as well as an expression.

We postulate that most of the adjectives found in evaluative expressions, besides their polarity and strength, incorporate semantic features which can be interpreted as arguments in the opinion analysis domain because they explain the polarity and the strength. For example, an expression in the hotel domain such as:
acceuil familial (English gloss: you are welcome as a family member) has the following features:
- positive orientation, strength: high,
- incorporated argument, with the probable interpretation: 'because the owners behave as if you were from their family'.
Obviously, the term 'family' could then be interpreted in a number of ways, but we do not need at this stage to go much further.

The extraction of the incorporated meaning, interpreted as an argument, raises major challenges in lexical semantics and lexical inference. In conceptual semantics, the semantics of an adjective is defined by either a set of features, in attribute value form, or, more or less equivalently, by a formula. Both modes of representations can be combined. In general, the semantics of the adjective is largely underspecified or higher order. Indeed the semantic interpretation largely depends on the semantics of the modified term, generally a noun. The full meaning is induced by a subtle combination of the semantics of both the adjective and the modified term. This means complex lexical developments even if some generalizations are possible. For example, *high* has almost an infinite number of senses that depends on the noun it combines with. Its basic meaning is simply e.g. 'performs better than average' applied to one or more properties of the noun.

Concerning the above example, 'familial' is a higher-order adjective which has the following representations:
(1) Communication domain: *(acceuil familial, conversation familiale, etc.)* globally means a communication act realized as if you were a family member. The modified nouns are predicative, e.g. $conversation(X, Y)$, the semantic represen-

tation of the adjective can then be:
$behave(X, in - family - of(Y, X))$
assuming that 'behave' and 'in-family-of' are defined as primitive terms.
(2) Concrete objects domain: *repas familial* (family-style meal) means a meal that has properties such as: casual, home-made, good and abundant, etc. Meal is not predicative: $meal(X)$, it has at least two facets: contents and atmosphere. Atmosphere being of communication type, it is represented as above. Besides a list of features, the contents feature can be represented by a formula as follows:
$meal(X) \wedge food(Y) - of(Y, X) \wedge good(Y) \wedge abundant(Y)$.

These small formulae (or their language paraphrase) constitute the arguments which can be extracted. These arguments support the evaluation provided by the customer by adding precise information to the polarity and strength. The main problem of this approach are feasibility and scalability. For a given domain, the number of adjectives used is in general relatively large, between 50 and 300. For each property, we observed an average of 40 adjectives with maximums around 90, including metaphorical uses and a large number of quasi-synonyms. This is obviously large. However, about 70% of the adjectives in a given domain are stable over all properties and have a fixed polarity and strength. About 10% have a variable polarity depending on the term they are combined with.

The last stage of the process is to construct a synthesis: given an entity (e.g. a hotel) and a property, and given a set of blogs, the challenge is to construct a synthesis of all the evaluative expressions which have been found. This synthesis is a set of arguments positively or negatively evaluating the property at stake, in other terms either supporting or attacking the statement 'property is good' or supporting or attacking each other.

3.2 Discourse relations as arguments

While the previous section requires local language analysis, which can be handled by local grammars, opinion analysis abound in statements which must be processed at discourse level. Reformulations, illustrations, elaborations (Mann et al. 1988) (Grosz et al. 1986) of various types abound with a rich linguistic structure, including emphasis and irony, with different argumentative purposes. Elaborations tend to reinforce an evaluation via a more detailed analysis of the reasons why the evaluation is positive or negative (e.g. ..., *in other words, free wifi*).
insonorisation élevée qui permet de se reposer après une dure journée de travail
(a high soundproofing that allows you to have a rest after a long working day).
The property 'soundproofing' of the hotel gets a positive value, associated with an elaboration which does not elaborate the soundproofing but one of its advantages in the present context, giving additional weight to that property. Considering our corpora on hotels and on banking products, it seems to us that the level of argumentation introduced by the elaboration relation is rather modest.

Illustrations, which also abound in opinion texts, are much more interesting. In general, the structure is the following:
property - polarity - illustration.
The polarity is optional: *location: 5 mns from Capitole and 10 mns from the station.*
The illustration gives the strength of the evaluation, possibly its orientation if there is no explicit polarity, and an argument that supports it:
well located (2 mns from the Capitole, 5 mns from Saint Sernin, close to the station, close to fancy restaurants, ...). The illustration is here between brackets, under the form of an enumeration of elements of interest for tourists. Language elements that indicate distance (in minutes or 'close' obviously need to be interpreted to get a positive or negative orientation). The illustration therefore explains why the hotel is well located (or not).

Identifying illustrations as arguments (and not just as mere enumerations) often requires domain knowledge. Touristic spots, food places and transportation facilities are identified as features of interest for tourists. The positive evaluation of the enumeration is induced e.g. from the spatial expressions that indicate proximity, which are, in our system, recognized by a local grammar. Proximity associated with touristic facilities is positively evaluated and constitutes an argument support. Besides the use of an ontology of the hotel domain and possibly touristic activity domain, inferential patterns that capture modes or strategies of evaluation are needed.

To further illustrate and generalize the above example, we developed a few, domain dependent, inferential schemas to identify illustrations which

behave as arguments. For example:
Room comfort (List of equipments in room): such a list indicates the level of comfort of the room: the evaluation is based on the level and amount of relevant room facilities.
Breakfast (List of food elements): such a list also indicates the quality of the breakfast. The evaluation is based on the proposed items, their originality, variety, etc. If the list is negative (e.g. no fruit juice, no pastries), then the polarity of the evaluation is inverted.
At the moment these remain quite basic. More corpus analysis should lead to the elaboration of higher level inferential patterns, but this is outside the scope of the present paper. The task is to investigate generalizations which would be domain independent that would capture generic uses of illustrations as an argument.

4 The lexicon of opinion analysis

Besides domain specific terms, in particular nouns denoting properties, we have categorized the different lexical units that structure evaluative expressions from the point of view of their polarity and strength in the domain of news editorial analysis (Bal and Saint-Dizier, 2008). The case of opinion analysis is relatively similar, with features which are much less prominent such as propositional attitudes or report verb semantics and pragmatics.

First, a polarity and strength lexicon of evaluative expressions (adjectives and other expressions) has been designed. For each expression, the following features are mentioned: syntactic category, polarity: which may be general or attribute dependent, in this latter case, polarity is coded by a pair (attribute name, polarity), this level also captures metaphorical uses, and strength (or persuasion force): which seems to be rather stable over domains.

Next, our lexicon contains pre-modifier terms which are basically adverbs of intensity *(very, somewhat, quite, etc.)*. About 55 such adverbs have been identified for French. Their orientation is described as a binary feature: increase or decrease. Then, we have identified three classes of intensifiers which have a kind of modal meaning: (1) emphasizers, with the following subclasses: Really (truly, genuinely, actually), Simply (merely, just, only, plainly), For sure (surely, certainly, sure, for certain, sure enough, undoubtedly), Of course (naturally); (2) amplifiers, with the following subclasses: Completely (all, altogether, entirely, totally, whole, wholly), Absolutely (totally and definitely, without question, perfectly, utterly), Heartily (cordially, warmly, with gusto and without reservation); (3) downtoners: Kind of (sort of, kind a, rather, to some extent, almost, all but), Mildly (gently).

Finally, a modal verb lexicon of those verbs that occur to soften opinions or make them relative to a certain view, introduces notions such as possibility, advice or necessity: *can, could, may, might, should, etc.*. These various lexical structures are associated with several local grammars as described above which are designed to recognize the structure of evaluative expressions be they basic (single adjective) or more complex (conjunction of terms, use of adverbs, etc.). Strength and polarity are compositionally computed from the terms that constitute the evaluation.

5 A formal framework for analyzing opinions

In this section, we propose a formal framework for modeling opinion analysis that can accommodate the previous observations. We consider a particular object (called target) on which some people have given their opinions. An opinion is generally given as a global rating on the object, and values associated with its attributes, and a set of arguments supporting this rating. Arguments highlight the positive (or the negative) features of the object on which the opinion is expressed. Let us consider the following opinion expressed on a digital camera: *It is a great digital camera for this century. The rotatable lens is great. It's very easy to use, and has fast response from the shutter. The LCD has increased from 1.5 to 1.8, which gives bigger view. But, it would be better if the model is designed for smaller size. I recommend this camera.*

The object here is the digital camera, the overall rating is "recommended", while the features are: the size, rotatable lens, response from the shutter, size of LCD. For instance, "it's easy to use" belongs to the arguments *pros* the digital camera while "it would be better if the model is designed for smaller size" is an argument against (or belongs to the *cons*) the camera.

Hence, we face a decision problem, namely, given an object O and information about O we should decide if this object should be recommended or not. We propose the following definitions in order to be able to deal with this particular decision problem.

Definition 1 (Recommendation domain). *A recommendation domain, RD, is a set that should contain at least two values representing the decision to recommend and not to recommend a given object.*

Example 1. *Recommendation domains can be either a boolean set* $\{YES, NO\}$*, or a set of qualitative decision values* $\{x_1, \ldots x_k\}$ *or a continuous interval* $[0, 1]$*, where 0 represents "not recommended" and 1 represents "recommended".*

We propose the following framework in order to aggregate opinions on a given subject:

Definition 2 (General opinion aggregation framework (GOAF)). *Given a target O, a set of agents,* $Ag = a_1, \ldots a_n$*, a set of features,* $F = f_1, \ldots, f_m$*, where each feature* f_j *is associated with a domain* D_j *(which is a set of possible values that can be assigned to the feature* f_j *of the object* O*).*
Let us denote the recommendation of agent a_i *about object O by* $r_i(O)$*, the global recommendation about the object O by* $r(O)$*, and let* $v_{i,j}$ *be the value attributed by agent* a_i *to the feature* f_j *of object O.*
The data can be represented as follows:

	f_1	...	f_j	...	f_m	*Target*
Ag \ domains	D_1	...	D_j	...	D_m	/
a_1	$v_{1,1}$	...	$v_{1,j}$	...	$v_{1,m}$	$r_1(O)$
⋮	⋮	⋮	⋮	⋮	⋮	⋮
a_i	$v_{i,1}$	...	$v_{i,j}$	...	$v_{i,m}$	$r_i(O)$
⋮	⋮	⋮	⋮	⋮	⋮	⋮
a_n	$v_{n,1}$	...	$v_{n,j}$	...	$v_{n,m}$	$r_n(O)$
Group	$v(f_1)$	...	$v(f_j)$	...	$v(f_m)$	$r(O)$

where each $v_{i,j} \in D_j$*.*

Some values of this table clearly depend from each other, namely, if the agent a_i is rational, then $r_i(O)$ should depend from the $v_{i,\_}$. Hence, we can assume that each rational agent a_i can be associated with an aggregation function $agreg_i$ defined as follows:

Definition 3 (MCA-function of an agent). *Let* a_i *be a rational agent and RD be a recommendation domain, a* multi-criteria aggregation function *for agent* a_i *is a function* mca_i *from* $D_1 \times \ldots \times D_j \times \ldots \times D_m$ *to RD linking the values of the features to the recommendation:*

$$\forall i \in [1, n] \quad r_i(O) = mca_i(v_{i,1}, \ldots v_{i,m})$$

The same kind of aggregation can be done in order to summarize a group of opinions about a given feature, note that each feature may be associated with a distinct aggregation function (similarly, agents do not necessarily have the same MCA-function).

Definition 4 (group aggregation). *Let* f_j *be a feature and* D_j *be its domain, a* group aggregation function *for the feature* f_j *is a function* $group_j$ *from* $(D_j)^n$ *to* D_j *linking the values given by agents to the feature* f_j *to only one value:*

$$\forall j \in [1, m] \quad v(f_j) = group_j(v_{1,j}, \ldots v_{n,j})$$

Definition 5 (Group MCA recommendation). *A group multicriteria recommendation can be defined by:*

- *either computing the MCA recommendation of each agent and then aggregates this result on the group of agent*
- *or computing the group values of the features and then making a multicriteria aggregation of these values.*

6 Applications and perspectives

The applications under development concern basic services : hotels, restaurants and e-commerce consumer opinions. A question-answering interface is being developed so that users can query the system only on one or a few properties, i.e. *is hotel X well located ?*. Besides these useful experimentations and developments, we are now investigating the e-reputation framework, of much importance for companies and public persons (we are having major elections in 2012), in particular using data from social networks, wikis and some rapidly evolving blogs. Then, given criteria and thresholds, alert signals can be sent to these companies or persons with an analysis of the reasons of opinion evolution, via arguments.

Finally, given that we can propose an analysis based on arguments, we can then model a network for opinion sharing via argumentation, analyzing support and attack situations, as developed in argumentation. The language part of this project has been implemented with the <TextCoop> platform (Saint-Dizier 2011, forthcoming). This platform is dedicated to discourse analysis and integrates lexical semantics and reasoning capabilities.

References

Ashley, K.,D., Desai, R., Levine, J.M., Teaching case-based argumentation concepts using dialectic arguments vs. didactic explanations, ITS 2002, Lecture notes in computer science, 2002.

Amgoud, L., Bonnefon, J.F., Prade, H., An Argumentation-based Approach to Multiple Criteria Decision, in 8th European Conference on Symbolic and Quantitative Approaches to Reasoning with Uncertainty, ECSQARU'2005, Barcelona, 2005.

Amgoud, L., Parsons, S., Maudet, N., Arguments, Dialogue, and Negotiation, in: 14th European Conference on Artificial Intelligence, Berlin, 2001.

Bal, K.B., Saint-Dizier, P. Towards Building Annotated Resources for Analyzing Opinions and Argumentation in News Editorials, LREC, Malta, 2008.

Baker, Mark C. Incorporation: A theory of grammatical function changing. Chicago, University of Chicago Press, 1988.

Bethard S., Yu H., Thornton A., Hatzivassiloglou V., Rafsky D., Automatic extraction of opinion propositions and their holders, Proceedings AAAI04, 2004.

Breck E., Choi Y., Cardie C., Identifying expressions of opinion in context. Twentieth International Joint Conference on Artificial Intelligence (IJCAI), 2007.

Cheng X., Xu F., Fine-grained opinion topic and polarity identification, Proceedings of LREC'08, marrakech, morocco, 2008.

Grosz, B., Sidner, C., Attention, intention and the structure of discourse, Computational Linguistics 12(3), 1986.

Keil, F.C., Wilson, R.A., Explanation and Cognition, Bradford Book, 2000.

Kim, s.m. and Hovy, E., Crystal: analyzing predictive opinions on the web. EMNLP 2007

Mann, W., Thompson, S., Rhetorical Structure Theory: Towards a Functional Theory of Text Organisation, TEXT 8 (3) pp. 243-281, 1988.

Mann, W., Thompson, S.A. (eds), Discourse Description: diverses linguistic analyses of a fund raising text, John Benjamins, 1992.

Marcu, D., The Rhetorical Parsing of Natural Language Texts, ACL 1997.

Marcu, D., Au unsupervised approach to recognizing Discourse relations, ACL 2002.

Miltasaki, E., Prasad, R., Joshi, A., Webber, B., Annotating Discourse Connectives and Their Arguments, new frontiers in NLP, 2004.

Pollock, J.L., Knowledge and Justification, Princeton university Press, 1974.

Potts, C., The expressive dimension. Theoretical linguistics 33(2):165-197, 2007

Redeker, G. (1990). Ideational and Pragmatic Markers of Discourse Structure, Journal of Pragmatics, vol. 14.

Reed, C., Generating Arguments in Natural Language, PhD dissertation, University College, London, 1998.

Saito, M., Yamamoto, K., Sekine, S., Using Phrasal Patterns to Identify Discourse Relations, ACL, 2006.

Takamura h., Inui,T., Okumura M., Extracting semantic orientations of words using spin model, Proceedings of the 43rd annual meeting on ACL, 2005.

Takechi, M., Tokunaga, T., Matsumoto, Y., Tanaka, H., *Feature Selection in Categorizing Procedural Expressions*, The Sixth International Workshop on Information Retrieval with Asian Languages (IRAL2003), pp.49-56, 2003.

Walton, D., Reed, C., Macagno, F., Argumentation Schemes, Cambridge University Press, 2008.

Wierzbicka, A., English Speech Act Verbs, Academic Press, 1987.

Wright, von G.H., Explanation and understanding, Cornell university Press, 2004.

Taking Refuge in Your Personal Sentic Corner

Erik Cambria
National University of Singapore
cambria@nus.edu.sg

Amir Hussain
University of Stirling
ahu@cs.stir.ac.uk

Chris Eckl
Sitekit Solutions Ltd.
chris.eckl@sitekit.net

Abstract

In a world in which web users are continuously blasted by ads and often compelled to deal with user-unfriendly interfaces, we sometimes feel like we want to evade from the sensory overload of standard web pages and take refuge in a safe web corner, in which contents and design are in harmony with our current frame of mind. Sentic Corner is an intelligent user interface that dynamically collects audio, video, images and text related to the user's current feelings and activities as an interconnected knowledge base, which is browsable through a multi-faceted classification website.

1 Introduction

In normal human cognition, thinking and feeling are mutually present – our emotions are often the product of our thoughts as well as our reflections are frequently the product of our sentiments. Emotions, in fact, are intrinsically part of our mental activity and play a key role in decision-making processes. They are special states shaped by natural selection to balance the reaction of our organism to particular situations, e.g., anger evolved for reaction, fear evolved for protection and affection evolved for reproduction.

In the new realm of Web 2.0 applications, the analysis of emotions has undergone a large number of interpretations and visualizations (WeFeelFine, 2011; Moodviews, 2011; Moodstats, 2011; Moodstream, 2011), which have often led to the development of emotion-sensitive systems and applications. Nonetheless, today web users still have to almost continuously deal with sensory-overloaded web pages, pop-up windows, annoying ads, user-unfriendly interfaces, etc. Moreover, even for websites uncontaminated by web spam, the affective content of the page is often totally unsynchronized with the user's emotional state. Web pages containing multimedia information inevitably carry more than just informative content. Behind every multimedia content, in fact, there is always an emotion. Sentic Corner exploits this concept to build a sort of parallel cognitive/affective digital world in which the most relevant multimedia contents associated to the users' current moods and activities are collected, in order to enable them, whenever they want to evade from sensory-rich, overwrought and earnest web pages, to take refuge in their own safe web corner.

The structure of the paper is the following: Section 2 presents related work on managing affective multimedia contents, Section 3 describes the AI and Semantic Web tools exploited within this work, Section 4 explains in detail the techniques and the methods hereby used to retrieve and manage semantically and affectively relevant multimedia contents, Section 5 illustrates the overall process for the creation of the affective multimedia environment, Section 6 presents an evaluation of the adopted tools and, eventually, Section 7 comprises concluding remarks and a description of future work.

2 Related Work

To our knowledge, there is still no published study on the task of automatically retrieving and displaying multimedia contents according to user's moods and activities, although the affective and semantic analysis of video, audio and textual contents have been separately investigated extensively (Srinivasan et al., 2005; Hanjalic, 2006; Schleicher et al., 2010; Cambria et al., 2011a). The most relevant commercial tool within this area is Moodstream (Moodstream, 2011), a mashup of

Proceedings of the Workshop on Sentiment Analysis where AI meets Psychology (SAAIP), IJCNLP 2011, pages 35–43, *Chiang Mai, Thailand, November 13, 2011.*

several forms of media, designed to bring users music, images, and video according to the mood they manually select on the web interface. Moodstream aims to create a sort of audio-visual ambient mix that can be dynamically modified by users by selecting from the presets of 'inspire', 'excite', 'refresh', 'intensify', 'stabilize', and 'simplify', e.g., mixtures of mood spectra on the Moodstream mixer such as happy/sad, calm/lively or warm/cool. Users can start with a preset and then mix things up including the type of image transition, whether they want more or less vocals in their music selection and how long images and video will stay, among other settings.

In Moodstream, however, songs are not played entirely but blended into one another every 30 seconds and, even if the user has control on the multimedia flow through the mood presets, he/she cannot actually set a specific mood and/or activity as a core theme for the audio-visual ambient mix. Sentic Corner, on the contrary, uses sentic computing (Cambria et al., 2010b), a new paradigm for the affective analysis of text, to automatically extract semantics and sentics, i.e., the cognitive and affective information, associated with user's status updates on micro-blogging websites and, hence, to retrieve relevant multimedia contents in harmony with his/her current emotions and motions.

3 Sentic Computing

Sentic computing has been recently proposed as a multi-disciplinary approach to opinion mining and sentiment analysis that exploits both computer and social sciences to better recognize, interpret and process opinions and sentiments over the Web. Specifically, sentic computing involves the use of AI and Semantic Web techniques, for knowledge representation and inference; mathematics, for carrying out tasks such as graph mining and multi-dimensionality reduction; linguistics, for discourse analysis and pragmatics; psychology, for cognitive and affective modeling; sociology, for understanding social network dynamics and social influence; finally ethics, for understanding related issues about the nature of mind and the creation of emotional machines.

In sentic computing, the analysis of text is based on common sense reasoning tools and affective ontologies. Differently from statistical classification, which generally requires large inputs and thus cannot appraise texts with satisfactory granularity, sentic computing enables the analysis of documents not only on the page or paragraph-level but also on the sentence and clause-level. Within this work, in particular, we use a novel emotion categorization model (section 3.1), a language visualization and analysis system (section 3.2) and a web ontology for human emotions (section 3.3).

3.1 The Hourglass of Emotions

The Hourglass of Emotions (Cambria et al., 2010c) is a novel affective categorization model in which sentiments are organized around four independent dimensions, whose different levels of activation make up the total emotional state of the mind. The Hourglass of Emotions, in fact, is based on the idea that the mind is made of different independent resources and that emotional states result from turning some set of these resources on and turning another set of them off (Minsky, 2006).

The primary quantity we can measure about an emotion we feel is its strength. But when we feel a strong emotion it is because we feel a very specific emotion. And, conversely, we cannot feel a specific emotion like 'fear' or 'amazement' without that emotion being reasonably strong. Mapping this space of possible emotions leads to an hourglass shape (Fig. 1).

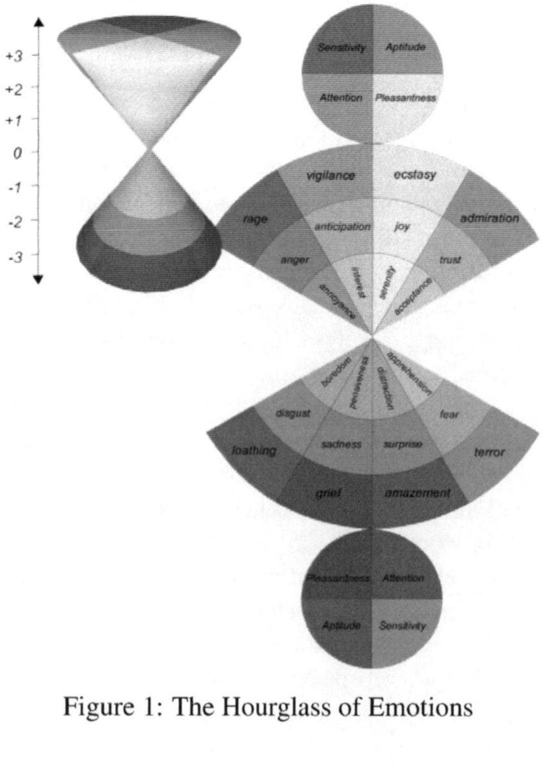

Figure 1: The Hourglass of Emotions

The Hourglass of Emotions is specifically designed to recognize, understand and express emotions in the context of human computer interaction (HCI). In the model, in fact, affective states are not classified, as often happens in the field of emotion analysis, into basic emotional categories, but rather into four independent and concomitant dimensions, Pleasantness, Attention, Sensitivity and Aptitude, in order to understand how much respectively the user is happy with the service provided, interested in the information supplied, comfortable with the interface and disposed to use the application. Each affective dimension, in particular, is characterized by six levels of activation (measuring the strength of an emotion), termed 'sentic levels', which determine the intensity of the expressed/perceived emotion as an $int \in [-3,3]$.

These levels are also labeled as a set of 24 basic emotions (Plutchik, 2001), six for each of the affective dimensions, in a way that allows the model to specify the affective information associated with text both in a dimensional and in a discrete form. The dimensional form, in particular, is called 'sentic vector' and it is a four-dimensional $float$ vector that can potentially express any human emotion in terms of Pleasantness, Attention, Sensitivity and Aptitude.

3.2 AffectiveSpace

AffectiveSpace (Cambria et al., 2009) is a multidimensional vector space built from ConceptNet (Havasi et al., 2007), a directed graph representation of common sense knowledge, and WordNet-Affect (Strapparava and Valitutti, 2004), a linguistic resource for the lexical representation of affective knowledge.

In particular, we use truncated singular value decomposition (TSVD) (Wall et al., 2003) in order to obtain a new matrix containing both hierarchical affective knowledge and common sense. The resulting matrix has the form $\tilde{A} = U_k \Sigma_k V_k^T$ and is a low-rank approximation of A, the original data. This approximation is based on minimizing the Frobenius norm of the difference between A and $\tilde{A}$ under the constraint $rank(\tilde{A}) = k$. For the Eckart–Young theorem it represents the best approximation of A in the mean-square sense, in fact:

$$\min_{\tilde{A}|rank(\tilde{A})=k} |A - \tilde{A}| = \min_{\tilde{A}|rank(\tilde{A})=k} |\Sigma - U^* \tilde{A} V| = \min_{\tilde{A}|rank(\tilde{A})=k} |\Sigma - S|$$

assuming that $\tilde{A}$ has the form $\tilde{A} = U S V^*$, where S is diagonal. From the rank constraint, i.e., S has k non-zero diagonal entries, the minimum of the above statement is obtained as follows:

$$\min_{\tilde{A}|rank(\tilde{A})=k} |\Sigma - S| = \min_{s_i} \sqrt{\sum_{i=1}^{n} (\sigma_i - s_i)^2} = \min_{s_i} \sqrt{\sum_{i=1}^{k} (\sigma_i - s_i)^2 + \sum_{i=k+1}^{n} \sigma_i^2} = \sqrt{\sum_{i=k+1}^{n} \sigma_i^2}$$

Therefore, $\tilde{A}$ of rank k is the best approximation of A in the Frobenius norm sense when $\sigma_i = s_i$ ($i = 1, ..., k$) and the corresponding singular vectors are same as those of A. If we choose to discard all but the first k principal components, common sense concepts and emotions are represented by vectors of k coordinates: these coordinates can be seen as describing concepts in terms of 'eigenmoods' that form the axes of AffectiveSpace, i.e., the basis e_0,...,e_{k-1} of the vector space (Fig. 2).

For example, the most significant eigenmood, e_0, represents concepts with positive affective valence. That is, the larger a concept's component in the e_0 direction is, the more affectively positive it is likely to be. Concepts with negative e_0 components, then, are likely to have negative affective valence. Thus, by exploiting the information sharing property of TSVD, concepts with the same affective valence are likely to have similar features – that is, concepts conveying the same emotion tend to fall near each other in AffectiveSpace. For example we can find concepts such as 'beautiful day', 'birthday party', 'laugh' and 'make person happy' very close in direction in the vector space, while concepts like 'sick', 'feel guilty', 'be laid off' and 'shed tear' are found in a completely different direction (nearly opposite with respect to the center of the space).

3.3 The Human Emotion Ontology

The Human Emotion Ontology (HEO) (Grassi, 2009) is conceived as a high level ontology for human emotions that supplies the most significant

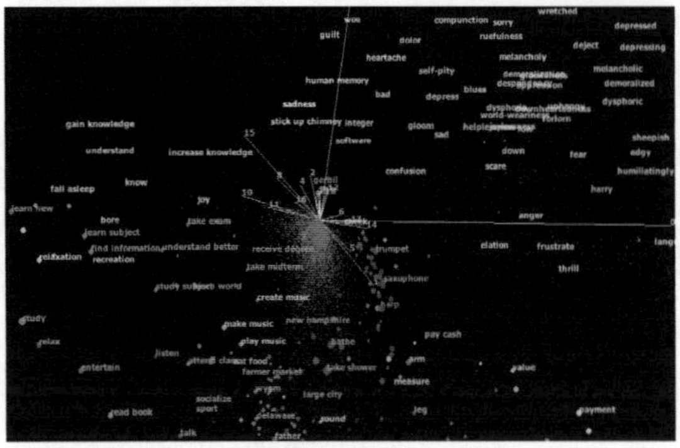

Figure 2: AffectiveSpace

concepts and properties, which constitute the centerpiece for the description of every human emotion. The main purpose of HEO is to create a description framework that could grant at the same time enough flexibility, by allowing the use of a wide and extensible set of descriptors to represent all the main features of an emotion, and interoperability, by allowing to map concepts and properties belonging to different emotion representation models.

HEO has been developed in ontology web language description logic (OWL DL) for its expressiveness and its inference power in mapping the different models used in the emotion description. OWL DL, in fact, allows a taxonomical organization of emotion categories and properties restriction in order to link emotion description made both by category and by dimension.

4 Corner Deviser

The main aim of the Corner Deviser is to process the semantics and sentics obtained through sentic computing in order to retrieve relevant multimedia contents from the Web and, hence, encode these in a Semantic Web aware format. In particular, the cognitive and affective information is processed through a technique that performs inference over multiple sources of data (section 4.1), a statistical method for the identification of common semantics (section 4.2), a technique that expands semantics through spreading activation (section 4.3).

The resulting semantics and sentics are then exploited to pull relevant music (Section 4.4), videos (Section 4.5), images (Section 4.6) and text (Section 4.7) from the Web and, eventually, encode these in RDF/XML (Section 4.8).

4.1 Blending

Blending (Havasi et al., 2009) is a technique that performs inference over multiple sources of data simultaneously, taking advantage of the overlap between them. It basically combines two sparse matrices linearly into a single matrix in which the information between the two initial sources is shared. When we perform SVD on a blended matrix, the result is that new connections are made in each source matrix taking into account information and connections present in the other matrix, originating from the information that overlaps.

By this method, we can combine different sources of general knowledge, or overlay general knowledge with domain-specific knowledge, such as medical, geological or financial knowledge.

4.2 CF-IOF Weighting

CF-IOF (concept frequency - inverse opinion frequency) (Cambria et al., 2010a) is a technique that identifies common domain-dependent semantics in order to evaluate how important a concept is to a set of opinions concerning the same topic.

Firstly, the frequency of a concept c for a given domain d is calculated by counting the occurrences of the concept c in the set of available d-tagged opinions and dividing the result by the sum of number of occurrences of all concepts in the set of opinions concerning d. This frequency is then multiplied by the logarithm of the inverse frequency of the concept in the whole collection of opinions, that is:

$$CF\text{-}IOF_{c,d} = \frac{n_{c,d}}{\sum_k n_{k,d}} \log \sum_k \frac{n_k}{n_c}$$

where $n_{c,d}$ is the number of occurrences of concept c in the set of opinions tagged as d, n_k is the total number of concept occurrences and n_c is the number of occurrences of c in the whole set of opinions. A high weight in CF-IOF is reached by a high concept frequency in a given domain and a low frequency of the concept in the whole collection of opinions.

4.3 Spectral Association

Spectral association (Havasi et al., 2010) is a technique that involves assigning values to 'seed concepts' and applying an operation that spreads their values across the ConceptNet graph.

This operation, an approximation of many steps of spreading activation, transfers the most activation to concepts that are connected to the key concepts by short paths or many different paths in common sense knowledge. In particular, we build a matrix C that relates concepts to other concepts, instead of their features, and add up the scores over all relations that relate one concept to another, disregarding direction.

Applying C to a vector containing a single concept spreads that concept's value to its connected concepts. Applying C^2 spreads that value to concepts connected by two links (including back to the concept itself). But what we would really like is to spread the activation through any number of links, with diminishing returns, so the operator we want is:

$$1 + C + \frac{C^2}{2!} + \frac{C^3}{3!} + ... = e^C$$

We can calculate this odd operator, e^C, because we can factor C. C is already symmetric, so instead of applying Lanczos' method to CC^T and getting the SVD, we can apply it directly to C and get the spectral decomposition $C = V \Lambda V^T$. As before, we can raise this expression to any power and cancel everything but the power of Λ. Therefore, $e^C = V e^{\Lambda} V^T$. This simple twist on the SVD lets us calculate spreading activation over the whole matrix instantly. As with the SVD, we can truncate these matrices to k axes and therefore save space while generalizing from similar concepts.

4.4 Sentic Tuner

The module for the retrieval of semantically and affectively related music is called Sentic Tuner. The relevant audio information is pulled from Stereomood, an emotional on-line radio that provides music that best suits users' mood and activities (Stereomood, 2011). In the web interface, music is played randomly through an on-line music player with the possibility for the user to play/stop/skip tracks.

In Stereomood, music tracks are classified according to some tags that users are supposed to manually choose in order to access a list of semantically or affectively related songs. These tags are either mood-tags (e.g., 'happy', 'calm', 'romantic', 'lonely' and 'reflective') or activity-tags (such as 'reading', 'just woke up', 'dressing up', 'cleaning' and 'jogging'), the majority of which represent cognitive and affective knowledge contained in AffectiveSpace as common sense concepts and emotional labels. The Sentic Tuner uses the mood-tags as centroids for blending and the activity-tags as seeds for spectral association, in order to build a set of affectively and semantically related concepts respectively, which will be used at run-time to match the concepts extracted from user's micro-blogging activity. The Sentic Tuner also contains a few hundreds $r\bar{a}gas$ (Sanskrit for moods), which are melodic modes used in Indian classical music meant to be played in particular situations (mood, time of the year, time of the day, weather conditions, etc.).

It is considered inappropriate to play $r\bar{a}gas$ at the wrong time (it would be like playing Christmas music in July, lullabies at breakfast or sad songs at a wedding) so these are played just when semantics and sentics exactly match time and mood specifications in the $r\bar{a}gas$ database. Hence, once semantics and sentics are extracted from natural language text through sentic computing, Stereomood API and the $r\bar{a}gas$ database are exploited to select the most relevant tracks to user's current feelings and activities.

4.5 Sentic TV

Sentic TV is the module for the retrieval of semantically and affectively related videos. In particular, the module pulls information from Jinni, a new site that allows users to search for video entertainment in many specific ways (Jinni, 2011).

The idea behind Jinni is to reflect how people really think and talk about what they watch. It is based on an ontology developed by film professionals and new titles are indexed with an innovative natural language processing (NLP) technology for analyzing metadata and reviews. In Jinni, users can choose from movies, TV shows, short films and on-line videos to find specific genres or what they are in the mood to watch. In particular, users can browse videos by topic, mood, plot, genre, time/period, place, audience and praise. Similarly to the Sentic Tuner, Sentic TV uses Jinni's mood-tags as centroids for blending and the topic-tags as seeds for spectral association in order to retrieve affectively and semantically related concepts respectively.

Time-tags and location-tags are also exploited in case relevant time-stamp and/or geo-location information is available within user's micro-blogging activity.

4.6 Sentic Slideshow

Sentic Corner also offers semantically and affectively related images through the Sentic Slideshow module. Pictures related to the user's current mood and activity are pulled from Fotosearch (Fotosearch, 2011), a provider of royalty free and rights managed stock photography which claims to be the biggest repository of images on the Web. Since Fotosearch does not offer a priori mood-tags and activity-tags, the CF-IOF technique is used on a set of 1000 manually tagged (according to mood and topic) tweets (Twitter, 2011), in order to find seeds for spectral association (topic-tagged tweets) and centroids for blending (mood-tagged tweets).

Each of the resulting concepts is used to retrieve mood and activity related images through the Fotosearch search engine. The royalty free pictures, eventually, are saved in an internal database according to their mood and/or activity tag, in a way that they can be quickly retrieved at run-time, depending on user's current feelings and thoughts.

4.7 Sentic Library

The aim of Sentic Library is to provide book excerpts depending on user's current mood. The module proposes random book passages users should read according to the mood they should be in while reading it and/or what mood they will be in when they have finished. The excerpt database is built according to '1001 Books for Every Mood: A Bibliophile's Guide to Unwinding, Misbehaving, Forgiving, Celebrating, Commiserating' (Ephron, 2008), a guide in which the novelist Hallie Ephron serves up a literary feast for every emotional appetite.

In the guide, books are labeled with mood-tags such as 'for a good laugh', 'for a good cry' and 'for romance', but also some activity-tags such as 'for a walk on the wild side' or 'to run away from home'. As for Sentic TV and Sentic Tuner, Sentic Library uses these mood-tags as centroids for blending and the topic-tags as seeds for spectral association.

4.8 Encoding

In order to effectively represent the retrieved audio, video, visual and textual multimedia information, we encode it in a Semantic Web aware format and store it in a Sesame triple-store, a purpose-built database for the storage and retrieval of RDF metadata (Sesame, 2009).

Sesame can be embedded in applications and used to conduct a wide range of inferences on the information stored, based on RDFS and OWL type relations between data. In addition, it can also be used in a standalone server mode, much like a traditional database with multiple applications connecting to it. In particular, we encode the data in RDF/XML using the descriptors defined by HEO and insert them into the triple-store, in a way that multimedia contents can be queried and results can be retrieved in a semantic aware format.

5 Sentic Corner Generation Process

The process for creating Sentic Corner comprises five main components (Fig. 3): a NLP module, which performs a first skim of the real-time fetched user tweets, a Semantic Parser, whose aim is to extract concepts from the lemmatized text, AffectiveSpace, for the extraction of semantics and sentics from the given concepts, the Corner Deviser, which exploits the cognitive and affective information obtained to retrieve and encode relevant multimedia, and the Exhibit (Exhibit, 2011) intelligent user interface (IUI), for the visualization of results.

In particular, the NLP module interprets all the affective valence indicators usually contained in tweets such as special punctuation, complete upper-case words, onomatopoeic repetitions, exclamation words, negations, degree adverbs and emoticons, and eventually lemmatizes text.

The Semantic Parser then deconstructs text into concepts and provides, for each of them, the relative frequency, valence and status, i.e., the concept's occurrence in the text, its positive or negative connotation, and the degree of intensity with which the concept is expressed.

The AffectiveSpace module projects the retrieved concepts into the vector space clustered wrt the Hourglass model sentic levels using a k-medoids approach (Cambria et al., 2011b), and infers the affective valence of these, in terms

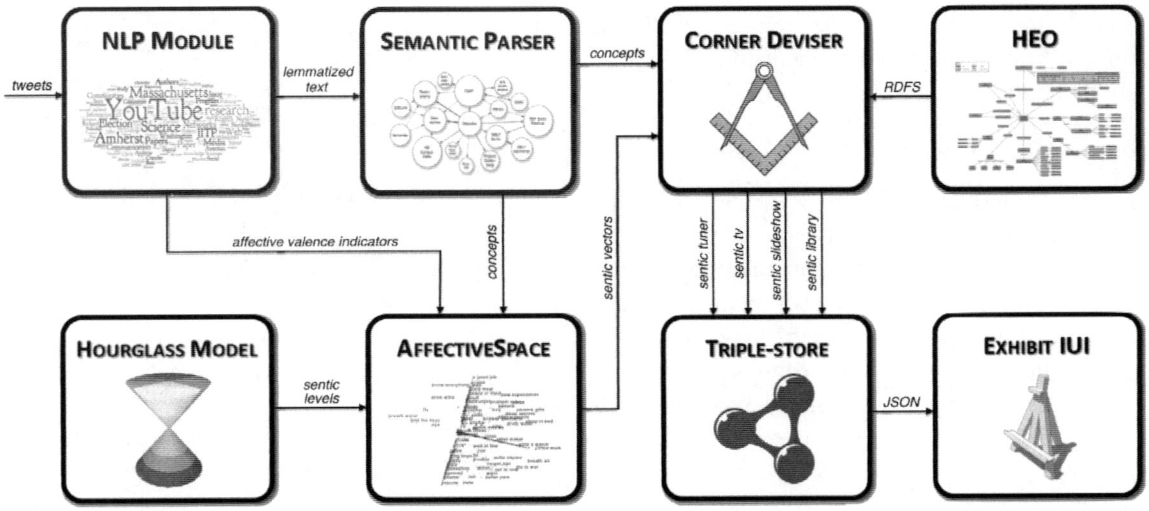

Figure 3: Sentic Corner Generation Process

of Pleasantness, Attention, Sensitivity and Aptitude, according to the positions they occupy in the space. The Corner Deviser exploits the semantic and sentic knowledge bases previously built by means of blending, CF-IOF and spectral association to find matches for the concepts extracted by the Semantic Parser and their relative affective information inferred by AffectiveSpace.

Such audio, video, visual and textual information (namely Sentic Tuner, Sentic TV, Sentic Slideshow and Sentic Library) is then encoded in RDF/XML according to HEO and stored in the triple-store. In case the sentics detected belong to the lower part of the Hourglass, the multimedia contents searched will have an affective valence opposite to the emotional charge detected, as Sentic Corner aims to restore the positive emotional equilibrium of the user, e.g., if the user is angry he/she might want to calm down.

The Exhibit IUI module, eventually, visualizes the contents of the Sesame database exploiting the multi-faceted categorization paradigm. Faceted classification allows the assignment of multiple categories to an object, enabling classifications to be ordered in multiple ways, rather than in a single taxonomic order. This allows to perform searches combining the textual approach with the navigational one. Faceted search, in fact, enables users to navigate a multi-dimensional information space by both writing queries in a text box and progressively narrowing choices in each dimension.

For Sentic Corner, in particular, we use SIMILE Exhibit API, a set of Javascript files that allows to easily create rich interactive web-pages including maps, timelines and galleries, with very detailed client-side filtering. Exhibit pages use the multi-faceted classification paradigm to display semantically structured data stored in a Semantic Web aware format, e.g., RDF or JavaScript object notation (JSON). One of the most relevant aspects of Exhibit is that, once the page is loaded, the web-browser also loads the entire data set in a lightweight database and performs all the computations (sorting, filtering, etc.) locally on the client-side, providing high performances.

The information contained in the triple-store is exported to the Exhibit IUI as a JSON file in order to make the data available for being browsed as a unique knowledge base (Fig. 4). In the web interface, multimedia contents are displayed in a dynamic gallery, which can be ordered according to mood and activity tags (in case they are not unique) plus other parameters such as title, genre, source, modality, etc.

The IUI allows to explore such information both by using the search box, to perform keyword-based queries, and by filtering the results using the faceted menus, i.e., by adding or removing constraints on the facet properties. The extracted affective information, moreover, is exploited to modify the design of the webpage in a way that the user always feels comfortable with the interface. If positive affective information is extracted, for example, a design with smooth edges windows and hot colors is adopted.

6 Evaluation

In order to test Sentic Corner's affect recognition capabilities, we evaluated the system with a corpus of mood-tagged blogs from LiveJournal (LJ) (LiveJournal, 2011), a virtual community of more than 23 millions users who keep a blog, journal or diary. One of the interesting features of this website is that LJ bloggers are allowed to label their posts with a mood tag, by choosing from more than 130 predefined moods or by creating custom mood themes. Since the indication of the affective status is optional, the mood-tagged posts are likely to reflect the true mood of the authors and, hence, form a good test-set for Sentic Corner.

In order to have full correspondence between LJ mood labels and Hourglass sentic levels, a pool of 10 students have been asked to map each of the 130 mood labels into the 24 emotional labels of the Hourglass model. All LJ accounts have Atom, RSS and other data feeds which show recent public entries, friend relationships and interests. Unfortunately, there is no possibility to get mood-tagged blog-posts via data feeds so we had to design our own crawler.

After retrieving and storing relevant data and metadata from 10,000 LJ posts, we extracted sentics through the Sentic Corner Generation Process and compared the output with the relative mood-tags, in order to calculate statistical classifications such as precision and recall. On average, each post contained around 140 words and, from it, about 4 affective valence indicators and 60 sentic vectors were extracted. According to this information, we assigned mood-labels to each post and compared these with the corresponding LJ mood-tags, obtaining very good accuracy for each of the mapped moods.

Among these, 'happy' and 'sad' posts were identified with particularly high precision (89% and 81% respectively) and decorous recall rates (76% and 68%). The F-measure values obtained, hence, were significantly good (82% and 74% respectively), especially if compared to the corresponding F-measure rates of the baseline methods (53% and 51% for keyword spotting, 63% and 58% for lexical affinity, 69% and 62% for statistical methods). In the future, we plan to perform also some usability tests in order evaluate the relevance of contents and design displayed, together with the overall user-friendliness of the interface.

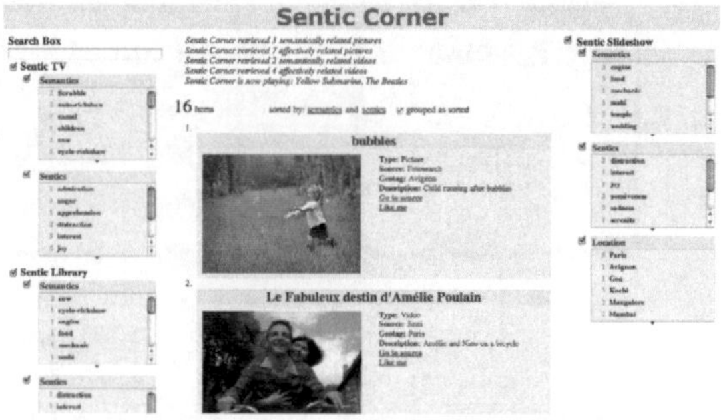

Figure 4: Sentic Corner web interface

7 Conclusion and Future Work

Today an average web user spends around 15 hours per week surfing the Net. Since most of the profit on the Web revolves around advertisement, users are too often blasted with sensory-overloaded web pages, pop-up windows and annoying ads. Within this work, we merged AI and Semantic Web techniques to build an intelligent user interface that dynamically collects audio, video, images and text related to the user's current feelings and activities as an interconnected knowledge base, which is browsable through a multi-faceted classification website.

Sentic Corner exploits the concept that behind every multimedia content there is always an emotion to build a sort of parallel cognitive/affective digital world in which all the multimedia contents are in harmony with user's current emotions and motions. Eventually, Sentic Corner represents a first step towards the development of sentic interfaces, i.e., next-generation intelligent applications capable of perceiving and expressing the cognitive and affective information associated with user interaction.

8 Acknowledgments

This work was undertaken during the first author's research visit to the National Laboratory of Pattern Recognition (NLPR), Institute of Automation, Chinese of Academy of Sciences (CAS) in Beijing (China), which was jointly funded by the Royal Society of Edinburgh (UK) and CAS.

References

Erik Cambria, Amir Hussain, Catherine Havasi, and Chris Eckl. 2009. AffectiveSpace: Blending Common Sense and Affective Knowledge to Perform Emotive Reasoning. In *WOMSA at CAEPIA*, Seville, Spain.

Erik Cambria, Amir Hussain, Tariq Durrani, Catherine Havasi, Chris Eckl, and James Munro. 2010a. Sentic Computing for Patient Centered Applications. In *IEEE ICSP10*, Beijing.

Erik Cambria, Amir Hussain, Catherine Havasi, and Chris Eckl. 2010b. Sentic Computing: Exploitation of Common Sense for the Development of Emotion-Sensitive Systems. volume 5967 of *Lecture Notes in Computer Science*, pages 148–156. Springer, Berlin Heidelberg.

Erik Cambria, Amir Hussain, Catherine Havasi, and Chris Eckl. 2010c. SenticSpace: Visualizing Opinions and Sentiments in a Multi-Dimensional Vector Space. volume 6279 of *Lecture Notes in Computer Science*, pages 385–393. Springer, Berlin Heidelberg.

Erik Cambria, Isabelle Hupont, Amir Hussain, Eva Cerezo, and Sandra Baldassarri. 2011a. Sentic Avatar: Multimodal Affective Conversational Agent with Common Sense. volume 6456 of *Lecture Notes in Computer Science*, pages 82–96. Springer-Verlag, Berlin Heidelberg.

Erik Cambria, Thomas Mazzocco, Amir Hussain, and Chris Eckl. 2011b. Sentic Medoids: Organizing Affective Common Sense Knowledge in a Multi-Dimensional Vector Space. volume 6677 of *Lecture Notes in Computer Science*, pages 601–610. Springer-Verlag, Berlin Heidelberg.

Hallie Ephron. 2008. *1001 Books for Every Mood: A Bibliophile's Guide to Unwinding, Misbehaving, Forgiving, Celebrating, Commiserating*. Adams Media, Avon.

Exhibit. 2011. http://simile-widgets.org/exhibit.

Fotosearch. 2011. http://fotosearch.com.

Marco Grassi. 2009. Developing HEO Human Emotions Ontology. volume 5707 of *Lecture Notes in Computer Science*, pages 244–251. Springer, Berlin Heidelberg.

Alan Hanjalic. 2006. Extracting Moods from Pictures and Sounds: Towards Truly Personalized TV. *IEEE Signal Processing Magazine*, 23(2):90–100.

Catherine Havasi, Robert Speer, and Jason Alonso. 2007. ConceptNet 3: a Flexible, Multilingual Semantic Network for Common Sense Knowledge. In *Proceedings of RANLP*, Borovets.

Catherine Havasi, Robert Speer, James Pustejovsky, and Henry Lieberman. 2009. Digital Intuition: Applying Common Sense Using Dimensionality Reduction. *IEEE Intelligent Systems*, 24(4):24–35.

Catherine Havasi, Robert Speer, and Justin Holmgren. 2010. Automated Color Selection Using Semantic Knowledge. In *Proceedings of AAAI CSK*, Arlington, USA.

Jinni. 2011. http://jinni.com.

LiveJournal. 2011. http://livejournal.com.

Marvin Minsky. 2006. *The Emotion Machine: Commonsense Thinking, Artificial Intelligence, and the Future of the Human Mind*. Simon & Schuster.

Moodstats. 2011. http://moodstats.com.

Moodstream. 2011. http://moodstream.com.

Moodviews. 2011. http://moodviews.com.

Robert Plutchik. 2001. The Nature of Emotions. *American Scientist*, 89(4):344–350.

Robert Schleicher, Shiva Sundaram, and Julia Seebode. 2010. Assessing Audio Clips on Affective and Semantic Level to Improve General Applicability. In *Fortschritte der Akustik - DAGA*, Berlin.

Sesame. 2009. http://openrdf.org.

Uma Srinivasan, Silvia Pfeiffer, Surya Nepal, Michael Lee, Lifang Gu, and Stephen Barrass. 2005. A survey of mpeg-1 audio, video and semantic analysis techniques. *Multimedia Tools and Applications*, 27(1):105–141.

Stereomood. 2011. http://stereomood.com.

Carlo Strapparava and Alessandro Valitutti. 2004. WordNet-Affect: an Affective Extension of WordNet. In *Proceedings of LREC*, Lisbon, Portugal.

Twitter. 2011. http://twitter.com.

Michael Wall, Andreas Rechtsteiner, and Luis Rocha. 2003. Singular Value Decomposition and Principal Component Analysis. In Daniel P. Berrar, Werner Dubitzky, and Martin Granzow, editors, *A Practical Approach to Microarray Data Analysis*, pages 91–109. Springer US.

WeFeelFine. 2011. http://wefeelfine.org.

Sense-level Subjectivity in a Multilingual Setting

Carmen Banea
University of North Texas
carmenbanea@my.unt.edu

Rada Mihalcea
University of North Texas
rada@cs.unt.edu

Janyce Wiebe
University of Pittsburgh
wiebe@cs.pitt.edu

Abstract

This paper explores the ability of senses aligned across languages to carry coherent subjectivity information. We start out with a manual annotation study, and then seek to create an automatic framework to determine subjectivity labeling for unseen senses. We identify two methods that are able to incorporate subjectivity information originating from different languages, namely co-training and multilingual vector spaces, and show that for this task the latter method is better suited and obtains superior results.

1 Introduction

Following the terminology proposed by (Wiebe et al., 2005), subjectivity and sentiment analysis focuses on the automatic identification of private states (opinions, emotions, sentiments, etc.) in natural language. While subjectivity classification labels text as either subjective or objective, sentiment or polarity classification further classifies subjective text as either positive, negative or neutral.

To date, a large number of text processing applications have used techniques for automatic sentiment and subjectivity analysis, including automatic expressive text-to-speech synthesis (Alm et al., 1990), tracking sentiment timelines in on-line forums and news (Balog et al., 2006; Lloyd et al., 2005), and mining opinions from product reviews (Hu and Liu, 2004). In many natural language processing tasks, subjectivity and sentiment classification has been used as a first phase filtering to generate more viable data. Research that benefited from this additional layering ranges from question answering (Yu and Hatzivassiloglou, 2003), to conversation summarization (Carenini et al., 2008), text semantic analysis (Wiebe and Mihalcea, 2006; Esuli and Sebastiani, 2006a) and lexical substitution (Su and Markert, 2010).

While research in English has underlined that the most robust subjectivity delineation occurs at sense and not at word level (Wiebe and Mihalcea, 2006), we are not aware of this consideration impacting research in other languages. For this reason, in this work we seek to analyze how subjectivity is maintained across sense aligned resources, and identify ways in which subjectivity at sense level may be employed in a multilingual framework to provide a strengthened automatic sense-level classification.

2 Related Work

Recently, resources and tools for sentiment analysis developed for English have been used as a starting point to build resources in other languages, via cross-lingual projections or monolingual and multilingual bootstrapping. Several directions were followed, focused on leveraging annotation schemes, lexicons, corpora and automated annotation systems. English annotation schemes developed for opinionated text lays the groundwork for research carried out by (Esuli et al., 2008) when annotating expressions of private state in Italian or by (Maks and Vossen, 2010) in Dutch. Sentiment and subjectivity lexicons such as the one included with the OpinionFinder distribution (Wiebe and Riloff, 2005), the General Inquirer (Stone et al., 1967), or the SentiWordNet (Esuli and Sebastiani, 2006b) were transferred into Chinese (Ku et al., 2006; Wu, 2008) and into Romanian (Mihalcea et al., 2007). English corpora manually annotated for subjectivity or sentiment such as MPQA (Wiebe et al., 2005), or the multi-domain sentiment classification corpus (Blitzer et al., 2007) were subjected to experiments in Spanish, Romanian, or Chinese upon automatic translation by (Banea et al., 2008b; Wan, 2009). Furthermore, tools developed for English were used to determine sentiment

Proceedings of the Workshop on Sentiment Analysis where AI meets Psychology (SAAIP), IJCNLP 2011, pages 44–50,
Chiang Mai, Thailand, November 13, 2011.

or subjectivity labeling for a given target language by transferring the text to English and applying an English classifier on the resulting data. The labels were then transferred back into the target language (Bautin et al., 2008; Banea et al., 2008b). These experiments are carried out in Arabic, Chinese, French, German, Japanese, Spanish, Romanian.

We are not aware of research that has considered leveraging subjectivity at word sense level, yet, in terms of methodology, the work closest to ours is the one proposed by (Wan, 2009), who constructs a polarity co-training system by using the multilingual views obtained through the automatic translation of product-reviews into Chinese and English. Unlike (Wan, 2009), we do not use any machine translation, and the labels employed are directly assigned by the annotators and not inferred based on stars. (Banea et al., 2008a) present a method to learn sentence level subjectivity by training classifiers on multilingual feature spaces and show that when considering features from multiple languages, the classification accuracy improves, even above that of the source language. We expand this method to allow for bootstrapping, thus enabling additional samples to be classified.

3 Sense Level Subjectivity Consistency Across Languages

While most multilingual research to date has focused on word, fragment, or document level subjectivity, this work seeks to examine sense-level subjectivity across languages. We aim to answer two questions. First, if we have a resource such as WordNet (Miller, 1995) aligned at sense level in two languages, is the subjectivity content consistent across equivalent senses in the two languages? Second, can we use a multilingual learning mechanism to automatically predict the subjectivity label of senses? We examine the first question in Section 3.1, and propose a framework for multilingual learning that responds to the second question in Section 3.2.

3.1 Annotation Study

For the purpose of this study we consider the English (Miller, 1995) and the Romanian (Tufiş et al., 2006) versions of WordNet, which contain 117659[1] and 58725[2] synsets, respectively. Both lexical resources are aligned at *synset* level, which represents a basic unit of meaning.

In order to add subjectivity information to this structure, we use the English annotated data from (Wiebe and Mihalcea, 2006) and (Akkaya et al., 2009), as well as a list of 48 additional words, for a total of 134 words encompassing 630 senses manually annotated for subjectivity. This data was then annotated by a native speaker of Romanian (who participated in previous subjectivity annotations studies) who was only presented with the gloss and the synset of each given sense from the Romanian WordNet. The agreement with the English annotations ranged from 90% (for the (Wiebe and Mihalcea, 2006) dataset) to 84% (for the (Akkaya et al., 2009) dataset), implying that subjectivity can strongly transfer across senses given manually aligned resources in different languages. However, we encountered several situations that may interfere with the subjective content of a sense, which are further explained below.

3.1.1 Differences between Languages

There were several examples where the subjectivity label changed between languages. Let us consider the following definitions of the fourth sense of the noun *argument* listed in Table 1. While this sense of *argument* is marked in the English data as subjective, the Romanian gloss and synset denote a "direct summary," which by definition disallows the expression of any subjective perspective. Therefore, in Romanian this sense is objective.

A similar scenario is posed by the fourth sense of the verb *decide* (see Table 1). While the English sense is labeled as objective, the Romanian sense directly implies a subjective decision, and therefore acquires a subjective label.

3.1.2 WordNet Granularity

In several cases, the same sense in WordNet may have both subjective and objective meanings. To exemplify, let us consider the first sense of the adjective *free*:

En gloss: not limited or hampered; not under compulsion or restraint; "free enterprise"; "a

[1] http://wordnet.princeton.edu/wordnet/man/wnstats.7WN.html

[2] http://www.racai.ro/wnbrowser/Help.aspx

	English	Romanian
argument		
Gloss	a summary of the subject or plot of a literary work or play or movie "the editor added the argument to the poem"	redare-prezentare pe scurt- scrisă sau orală- a ideilor unei lucrări- ale unei expuneri etc. $(translation)$ short summary, oral or in writing, of the ideas presented in a literary work
Synset	argument, literary argument	rezumat $(translation)$ summary
decide		
Gloss	influence or determine "The vote in New Hampshire often decides the outcome of the Presidential election"	a exercita o influenţă - a determina $(translation)$ to exercise influence - to determine
Synset	decide	influenţa; decide; hotărî $(translation)$ influence; decide; determine

Table 1: *Differences between languages.* Definitions and synonyms of the fourth sense of the noun *argument* and the fourth sense of verb *decide* as provided by the English and Romanian WordNets; for Romanian we also provide the manual translation into English.

free port"; "a free country"; "I have an hour free"; "free will"; "free of racism"; "feel free to stay as long as you wish"; "a free choice"
Ro gloss: (Despre oameni) Care are posibilitatea de a acţiona după voinţa sa - de a face sau de a nu face ceva; $(translation)$ (About people) Someone who can act according to his will - who can do or not do something

While the English sense can have both subjective and objective uses, the Romanian sense is subjective, as it further enforces the constraint that the context of the word should refer to people.

From these examples, we notice that a perfect sense to sense mapping among languages is impossible, as a particular sense may denote additional meanings and uses in one language compared to another, thus rendering a perfect parallel sense boundary permeable. However, for about 90% of the senses the subjective meaning does hold across languages, implying that this information could be leveraged in an automatic fashion to provide additional clues for the subjectivity labelling of unseen senses.

3.2 Multilingual Subjectivity Sense Learning

In this section we explore ways to use a multilingual learning mechanism to automatically predict the subjectivity of a word sense. We are experimenting with two different methods, one based on co-training using monolingual feature spaces, and one based on machine learning applied to a multilingual vector space.

We start by considering the intersection of the Romanian and English WordNets, so that we can have equivalent definitions in both languages. We then generate vector representations for two monolingual models (one in English and one in Romanian), and one multilingual model (comprising both Romanian and English features). These are composed of unigrams extracted from the synset and the gloss of a given sense, appended with a binary weight. The synset is stripped of any sense identifying features in order not to favor the classifier. To exemplify, we provide below the sparse vector representation of the fourth sense of the noun *argument* (see Table 1):

English vector: <a_{en} 1, summary 1, of 1, the 1, subject 1, or 1, plot 1, literary 1, work 1, play 1, movie 1, editor 1, added 1, argument 1, to 1, poem 1>
Romanian vector: <redare 1, prezentare 1, pe 1, scurt 1, scrisa 1, orala 1, a_{ro} 1, ideilor 1, unei 1, lucrari 1, ale 1, expuneri 1, etc 1, rezumat 1>
Multilingual vector: <a_{en} 1, summary 1, of 1, the 1, subject 1, or 1, plot 1, literary 1, work 1, play 1, movie 1, editor 1, added 1, argument 1, to 1, poem 1, redare 1, prezentare 1, pe 1, scurt 1, scrisa 1, orala 1, a_{ro} 1, ideilor 1, unei 1, lucrari 1, ale 1, expuneri 1, etc 1, rezumat 1>

In the first method, based on the co-training algorithm proposed by (Wan, 2009), we consider the manually annotated training data in each of the languages individually, and we learn two monolingual classifiers (see Figure 1). We then allow the machine learners to individually predict a class for every sample in the unlabeled data, and at every iteration create a set with the top n most confident examples where both classifiers agree, and their confidence is higher than a given threshold. As long as the set has at least one sample, at the next iteration the monolingual English vectors and the aligned Romanian vectors are added to their respective training set with the newly predicted label, and removed from the test data. The process repeats until no confident examples can be added. Although the method differs from the original co-training mechanism proposed by (Blum and Mitchell, 1998), since it enforces that the classifiers agree before adding their predictions to the next train set, we believe this was a necessary modification given the low accuracy attained by the Romanian classifier by itself (68%). Through this additional agreement constraint, we ensure that only samples that have a high probability of being labeled correctly are added, therefore reducing noise propagation across iterations. At the same time, we are able to learn new information from the features co-occurring with those that participated in the previous classification step.

For the second method, we create a multilingual feature space based on the model proposed in (Banea et al., 2010). Instead of using the monolingual vectors described above, we enrich the feature space by merging together two aligned vector space representations (see the multilingual vector example above), thus allowing the system to simultaneously use both Romanian and English features in order to decide the subjectivity of a given sense. At every iteration we select the most confident n samples, and add them to the training set, while discarding them from the test set for the next iteration.

For all the experiments presented in this paper we use support vector machines (the LibSVM implementation (Fan et al., 2005)) with default parameters and probability estimates enabled. As we are interested in an accurate classification of the senses, we chose a threshold level of 0.8, and at every iteration we add the most confident $n = 40$ samples to the previous training set.

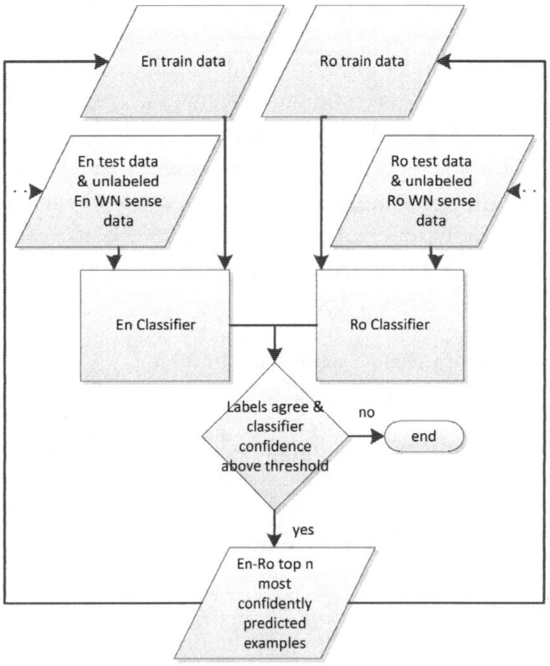

Figure 1: Co-training

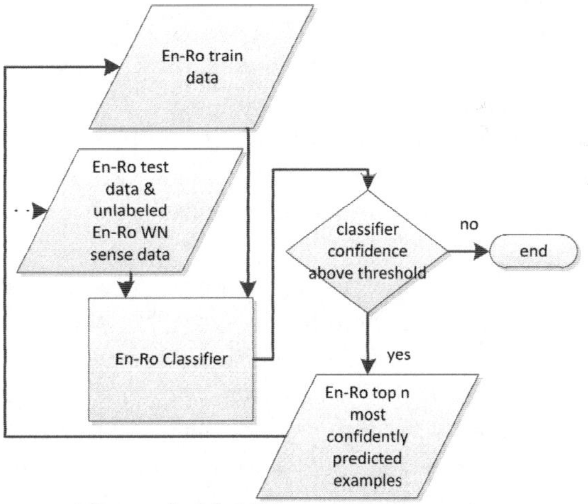

Figure 2: Multilingual bootstrapping

3.2.1 Datasets

We use the manually annotated data described in Section 3.1, and we filter out 20 examples that were labeled as both objective and subjective, since they could confuse the classifiers and prevent them from making strong predictions. We then split the labeled data into three subsets to enable a three-fold cross validation. Note that we enforce that all the senses belonging to a given word be found in either the test or the training set, but never in both. This was done to ensure that the classifier would not have an unfair advantage due to finding similar senses in the training data. For this reason, the fold sizes are not perfectly equal. Furthermore, for every fold, each iteration is evaluated on the immutable test set corresponding to that fold, which has manually assigned labels in English and Romanian. In order to generate a running test set, which is modified after every iteration, we append the remaining unlabeled WordNet senses to the corresponding test set for the fold (see Figures 1 and 2).

3.2.2 Results and Discussions

Figure 3 presents the results obtained using the monolingual co-training algorithm over 40 iterations. The accuracies obtained at position 0 represent the baseline for a simple monolingual classifier with no co-training. Unlike the increasing accuracy with the number of iterations obtained by (Wan, 2009) when applying a similar method to sentiment classification of reviews, we were unable to surpass these baselines. We attribute this behavior to the small size of the training set (approximately 400 samples in our case versus 8000 product reviews in (Wan, 2009)) and the type of data itself (product reviews are longer and often contain a full paragraph of text, while senses may comprise an average of ten words). The overall accuracy is slowly decreasing from 0.73 to 0.62 for English and from 0.68 to 0.54 for Romanian. The same trend is observed for class precision, recall and F-measure.

When employing a simple SVM classifier trained on a multilingual space, the accuracy increases from 0.73 for English and 0.62 for Romanian to 0.76 when both languages are simultaneously used, thus providing an error reduction of 11.34% and 25.74% with respect to the monolingual English and Romanian models, respectively. Since the English WordNet is more complete (longer glosses and richer synsets), its corresponding monolingual model is able to capture sufficient information and thus provide a robust subjectivity classification on its own. However, upon training on a multilingual representation of the data, features from both languages synergistically work together to achieve better results than what would be individually possible. These results further confirm the improving trend we noticed in (Banea et al., 2010) when training classifiers on incrementally more languages.

We also attempted to bootstrap the multilingual classifier (see Figure 4), but its performance degrades faster than when using the co-training method, and after only 3 iterations the confidence of the classifier drops below the threshold and the process terminates. It may be beneficial to add fewer instances to the training set at each iteration in order to introduce less noise and thus obtain a more robust classifier. This is a setting that we intend to explore in the future, however for the current experiments, in order to equitably compare the two methods, we kept all the parameters equal.

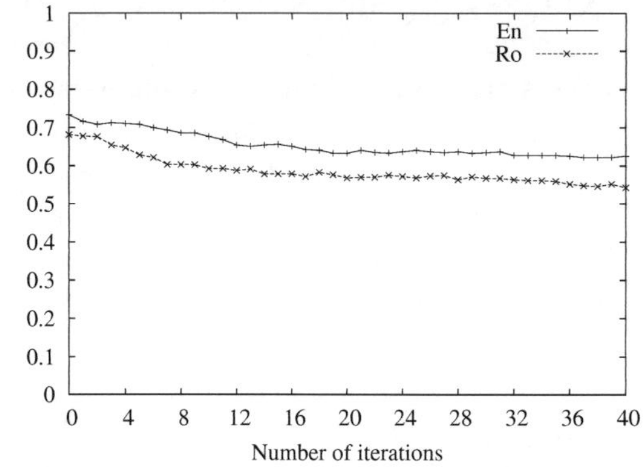

Figure 3: Macro-accuracy for co-training

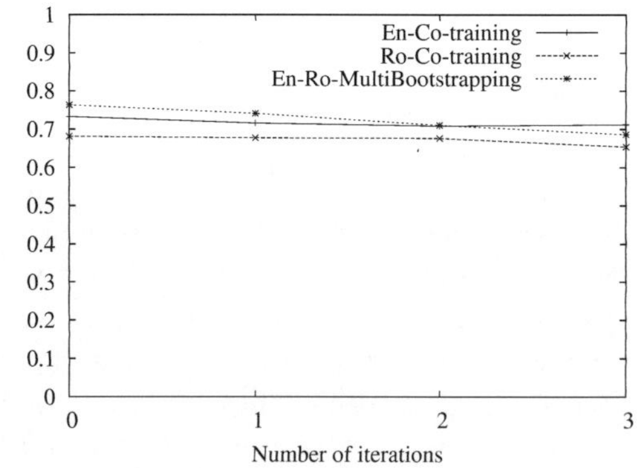

Figure 4: Macro-accuracy for multilingual bootstrapping versus monolingual co-training

4 Conclusion

We performed a manual annotation study for subjectivity at sense level and we showed that the subjectivity content of a sense does carry across language boundaries in about 90% of the cases, implying that this information is robust enough to be learned automatically. We then proposed and applied a framework that is able to jointly exploit the subjectivity information originating from multiple languages. We demonstrated that a multilingual feature space is able to capture more information and outperform a monolingual based model, suggesting that future research should use a similar representation.

Acknowledgments

This material is based in part upon work supported by National Science Foundation awards #0917170 and #0916046. Any opinions, findings, and conclusions or recommendations expressed in this material are those of the authors and do not necessarily reflect the views of the National Science Foundation.

References

Cem Akkaya, Janyce Wiebe, and Rada Mihalcea. 2009. Subjectivity Word Sense Disambiguation. In *Proceedings of the 2009 Conference on Empirical Methods in Natural Language Processing*, pages 190–199, Singapore, August.

Cecilia Ovesdotter Alm, Dan Roth, and Richard Sproat. 1990. Emotions from text: machine learning for text-based emotion prediction. *Intelligence*.

Krisztian Balog, Gilad Mishne, and Maarten De Rijke. 2006. Why Are They Excited? Identifying and Explaining Spikes in Blog Mood Levels. In *Proceedings of the 11th Conference of the European Chapter of the Association for Computational Linguistics (EACL-2006)*, Trento, Italy.

Carmen Banea, Rada Mihalcea, and Janyce Wiebe. 2008a. A Bootstrapping method for building subjectivity lexicons for languages with scarce resources. In *Proceedings of the Learning Resources Evaluation Conference (LREC 2008)*, Marrakech, Morocco.

Carmen Banea, Rada Mihalcea, Janyce Wiebe, and Samer Hassan. 2008b. Multilingual subjectivity analysis using machine translation. In *Proceedings of the 2008 Conference on Empirical Methods in Natural Language Processing (EMNLP-2008)*, pages 127–135, Honolulu, Hawaii.

Carmen Banea, Rada Mihalcea, and Janyce Wiebe. 2010. Multilingual Subjectivity: Are More Languages Better ? In *Proceedings of the International Conference on Computational Linguistics (COLING 2010)*, Beijing, China.

Mikhail Bautin, Lohit Vijayarenu, and Steven Skiena. 2008. International sentiment analysis for news and blogs. In *Proceedings of the International Conference on Weblogs and Social Media (ICWSM-2008)*, Seattle, Washington.

John Blitzer, Mark Dredze, and Fernando Pereira. 2007. Biographies, Bollywood, Boom-boxes and Blenders: Domain Adaptation for Sentiment Classification. In *Proceedings of the 45th Annual Meeting of the Association of Computational (ACL-2007)*, pages 440–447, Prague, Czech Republic. Association for Computational Linguistics.

Avrim Blum and Tom Mitchell. 1998. Combining labeled and unlabeled data with co-training. In *COLT: Proceedings of the Workshop on Computational Learning Theory*, pages 92–100. Morgan Kaufmann.

Giuseppe Carenini, Raymond T Ng, and Xiaodong Zhou. 2008. Summarizing Emails with Conversational Cohesion and Subjectivity. In *Proceedings of the Association for Computational Linguistics: Human Language Technologies (ACL- HLT 2008)*, pages 353–361, Columbus, Ohio.

Andrea Esuli and Fabrizio Sebastiani. 2006a. Determining Term Subjectivity and Term Orientation for Opinion Mining. In *Proceedings of the 11th Meeting of the European Chapter of the Association for Computational Linguistics (EACL-2006)*, volume 2, pages 193–200, Trento, Italy.

Andrea Esuli and Fabrizio Sebastiani. 2006b. SentiWordNet: A Publicly Available Lexical Resource for Opinion Mining. In *Proceedings of the 5th Conference on Language Resources and Evaluation*, pages 417–422.

Andrea Esuli, Fabrizio Sebastiani, and Ilaria C Urciuoli. 2008. Annotating Expressions of Opinion and Emotion in the Italian Content Annotation Bank. In *Proceedings of the Sixth International Language Resources and Evaluation (LREC-2008)*, Marrakech, Morocco.

Rong-En Fan, Pai-Hsuen Chen, and Chih-Jen Lin. 2005. Working set selection using the second order information for training SVM. *Journal of Machine Learning Research*, 6:1889—-1918.

Minqing Hu and Bing Liu. 2004. Mining and Summarizing Customer Reviews. In *Proceedings of ACM Conference on Knowledge Discovery and Data Mining (ACM-SIGKDD-2004)*, pages 168–177, Seattle, Washington.

Lun-wei Ku, Yu-ting Liang, and Hsin-hsi Chen. 2006. Opinion Extraction, Summarization and Tracking in News and Blog Corpora. In *Proceedings of AAAI-2006 Spring Symposium on Computational Approaches to Analyzing Weblogs*, number 2001, Boston, Massachusetts.

Levon Lloyd, Dimitrios Kechagias, and Steven Skiena. 2005. Lydia : A System for Large-Scale News Analysis (Extended Abstract) News Analysis with Lydia. In *Lecture Notes in Computer Science*, pages 161–166. Springer, Berlin / Heidelberg.

Isa Maks and Piek Vossen. 2010. Annotation scheme and gold standard for Dutch subjective adjectives. In *Proceedings of the 7th conference on International Language Resources and Evaluation (LREC'10)*, pages 1327–1334, Valletta, Malta.

Rada Mihalcea, Carmen Banea, and Janyce Wiebe. 2007. Learning Multilingual Subjective Language via Cross-Lingual Projections. In *Proceedings of the 45th Annual Meeting of the Association of Computational Linguistics (ACL-2007)*, pages 976–983, Prague, Czech Republic.

George A. Miller. 1995. WordNet: a Lexical database for English. *Communications of the Association for Computing Machinery*, 38(11):39—-41.

Philip J Stone, Marshall S Smith, Daniel M Ogilivie, and Dexter C Dumphy. 1967. *The General Inquirer: A Computer Approach to Content Analysis. /*. The MIT Press, 1st edition.

Fangzhong Su and Katja Markert. 2010. Word sense subjectivity for cross-lingual lexical substitution. In *Proceedings of Human Language Technologies: The 2010 Annual Conference of the North American Chapter of the Association for Computational Linguistics (HLT'10)*, pages 357—-360, Los Angeles, CA, USA.

Dan Tufiş, Verginica Mititelu Barbu, Luigi Bozianu, and Cătălin Mihăilă. 2006. Romanian Wordnet: current state, new developments and applications. In *Proceedings of the 3rd Conference of the Global WordNet Association (GWC'06)*, pages 337–344, Seogwipo, Jeju Island, Republic of Korea.

Xiaojun Wan. 2009. Co-Training for Cross-Lingual Sentiment Classification. In *Proceedings of the 47th Annual Meeting of the Association for Computational Linguistics and the 4th International Joint Conference on Natural Language Processing of the Asian Federation of Natural Language Processing (ACL-IJCNLP 2009)*, Singapore.

Janyce Wiebe and Rada Mihalcea. 2006. Word Sense and Subjectivity. In *Proceedings of the joint conference of the International Committee on Computational Linguistics and the Association for Computational Linguistics (COLING-ACL-2006)*, Sydney, Australia.

Janyce Wiebe and Ellen Riloff. 2005. Creating Subjective and Objective Sentence Classifiers from Unannotated Texts. In *Proceeding of CICLing-05, International Conference on Intelligent Text Processing and Computational Linguistics*, pages 486–497, Mexico City, Mexico.

Janyce Wiebe, Theresa Wilson, and Claire Cardie. 2005. Annotating Expressions of Opinions and Emotions in Language. *Language Resources and Evaluation*, 39(2-3):165–210.

Yejun Wu. 2008. Classifying attitude by topic aspect for English and Chinese document collections.

Hong Yu and Vasileios Hatzivassiloglou. 2003. Towards answering opinion questions: Separating facts from opinions and identifying the polarity of opinion sentence. In *Proceedings of the Conference on Empirical Methods in Natural Language Processing (EMNLP-2003)*, pages 129–136, Sapporo, Japan.

Applying Sentiment-oriented Sentence Filtering to Multilingual Review Classification

Takashi Inui and **Mikio Yamamoto**
Graduate School of Systems and Information Engineering
University of Tsukuba
1-1-1 Tenoudai, Tsukuba, Ibaraki 305-8573, JAPAN
{inui,myama}@cs.tsukuba.ac.jp

Abstract

A method for multilingual review classification is described. In this classification task, machine translation techniques are used to remove language gaps in the dataset, but many translation errors occur as a side-effect. These errors cause a decrease in the review classification performance. To resolve this problem, we introduce a sentiment-oriented sentence filtering module to the process of multilingual review classification. Experimental results showed that the proposed method achieved 81.7% classification accuracy for the evaluation data.

1 Introduction

People can nowadays easily disseminate information including their personal subjective opinions on products and services on the Internet. The massive amounts of this type of information are beneficial for both product companies and users who are planning to purchase and use the products. The information is mainly presented in a textual form, so in the research field of natural language processing, many researchers have focused on developing techniques for *sentiment analysis* (or *opinion mining*) (Pang and Lee, 2008; Tang et al., 2009).

One fundamental technique in sentiment analysis (opinion mining) is to classify review texts. Unlike the conventional topic-based text classification task, classifiers for review classification must discriminate between *positive* and *negative* aspects of opinions in a review text. In the review classification task, supervised machine learning methods such as Naive Bayes and Support Vector Machines have been mostly applied (Pang et al., 2002; Mullen and Collier, 2004; Whitelaw et al., 2005). These supervised approaches have achieved good performance, but they have a crucial issue: they require a large amount of labeled data, which involves the high cost of manual annotation.

Approaches to reduce or avoid the cost of annotation have been proposed, such as semi-supervised and substitutional data approaches. Semi-supervised approaches (e.g., that by Aue and Gamon (2005)) provide a simple solution by combining labeled and unlabeled data. Substitutional data approaches provide substitutional labeled data, available at low costs, instead of pure labeled data. The tasks of domain adaption (Blitzer et al., 2007) and multilingual text classification (Banea et al., 2008; Wan, 2009; Banea et al., 2010) are special cases of substitutional approaches.

In this paper, we examine the effectiveness of applying a sentence filtering module to multilingual document classification, especially to multilingual review classification. In multilingual review classification, machine translation techniques are usually used to remove language gaps in the dataset. But, even if one can use the state-of-the-art machine translation techniques, many translation errors occur as a side-effect. These errors cause a decrease in the review classification performance. In this study, to resolve this problem, we introduce a sentiment-oriented sentence filtering module to the process of multilingual review classification. we focus on the quality rather than the quantity of the training data, and attempt to filter out some worthless sentences from the dataset.

The rest of this paper is organized as follows. First, we provide an overview of multilingual review classification in Section 2. In addition, an issue essentially related to the task of multilingual review classification is presented. In Section 3, we explain our sentiment-oriented sentence filtering method. In Section 4, we report on our experi-

Proceedings of the Workshop on Sentiment Analysis where AI meets Psychology (SAAIP), IJCNLP 2011, pages 51–58,
Chiang Mai, Thailand, November 13, 2011.

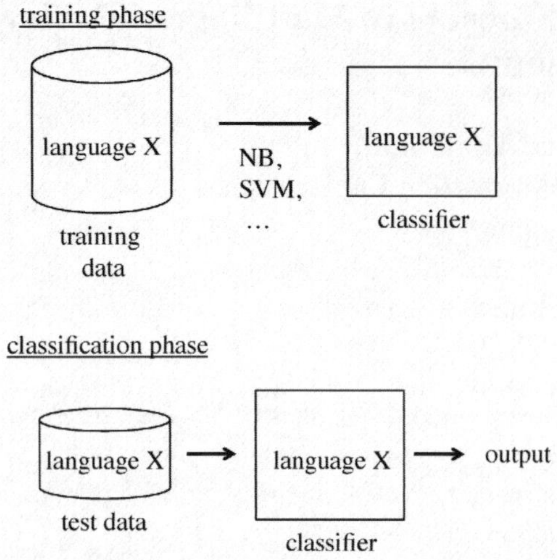

Figure 1: Monolingual review classification

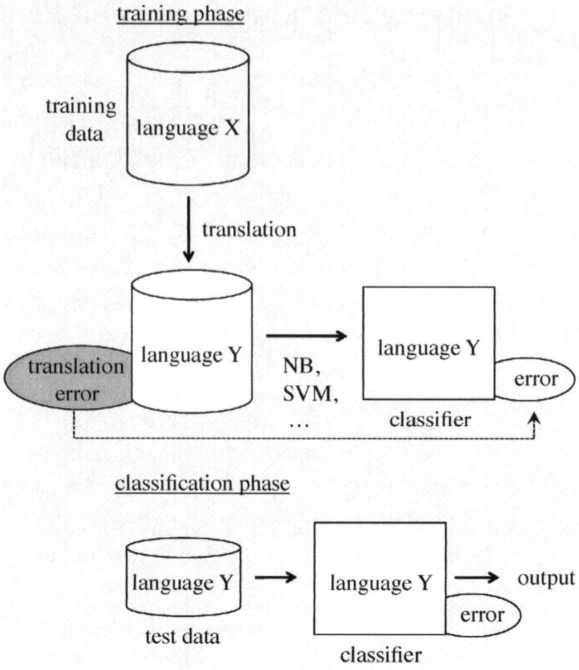

Figure 2: Multilingual review classification

ments investigating the effectiveness of applying our filtering method to multilingual review classification.

2 Multilingual Review Classification

2.1 Overview

Figure 1 shows an ordinary processing flow of text (review) classification with monolingual data. In a monolingual setting, in both the training phase and classification phase, text documents in the dataset are described in the same language (language *X* in Figure 1). Figure 2, in contrast, shows a multilingual setting for review classification. In this setting, text documents in the classification phase are described in a different language, *Y*, from *X*.

To remove the language gap between the training and test datasets, machine translation (MT) techniques are used in the training phase. By translating text documents in the dataset from the source language *X* into the target language *Y*, an MT system automatically generates a substitutional dataset in which text documents are described in the target language *Y*[1].

2.2 The issue

Here, the MT system succeeds in removing the language gap between *X* and *Y*. However, many translation errors occur in the dataset as a side-effect. In general, a text classifier uses information about word distributions over the dataset. When there are erroneous translations in the dataset, a situation is invoked in which the distributions of each word in the dataset differ between the training data and the test data. As a result, these errors cause increase of text classification errors indirectly (dotted line in Figure 2).

[1]Note that even though a small amount of original labeled documents is described (i.e., not translated) in language *Y* in general cases, this is omitted in Figure 2 for simplicity.

3 Applying Sentiment-oriented Sentence Filtering

In this section, our method for reducing the influences of translation errors is proposed. In the proposed method, documents translated by an MT system are then compressed by a sentiment-oriented sentence filtering module. We begin with discussion about our key idea of the proposed method, and then explain our sentiment-oriented sentence filtering.

3.1 Key idea

Consider the relationship between a labeled dataset for training a text classifier and its classification accuracy. In a general case, the larger the labeled training dataset, the better the performance of the text classifier. However, in the case of multilingual review classification, this relationship does not hold due to the translation errors be-

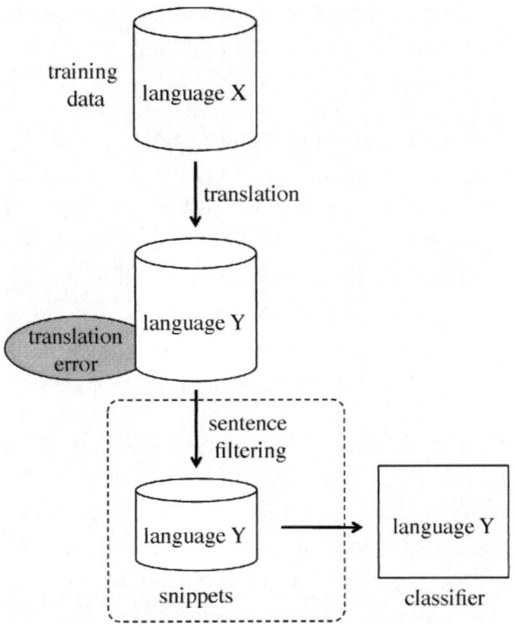

Figure 3: Multilingual review classification with sentence filtering

cause if the labeled data increase, the translation errors included in them may also increase. That is, the number of translation errors may be proportional to the number of labeled documents.

According to the above discussion, we focused our attention on the *quality* rather than the *quantity* of the labeled data. To achieve this change of focus, we introduce a sentence filtering module after the machine translation step. Figure 3 shows the training phase of multilingual review classification with the sentence filtering module. In the sentence filtering module, a translated document is compressed into a snippet consisting of important parts of the translated document for the review classification task. Since the generated snippet is shorter than the input document, and recalling that the number of translation errors may be proportional to the quantity of the dataset, applying sentence filtering should help to prevent errors being incorporated into the dataset.

3.2 Sentiment-oriented sentence filtering

Our sentence filtering module aims to generate text snippets by excluding translation errors from the input translated documents. To do so, we developed a sentiment-oriented sentence filtering method.

We need to develop criteria by which sentences should be extracted. The most direct approach is that *all sentences correctly translated are extracted and all remaining erroneous sentences are excluded.* This may work well, but it is infeasible because detecting whether a sentence is correctly translated is difficult.

Instead, we consider an alternative approach based on sentiment information. Pang et al. (2004) found that an important factor for a review classification task is whether each sentence in a document to be classified holds subjective aspects. Generally, subjective sentences contribute to the performance of review classification, while objective sentences do not. According to this finding, we adopted the following sentence filtering criteria: *all sentences holding subjective aspects are extracted and all remaining objective sentences are excluded.* We consider that objective sentences with translation errors are not only unnecessary but also harmful for the multilingual review classification.

In this study, we detect a sentence S_Y as holding subjective aspects when all the following conditions are fulfilled.

(1) S_Y includes at least one polarity word,

(2) A sentence S_X, which has a translation relation to S_Y, also includes at least one polarity word,

(3) All the polarity words in S_X and S_Y have the same sentiment polarity.

Condition (1) is commonly used in the field of sentiment analysis (Kim and Hovy, 2005). Conditions (2) and (3), on the other hand, are originally derived from the translation process in the multilingual review classification. By adding these two conditions, we achieve more robust subjectivity detection. Figure 4 shows an example of the sentence filtering process. Sentences S_{Y2} and S_{Y4} fulfill all the conditions and thus are extracted. Sentences S_{Y1} and S_{Y3} are excluded. S_{Y1} violates condition (1): it has no polarity words. S_{Y3} violates condition (3): although S_{Y3} has a negative polarity word, S_{X3} has a positive polarity word. In this example, one can see that the snippet generated keeps almost all the subjective information and also that it succeeds in eliminating parts of erroneous translations.

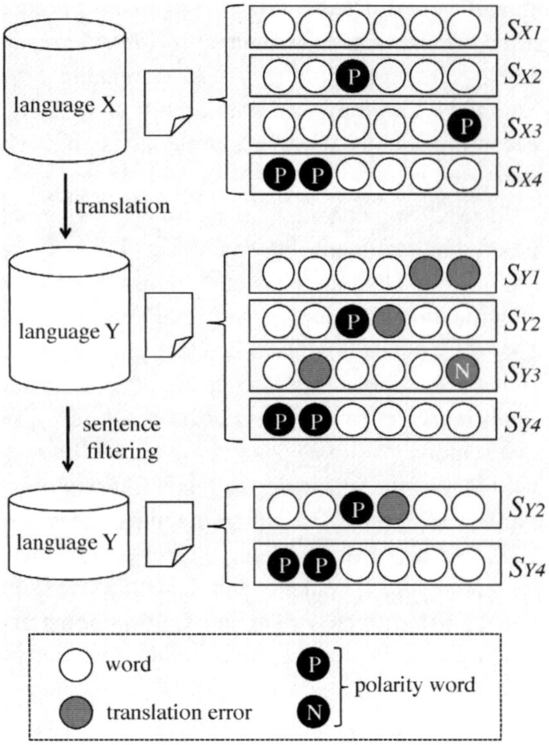

Figure 4: Example of sentence filtering process

4 Evaluation

We conducted experiments for investigating the effectiveness of applying our sentiment-oriented sentence filtering method to the multilingual review classification.

4.1 Experimental settings

4.1.1 Multilingual review classification methods

Review classification methods that enable handling of multilingual data have been proposed. We adopted those proposed by Banea et al. (2008) and Wan (2009) in our experiments, since theirs are well-known and standard methods.

Banea's method (2008) has two classification models that are dependent on the running position of the MT system.

Training data Translation Model (TrTM) This model is actually shown in Figure 2. A text classifier is learned using a dataset described in the target language. To do so, before the text classifier is learned, documents (reviews) in the training dataset that are described in the source language are translated into the same language as those in the test dataset. We do not need to do anything with the test dataset.

Test data Translation Model (TeTM) This is a reverse version of TrTM. A text classifier is learned using a dataset described in the source language. In this model, documents in the test dataset are translated into the same language as that in the training dataset before the classification phase is run. We do not need to do anything with the training dataset.

Wan's method (2009) combines the above two models through the multi-viewpoint style co-training approach proposed by Blum and Mitchell (1998). Here, the source language and the target language are considered as each viewpoint. The sets of features extracted from dataset described in each language are simultaneously used in the co-training framework. This method iteratively runs TrTM and TeTM. For each iteration, two sets of additional unlabeled review dataset, one is described in the target language and another is the same dataset but is translated into the source language, are applied as input to TrTM/TeTM to predict their (temporal) class label. Of all predicted review data, a subset confidently predicted is added into the original labeled training dataset. We call this method the **Co-training Model** in the remainder of this paper.

The sentence filtering mentioned in the previous section is a preprocessing stage of multilingual review classification. Therefore, each classification model (TrTM, TeTM, and Co-training) is able to run without any modifications. We can directly use the snippets as elements of the training/test dataset.

4.1.2 Dataset

Works on sentiment analysis have usually been carried out in English because there is a large amount of English linguistic resources available for sentiment analysis. Thus, in this study we set English as a source language and Japanese as a target language.

We collected reviews for use in our experiments from one of the most popular global e-commerce sites, Amazon. We accessed Amazon.com ("http://www.amazon.com/") for English reviews and Amazon.co.jp ("http://www.amazon.co.jp/") for Japanese reviews.

Table 1: Number of English/Japanese polarity words

polarity words	all	positive	negative
English	1,392	609	783
Japanese	724	340	384

Table 2: Number of documents/sentences including a polarity word

data type	#documents		#sentences	
English	9,738/10,000	(97%)	51,661/82,310	(63%)
EtoJ	8,283/10,000	(83%)	26,424/82,310	(32%)
Japanese	955/ 1,000	(96%)	3,498/ 7,466	(47%)
JtoE	985/ 1,000	(99%)	5,017/ 7,466	(67%)

First, we prepared a common product list. This is a list of products that can be purchased through both Amazon.com and Amazon.co.jp. We used in this study a list of MP3 audio players, such as "iPod (Apple)" and "Walkman (Sony)". Second, we retrieved and crawled a set of reviews by using the above list from Amazon.com and Amazon.co.jp. All crawled reviews hold an up-to-five-star user rating. We regarded reviews holding four or five stars as positive reviews and those holding one or two stars as negative reviews. As a result, we obtained 1,000 Japanese reviews (500 positive / 500 negative reviews), and 10,000 English reviews (5,000 positive / 5,000 negative reviews). In our setting, the source language was English. The volume of English reviews was 10 times that of Japanese ones. All reviews were original, and there were no duplicates.

4.1.3 Polarity dictionary

We need to prepare a set of polarity words to run sentiment-oriented sentence filtering. We used a polarity dictionary generated as follows.

1) We constructed initial polarity dictionaries by using the methods by Takamura et al. (2005b) and Takamura et al. (2005a) [2]. In these methods, the English polarity dictionary is constructed based on WordNet (1998) information, and the Japanese polarity dictionary is constructed based on Iwanami Japanese-language dictionary (1994), respectively. Each method output a set of word/polarity pairs with a confidence level.

2) We manually corrected words with a high confidence level, and we eliminated words with a low confidence level from the initial dictionary.

Table 1 shows the number of English/Japanese polarity words in our dictionary.

Table 2 shows the number of documents/sentences including a polarity word in the dataset. The abbreviation EtoJ means English documents were translated to Japanese. The abbreviation JtoE means translation in the opposite direction. On the document level, excepting the case of EtoJ (83%, slightly low percentage), almost all documents (reviews) included at least one polarity word. This means that the set of polarity words used in the experiments has wide coverage.

4.1.4 Other settings

We used as a machine translation system the Excite automatic translation service[3]. This site provides rule-based machine translation between English and Japanese (both EtoJ and JtoE).

For learning review classifiers, we used a linear kernel support vector machine (SVM) and the software package Classias[4] for training SVM classifiers. Unigram-based binary feature vectors were constructed. As the tokenization process (recognizing word separations) for Japanese reviews, we used a well-known Japanese NLP programming software package, MeCab[5]. All English words in

[2]The essential part of the above both papers is the same. The difference is only that language for the input. In the (Takamura et al., 2005b) the authors introduced for the English polarity dictionary, and in the (Takamura et al., 2005a) introduced for the Japanese polarity dictionary.

[3]http://www.excite.co.jp/world/

[4]http://www.chokkan.org/software/classias/index.html.en

[5]http://mecab.sourceforge.net/

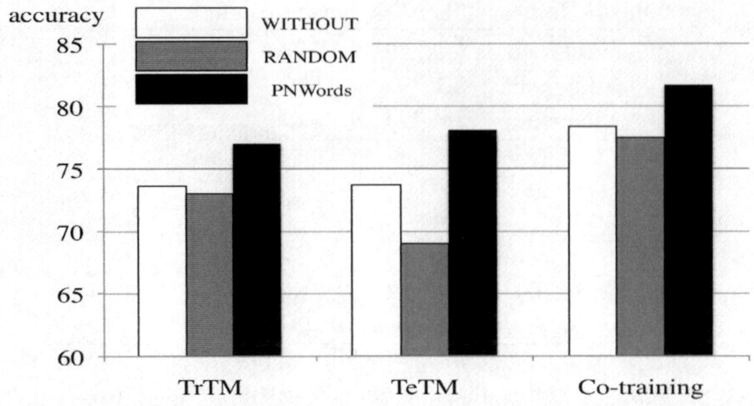

Figure 5: Effects of sentence extraction

the dataset were lower-cased.

We used ten-fold cross-validation for the evaluation.

4.2 Experimental results

The experimental results are shown in Table 3 (see also Figure 5). The value in each cell indicates the classification accuracy. Each column shows the multilingual review classification method, and each row shows the sentence extraction method in the sentence filtering step. **PNWords** is the sentence extraction method described in Section 3, i.e., our proposed method. The others are baseline methods for comparison. **WITHOUT** means that the sentence filtering step was skipped at the training phase of text classifiers; all sentences in the reviews in the training dataset were used in the training phase. **RANDOM** means that snippets were generated by randomly extracting K percent of sentences from the original reviews in the dataset. We set K=50 in the experiments. Unlike WITHOUT and PNWords, RANDOM had essentially randomness. Therefore, we prepared five sets of snippets by running RANDOM five times and then measured five accuracy values. The average accuracy is shown in Table 3.

We also developed a system which was trained on documents written in Japanese in order to see what is the accuracy of the system when a MT is not used. The accuracy of this system is 77.9%.

To investigate the performances of the three multilingual classification methods, we first ignored the effects of sentence filtering modules and simply compared the accuracies of the first row, i.e., the results obtained by WITHOUT. Table 3

Table 3: Effects of sentence extraction

	TrTM	TeTM	Co-training
WITHOUT	73.6	73.7	78.4
RANDOM	73.0	69.0	77.5
PNWords	77.0	78.1	**81.7**

shows that the accuracy of Co-training is higher than that of both TrTM and TeTM. Thus, the co-training model is considered to have an advantage over both TrTM and TeTM. This result corresponds with those reported by Wan (2009). We confirmed that Wan's co-training method outperforms TrTM and TeTM in a multilingual review classification problem.

Next, we investigated the effectiveness of the proposed sentence filtering method. In comparing WITHOUT and RANDOM for each multilingual review classification method, when the sentence filtering step with the RANDOM method was added to the training phase of text classifiers, the classification accuracy worsened rather than improved. One can see that extracting sentences without thought (namely, at random) does not contribute to improvement of the text classification performance. Last, in comparing WITHOUT and PNWords, one can see that PNWords outperforms WITHOUT for all the multilingual review classification methods and that the combination of Co-training and PNWords achieves the best performance. From the results, we can conclude that our sentiment-oriented sentence filtering method can improve multilingual review classification.

5 Related Works

Several methods of monolingual document-level sentiment classification have been proposed. In the early works in this field, such as by Pang et al. (2002), Mullen and Collier (2004), and Gamon (2004), the interest was in simply applying machine learning approaches. The latest works in this field have discussed some specific features for sentiment analysis. For example, Li et al. (2009) and Dasgupta and Ng (2010) considered shifting polarity and ambiguous polarity in documents.

The multilingual setting is also a recent topic. As described in Section 4, Banea et al. (2008) proposed a simple solution using machine translation. Wan (2009) extended Banea's work, and applied for English/Chinese reviews. Denecke (2008) also proposed a similar method for English/German reviews. He used SentiWordNet[6], which is an enhanced lexical resource for sentiment analysis and opinion mining.

In the word-level multilingual sentiment classification area, Mihalcea et al. (2007) proposed two methods for translating polarity words using bilingual dictionaries and a parallel corpus. Scheible (2010) proposed a graph-based approach to obtain translation information of polarity words. He used English/German dataset.

In the sentence-level multilingual sentiment classification area, Banea et al. (2010) conducted experiments with six languages (English, Arabic, French, German, Romanian and Spanish) , and reported that one can predict sentence-level subjectivity in languages other than English, by leveraging on a manually annotated English dataset, with 71.3% (for Arabic) to 73.66% (for Spanish).

6 Conclusion

We investigated the effectiveness of applying our sentiment-oriented sentence filtering method to reduce the influence of translation errors in multilingual document-level review classification. Our filtering method can improve the performance of multilingual review classification. Experimental results showed that the proposed method achieved 81.7% classification accuracy.

The following issues will need to be addressed to refine our method.

- In this study, we treated sentence-level linguistic units to reduce the influence of translation errors. In the future, we will also investigate performances when extracting fine-grained linguistic units, such as words and phrases. For example, Wei and Pal (2010) attempted to apply structural correspondence learning (Blitzer et al., 2006; Blitzer et al., 2007) to find a low dimensional document representation.

- We applied the proposed method only to English/Japanese dataset. Additional experiments with other languages should be conducted for further and more sophisticated data analysis.

- Yang et al. (2009) handled heterogeneous data in a framework of transfer learning (Pan and Yang, 2010). The relationship between our approach and transfer learning would be interesting to examine.

[6] http://sentiwordnet.isti.cnr.it/

References

Anthony Aue and Michael Gamon. 2005. Customizing sentiment classifiers to new domains: a case study. In *Proceedings of Recent Advances in Natural Language Processing*.

Carmen Banea, Rada Mihalcea, Janyce Wiebe, and Samer Hassan. 2008. Multilingual subjectivity analysis using machine translation. In *Proceedings of the Conference on Empirical Methods in Natural Language Processing*, pages 127–135.

Carmen Banea, Rada Mihalcea, and Janyce Wiebe. 2010. Multilingual subjectivity: Are more languages better? In *Proceedings of the 23rd International Conference on Computational Linguistics*, pages 28–36.

John Blitzer, Ryan McDonald, and Rernando Pereira. 2006. Domain adaptation with structural correspondence learning. In *Proceedings of the Conference on Empirical Methods in Natural Language Processing*, pages 120–128.

John Blitzer, Mark Dredze, and Fernando Pereira. 2007. Biographies, bollywood, boom-boxes and blenders: Domain adaptation for sentiment classification. In *Proceedings of the 45th Annual Meeting of the Association for Computational Linguistics*, pages 440–447.

Avrim Blum and Tom Mitchell. 1998. Combining labeled and unlabeled data with co-training. In *Proceedings of the eleventh annual conference on Computational learning theory*, pages 92–100.

Sajib Dasgupta and Vincent Ng. 2010. Mine the easy and classify the hard: Experiments with automatic sentiment classification. In *Proceedings of the 47th Annual Meeting of the Association for Computational Linguistics*, pages 701–709.

Kerstin Denecke. 2008. Using SentiWordNet for multilingual sentiment analysis. In *Proceedings of the ICDE Workshop on Data Engineering for Blogs, Social Media, and Web 2.0*, pages 507–512.

C. Fellbaum. 1998. *WordNet: An Electronic Lexical Database*. The MIT Press.

Michael Gamon. 2004. Sentiment classification on customer feedback data: Noisy data, large feature vectors, and the role of linguistic analysis. In *Proceedings of the 18th International Conference on Computational Linguistics*.

Soo-Min Kim and Eduard Hovy. 2005. Automatic detection of opinion bearing words and sentences. In *Proceedings of the 2nd International Joint Conference on Natural Language Processing*, pages 61–66.

Shoushan Li, Sophia Yat Mei Lee, Ying Chen, Chu-Ren Huang, and Guodong Zhou. 2009. Sentiment classification and polarity shifting. In *Proceedings of the 23rd International Conference on Computational Linguistics*.

Rada Mihalcea, Carmen Banea, and Janyce Wiebe. 2007. Learning multilingual subjective language via cross-lingual projections. In *Proceedings of the 45th Annual Meeting of the Association for Computational Linguistics*.

Tony Mullen and Nigel Collier. 2004. Sentiment analysis using support vector machines with diverse information sources. In *Proceedings of the Conference on Empirical Methods in Natural Language Processing*, pages 412–418.

M. Nishio, E. Iwabuchi, and S. Mizutani. 1994. *Iwanami Japanese-language dictionary*. Iwanami Shoten.

Sinno Jialin Pan and Qiang Yang. 2010. A survey on transfer learning. *IEEE Transactions on Knowledge and Data Engineering*, 22(10):1345–1359.

Bo Pang and Lillian Lee. 2004. A sentimental education: Sentiment analysis using subjectivity summarization based on minimum cuts. In *Proceedings of the 42th Annual Meeting of the Association for Computational Linguistics*, pages 271–278.

Bo Pang and Lillian Lee. 2008. *Opinion Mining and Sentiment Analysis*. Now Publishers Inc.

Bo Pang, Lillian Lee, and Shivakumar Vaithyanathan. 2002. Thumbs up? sentiment classification using machine learning techniques. In *Proceedings of the Conference on Empirical Methods in Natural Language Processing*, pages 76–86.

Christian Scheible. 2010. Sentiment translation through lexicon induction. In *Proceedings of the ACL 2010 Student Research Workshop*, pages 25–30.

Hiroya Takamura, Takashi Inui, and Manabu Okumura. 2005a. Extracting semantic orientation of words using spin model. In *IPSJ SIG Note (NL-168-22)*, pages 141–148. (In Japanese).

Hiroya Takamura, Takashi Inui, and Manabu Okumura. 2005b. Extracting semantic orientations of words using spin model. In *Proceedings of the 43rd Annual Meeting of the Association for Computational Linguistics*, pages 133–140.

Huifeng Tang, Songbo Tan, and Xueqi Cheng. 2009. A survey on sentiment detection of reviews. *Expert Systems with Applications*, 36(7):10760–10773.

Xiaojun Wan. 2009. Co-training for cross-lingual sentiment classification. In *Proceedings of the 47th Annual Meeting of the Association for Computational Linguistics*, pages 235–243.

Bin Wei and Christopher Pal. 2010. Cross lingual adaptation: An experiment on sentiment classifications. In *Proceedings of the 48th Annual Meeting of the Association for Computational Linguistics*, pages 258–262.

Casey Whitelaw, Navendu Garg, and Shlomo Argamon. 2005. Using appraisal groups for sentiment analysis. In *Proceedings of the ACM 14th Conference on Information and Knowledge Management*.

Qiang Yang, Yuqiang Chen, Gui rong Xue, Wenyuan Dai, and Yong Yu. 2009. Heterogeneous transfer learning for image clustering via the social web. In *Proceedings of the ACL-IJCNLP*, pages 1–9.

Analyzing Emotional Statements – Roles of General and Physiological Variables

Dipankar Das
Computer Science & Engineering
Department, Jadavpur University, India
dipankar.dipnil2005@gmail.com

Sivaji Bandyopadhyay
Computer Science & Engineering
Department, Jadavpur University, India
sivaji_cse_ju@yahoo.com

Abstract

The present task collects different statistics of emotions based on the combinations of general variables (*intensity, timing and longevity*) and physiological variables (*psycho-physiological arousals*) from the situational statements of the ISEAR (International Survey on Emotion Antecedents and Reactions) dataset. The individual as well as combinational roles of different variables are analyzed. Some interesting observations and insights are found with respect to emotions. The statements of similar emotions are clustered according to different combinations of the variables. Each of the statements of a cluster is passed through two types of emotion tagging systems, a lexicon based baseline system followed by a supervised system. Due to the difficulty of incorporating knowledge regarding physiological variables, the supervised system only considers the roles of general variables from textual statements. The roles of the general variables are played by intensifiers, modifiers and explicitly specified *temporal* and *causal* discourse markers. The evaluation indicates that the supervised system based on general variables produces satisfactory results in identifying emotions.

1 Introduction

There exist several frameworks from various fields of academic study, such as cognitive science, linguistics and psychology that can inform and augment analyses of sentiment, opinion and emotion (Read and Caroll, 2010). Emotion is a complex psycho-physiological experience of an individual's state of mind as interacting with biochemical (internal) and environmental (external) influences. In humans, emotion fundamentally involves physiological arousal, expressive behaviors and conscious experience (Myers, 2004). Emotions, of course, are not linguistic objects/entities. However the most convenient access to emotions is through the language (Strapparava and Valitutti, 2004). Natural language texts not only contain informative contents, but also some attitudinal private information including emotions. But, the identification of emotions from texts is not an easy task due to its restricted access in case of objective observation or verification (Quirk *et al.*, 2007). Moreover, the same textual content can be presented with different emotional slants (Grefenstette *et al.*, 2004). Ekman (1993), for instance, derived a list of six basic emotions from subjects' facial expressions which Strapparava and Mihalcea (2007) employed as classes in an affect recognition task. There are several other theories on emotion classes. But, the debate is concerned with some basic and complex categories, where the complex emotions could arise from cultural conditioning or association combined with the basic emotions.

In the present task, the corpus is obtained from the International Survey of Emotion Antecedents and Reactions (ISEAR) dataset (Scherer, 2005). The survey was conducted in 1990s across 37 countries and had almost about 3000 respondents. This dataset contains psychological statements of about 3~4 sentences pre-classified into seven categories of emotion (*anger, disgust, fear, guilt, joy, sadness* and *shame*). The respondents were instructed to describe a situation or event in which they felt the emotion. Thus, we have clustered the situational statements into their corresponding emotion classes based on three general and three physiological variables. The *intensity* (INTS), *timing* (WHEN) and *longevity* (LONG) of the feeling were considered as general variables whereas *Ergotropic Arousal* (ERGO) (e.g.,

Proceedings of the Workshop on Sentiment Analysis where AI meets Psychology (SAAIP), IJCNLP 2011, pages 59–67, *Chiang Mai, Thailand, November 13, 2011.*

change in breathing, heart beating faster etc.), *Trophotropic Arousal* (TROPHO) (e.g., *lump in throat, crying* etc.) and *Felt temperature* (TEMPER) (e.g., *feeling hot, warm, cold/shiver*) proposed by Gellhorn (1970) have been considered as physiological variables.

The individual statistics based on general and physiological variables show various interesting insights of the variables from the perspective of emotion (e.g., low *intensity* for emotion classes of *shame* and *guilt* and high for *joy*, *fear* and *sadness*). The statistics that are acquired based on the combinations of different variables also elicit some crucial properties for a comparative analysis of emotions (e.g., people feel *warm* and *lump in throat* in case of *joyous* situation). Therefore, the statements containing one or more sentences are clustered into the seven emotion classes according to different combinations of the general and physiological variables.

The sentences are then passed through the preprocessing steps followed by the identification of emotional words based on the *WordNet Affect* lists (Strapparava and Valitutti, 2004). The word level emotion tags are assigned as sentence and statement level emotion tags. Multiple emotion tags assigned by the system for each of the statements are compared against its corresponding single annotated emotion tag. The baseline system based on *WordNet Affect lists* achieves the average *Precision*, *Recall* and *F-Score* values of 58%, 47.4% and 50.6% respectively on 5120 sentences with respect to five emotion classes.

The word as well as phrase level emotion expressions are identified using Support Vector Machine (SVM) based supervised system (Das and Bandyopadhyay, 2010). The system achieves average *Precision*, *Recall* and *F-Score* values of 69%, 45.8% and 55.05% respectively. The sentential emotion tags are assigned based on the identified emotional expressions and intensity clues. Two types of explicit discourse markers such as *temporal* (e.g., '*when*' '*while*') and *causal* (e.g., '*as*', '*because*') are employed for identifying emotions at statement level. It has been found that the incorporation of the *intensity* and discourse level clues improves the *Precision* (70.04%), *Recall* (65.3%) and *F-Score* (68.03%) values respectively. The errors are due to the problem in identifying the textual clues in support of the physiological variables. But, it has been observed that the general variables play the significant roles in identifying emotions.

The rest of the paper is organized as follows. Section 2 describes the related work. The statistics of emotions based on various general and physiological variables are discussed in Section 3. The baseline and supervised systems for emotion identification are described in Section 4. Evaluation results along with error analysis are specified in Section 5. Finally Section 6 concludes the paper.

2 Related Work

The characterization of the words and phrases according to their emotive tones was attempted by several researchers (Turney, 2002). Following the terminology proposed by (Wiebe *et al.*, 2005), subjectivity analysis focuses on the automatic identification of private states, such as opinions, emotions, sentiments, evaluations, beliefs and speculations in natural language. Natural language domains such as News (Strapparava and Mihalcea, 2007) and Blogs (Mishne and Rijke, 2006) are also becoming a popular, communicative and informative repository of text based emotional contents in the Web 2.0 for mining and summarizing opinion at word, sentence and document level granularities (Ku *et al.*, 2006). The model proposed in (Neviarouskaya *et al.*, 2007) processes symbolic cues and employs NLP techniques to estimate the affects in text. Machine learning techniques were used either to predict text-based emotions based on the SNoW learning architecture (Alm *et al.*, 2005) or to identify the mood of the authors during reading and writing (Yang *et al.*, 2009).

The ISEAR corpus was used in (Boldrini *et al.*, 2010) for the experiments concerning emotional expressions and fine-grained analysis of affect in text. Their aim was to build the subjectivity expression models and they did not explore the intensity or physiological variables in case of identifying emotions.

Psychiatric query document retrieval can assist individuals to locate query documents relevant to their depression-related problems efficiently and effectively (Yeh *et. al.*, 2008). A DSM-IV based screening tool for Adult psychiatric disorders in Indian Rural health Centre has been discussed in (Chattopadhyay, 2006). One promising related task in the of emotion and psychology literature has been proposed in (Yu *et al.*, 2007). The authors use high-level topic information extracted from consultation documents that include *negative life events*, *depressive symptoms* and *semantic relations* between symptoms to identify the similarities between the documents corresponding to a query.

3 Analysis of Emotion Variables

3.1 Roles of the General Variables

Emotions generally appear in natural language texts along with *intensity* (INTS). Four different types of *intensity* (*not very, moderately intense, intense and very intense*) are annotated in the ISEAR dataset. The other two emotion variables that are closely associated with *intensity* are *timing* (WHEN) and *longevity* (LONG) of the emotional feeling. Four different values were assigned for the *timing* (e.g., *days ago, weeks ago, months ago, years ago*) in the dataset. Similarly, four values were assigned for the *longevity* (*a few minutes, an hour, several hours, a day or more*). These variables are termed as general variables in our present discussion.

In case of identifying emotions, the last two variables (*timing* and *longevity*) in association with *intensity* play the important roles rather than their individual appearances. Hence, the statements of the dataset are clustered into seven emotion classes based on the *intensity* variable alone and the combined relation of *intensity* with *timing* and *longevity*. The frequencies of the emotional statements in each of the emotion classes based on *intensity*, the combinations of *intensity* with *timing* and *longevity* are shown in Figure 1, Figure 2 and Figure 3 respectively.

It has been observed that emotions vary along with intensity but the variations of the emotion classes are not similar from the perspective of *intensity*. From the frequency information as shown in Figure 1, it is found that *intensity* is comparatively high in *sadness, fear, joy* and *anger* but is low in case of *guilt, disgust* and *shame*.

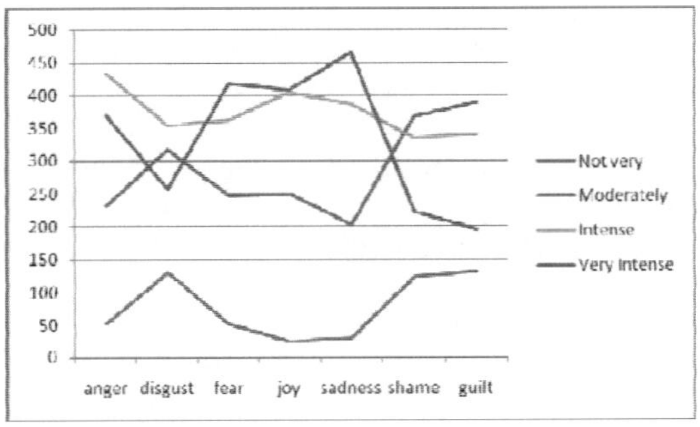

Figure 1: Frequencies of instances (Emotion Statements) in seven emotion classes based on Intensity (INTS).

We have mentioned earlier that *intensity* plays a crucial role in association with the *timing* and *longevity* for identifying different emotional slants. The variations of emotions with respect to different combinations of *intensity* and *timing* are shown in Figure 2. The events that have taken place usually before a year elicit *sadness* and *fear* with very high *intensity* and *shame* and *guilt* with relatively moderate *intensity*. In case of *very intense* events, *shame* increases exponentially with respect to time.

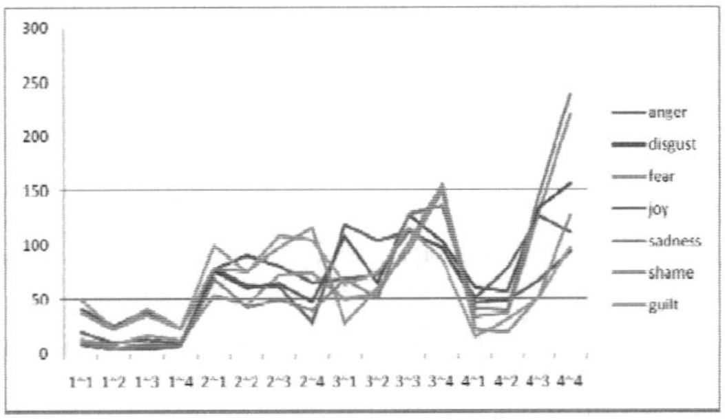

Figure 2: Frequencies of instances (Emotion Statements) in seven emotion classes based on Intensity (INTS) and Timing (WHEN) [INTS ~ WHEN]

On the other hand, the *intensity* also varies with *longevity* or duration of the emotional feeling. The frequencies of different emotions based on the combination of *intensity* and *longevity* are shown in Figure 3. The emotions that persist with very high *intensity* for several years in comparison with other emotions are *sadness* and *joy*. The *moderately intense* emotions that persist for several months or years are *shame* and *guilt*. In case of low *intensity*, *guilt* emotion persists for longer time in comparison with other emotions.

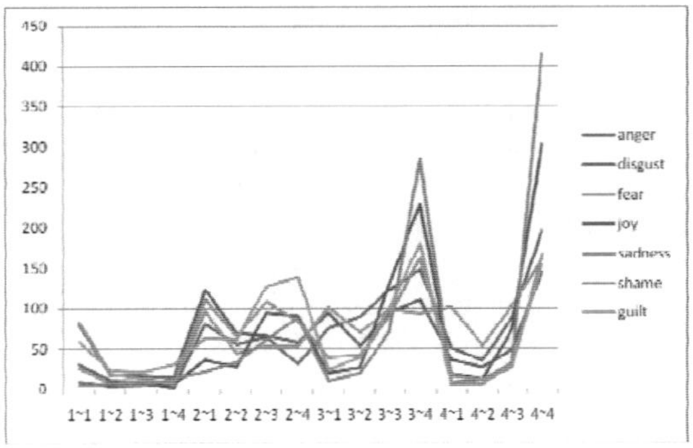

Figure 3: Frequencies of instances (Emotion Statements) in seven emotion classes based on Intensity (INTS) and Longevity (LONG) [INTS ~ LONG]

3.2 Roles of the Physiological Variables

It is observed that not only the *intensity* but some physiological variables also help in identifying the emotions. Three types of symptoms or *arousals* namely, *Ergotropic Arousal* (ERGO) (e.g., *change in breathing, heart beating faster, muscles tensing/trembling* and *perspiring/moist hands*), *Trophotropic Arousal* (TROPHO) (e.g., *lump in throat, stomach troubles* and *crying/sobbing*) and *felt temperature* (TEMPER) (e.g., *feeling cold/shivering, feeling warm/pleasant, feeling hot/cheeks burning*) as proposed by Gellhorn (1970) are mentioned in the ISEAR corpus. The symptoms are termed as physiological variables for studying the nature of emotions. The frequencies of the emotional statements in each of the emotion classes based on the individual physiological variables are shown in Figure 4, Figure 5 and Figure 6 respectively. Their combinations are shown in Figure 7, Figure 8 and Figure 9 respectively.

It is observed from Figure 4 that, in case of *fear* and *anger*, the *heart beat* becomes *faster* and *muscles* are *tensed.* But, the *perspiring* along with *moist hands* are the noticeable symptoms that differentiate *fear* from any other emotions. *Change in breathing* is *faster* in case of *anger, joy* and *shame.*

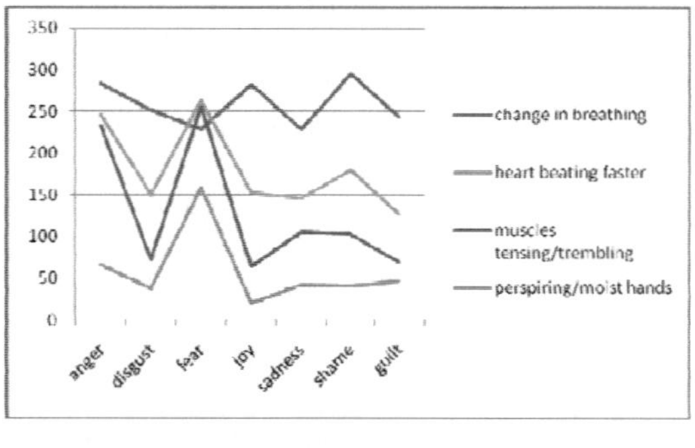

Figure 4: Frequencies of instances (Emotion Statements) in seven emotion classes based on *Ergotropic Arousal* (ERGO)

One crucial fact can be recognized if we analyse the impact of *Trophotropic* variables from the perspective of *sadness* (as shown in Figure 5). *Stomach troubles* and *crying/sobbing* are recognized as the general symptoms for *sadness*. The *lump in throat* is low for *sadness* but high for *joy*. *Stomach troubles* are low for *joy* but persist more or less in all other emotions such as *anger, disgust, fear, shame* and *guilt*. The frequency information also identifies the support of *crying/sobbing* for *fear* in addition to *sadness*.

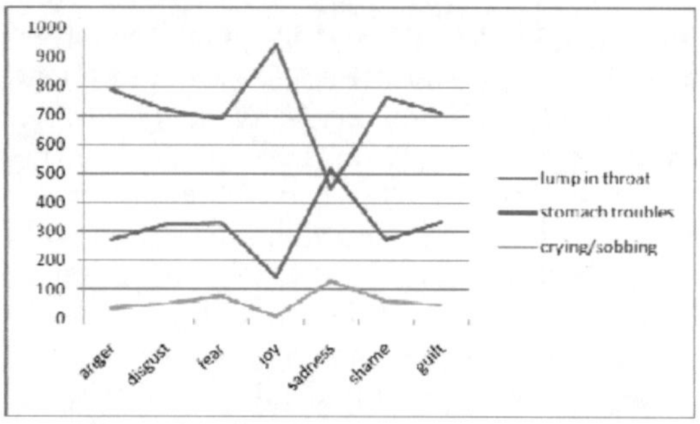

Figure 5: Frequencies of instances (Emotion Statements) in seven emotion classes based on *Trophotropic Arousal* (TROPHO)

The other important physiological variable that helps in identifying the nature of emotions is *felt temperature* (as shown in Figure 6). People feel *warm* and *pleasant* in case *joy* only. Any kind of *temperature* symptom is observed in *joy* rather than other emotions. The symptom of *hot feeling* and *cheeks burning* are the distinguishable symptoms for identifying *shame* and *anger*. It is also found that people feel *cold* and even *shiver* in case of *fear* and *sadness*.

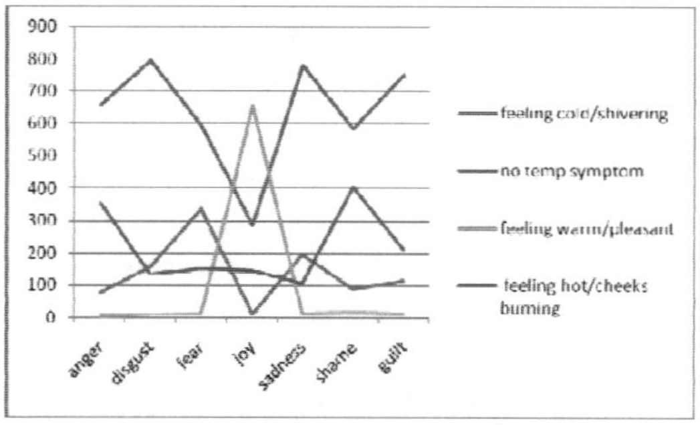

Figure 6: Frequencies of instances (Emotion Statements) in seven emotion classes based on *Felt temperature* (TEMPER)

Though the characteristic curves for different emotions are equivalent and similar with respect to the combination of *Ergotropic* and *Trophotropic* variables (as shown in Figure 7), the slight distinctions prevail for *fear, joy* and *sadness*. The *heart beating* fastens and *muscles* are tensed along with *lump in throat* in case of *fear* and *sadness*. *Perspiring* and *lump in throat* also happen in *fear* emotion.

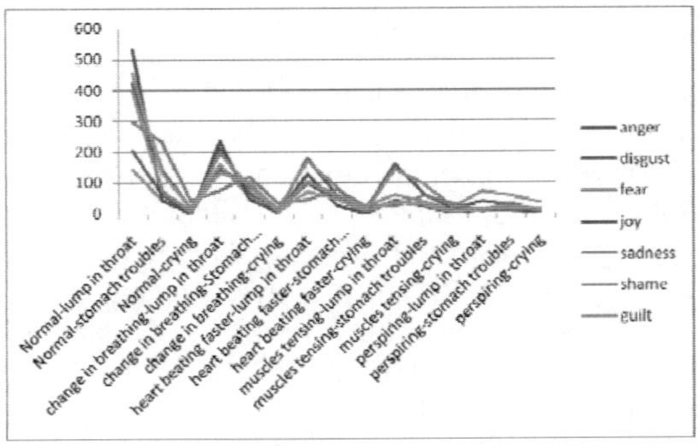

Figure 7: Frequencies of instances (Emotion Statements) in seven emotion classes based on *Ergotropic* (ERGO) and *Trophotropic* (TROPHO) *Arousals*

Figure 8 shows the impact of the *Ergotropic* variables along with *felt temperature* in characterizing different emotions. It is observed that the *change in breathing* and *faster heart beating* with *warm* feeling is identified as the distinguishing features for *joy*. People generally feel *hot* and experience *tensed muscles* in case of *sadness* whereas they feel *cold* and *perspire* in *fear*.

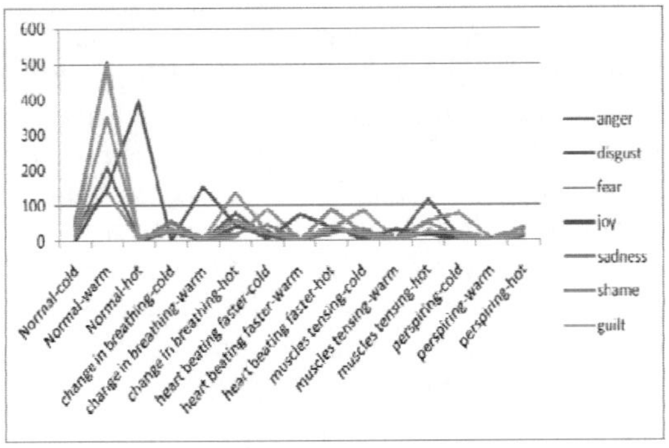

Figure 8: Frequencies of instances (Emotion Statements) in seven emotion classes based on *Ergotropic Arousal* (ERGO) and *Felt temperature* (TEMPER)

The frequencies based on the combination of *Trophotropic Arousal* and *felt temperature* for identifying emotions are shown in Figure 9. *Warm* feeling and *lump in throat* are generally seen in case of *joy* whereas *hot feeling* is observed in case of *shame* and *sadness*. *Stomach troubles* and *cold feeling* are identified as the general symptoms for *sadness* and *fear*.

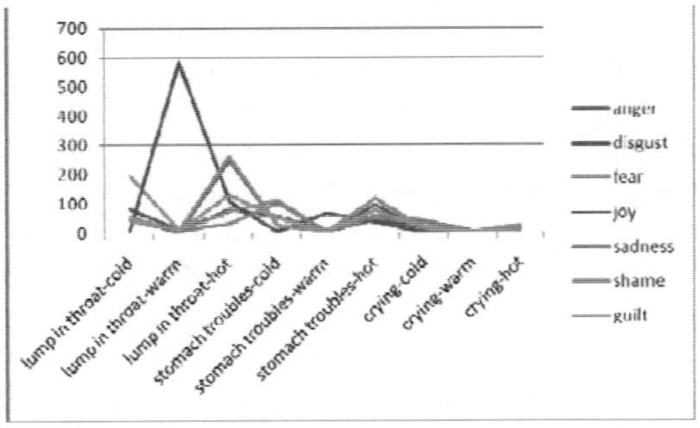

Figure 9: Frequencies of instances (Emotion Statements) in seven emotion classes based on *Trophotropic Arousal* (TROPHO) and *Felt temperature* (TEMPER)

4 Emotion Tagging

While analyzing the interdependent and interactive roles between emotions and the variables it is observed that the identification of the textual clues related to the physiological variables is difficult. On the other hand, the textual hints related to emotions (e.g., *intensifiers*, *modifiers* etc.) and the general variables are also taken into consideration for developing the emotion tagging systems. Each of the sentences is passed through two different systems, a lexicon based baseline system followed by machine learning based supervised system. The baseline system aims to identify emotions without including any knowledge of the textual clues related to the general variables whereas the supervised system identifies emotions by incorporating the hints that are explicitly present in the text and are related to the variables.

The corpus obtained from the International Survey of Emotion Antecedents and Reactions (ISEAR) dataset (Scherer, 2005) contains the psychological statements of seven different emotions. Thus, we have clustered the statements into seven emotion classes based on the combinations of different variables and employed them for identifying emotions.

4.1 Clustering of Emotional Statements

The emotional statements are clustered based on the individual and combinational appearances from the perspective of general and physiological variables. In our present attempt, only the unary and binary combinations of the variables are considered for clustering the statements.

The frequencies or the number of statements in each cluster are shown in the figures 1 through 5. A total of 12 different clusters are identified for six individual variables and their combinations. But, our next motivation is to automatically recognize the emotions from each of the statements of a cluster. Each of the statements generally contains 3~4 sentences on an average. Therefore, we have passed each of the sentences of a cluster for sentence level emotion tagging.

4.2 Preprocessing

A set of standard preprocessing techniques is carried out, *viz.*, *tokenizing, stemming* and *stop word removal* for each of the statements of a cluster. Tools provided by *Rapidminer's text plugin*[1] were used for these tasks.

4.3 Lexicon based Baseline Model

The emotion word lists, *WordNet Affect* (Strapparava and Valitutti, 2004) is available for only Ekman's (1993) six basic emotions (*anger, disgust, fear, joy, sadnesss* and *surprise*) in English. But, no such wordlist is available for the emotions like *shame* and *guilt*. Therefore, in our present attempt, we have only focused on the Ekman's five emotions (*anger, disgust, fear, joy* and *sadness*) that are present in the ISEAR dataset. The five lists of *WordNet Affect* are used to obtain the affect words that are present in the emotional expressions. These affect words in turn contribute towards identifying the sentential and statement level emotion tags.

The algorithm is that, if a word in a statement is present in any of the *WordNet Affect* lists; the statement is tagged with the emotion label corresponding to that affect list. But, if no word is found in any of the five lists, each word of the statement is passed through the morphological process to identify its root form which is again searched in the *WordNet Affect* lists. If the root form is found in any of the five *WordNet Affect* lists, the statement is tagged accordingly. Otherwise, the statement is tagged as non-emotional or *neutral*. A single statement is tagged with multiple emotions based on the affect words contained in that statement. But, the evaluation has been carried out with respect to the single annotated emotion. The Recall of the system has been calculated if at least one of the Ekman's five emotions is assigned by the system and the Precision has been calculated if any of the system assigned emotions matches with the annotated emotion.

[1] http://rapid-i.com/content/blogcategory/38/69/

4.4 SVM based Supervised Model

The Support Vector Machine (SVM) (Cortes and Vapnik, 1995) based supervised framework has been used to extract the emotional expressions as well as to tag the sentences with emotions. Considering the approach described in (Das and Bandyopadhyay, 2010), the emotion tagging is done at statement level. For emotional expressions, the task is to label any of the five emotion tags to a single word or a sequence of words in a sentence. Other words are tagged as *neutral*. Finally, the statement level emotion tagging is carried out based on the emotional expressions along with *intensity* and other discourse level clues.

The identification of the basic features is straightforward. This includes the identification of *Emotion/Affect Words of WordNet Affect*, *Parts-of-Speech* (*verb, noun, adjective* and *adverb*) (Das and Bandyopadhyay, 2010). But, it is difficult to identify the textual clues in support of the physiological variables. Thus, the *intensity* feature along with *temporal* and *causal* discourse markers is employed in the supervised system to compensate the roles of the *general* variables.

Intensity Clues: The Intensity clues are the *Intensifiers* that are identified by the *Stanford dependency relations amod*() (adjectival modifier), *advmod*() (adverbial modifier), JJ (adjective) and RB (adverb). If the intensifier is found in the *SentiWordNet* (Baccianella *et al.*, 2010), then the positive and negative scores of the intensifier are retrieved from the *SentiWordNet* (Baccianella *et al.*, 2010). The intensifier is classified as either positive (pos) ($INTF_{pos}$) or negative (neg) ($INTF_{neg}$) for which the average retrieved score is higher.

Punctuation Symbols, *Capitalized Phrases*, *Conjuncts* and *Negations* are also employed as features during the training and the testing. The following discourse level features play an important role in identifying the emotions at statement level.

Discourse Clues: The present task aims to identify only the explicit *discourse markers* that are tagged by *conjunctive_*() or *mark_*() type dependency relations of the parsed constituents (e.g. *as*, *because*, *while*, *whereas*). Two types of discourse markers are identified, temporal and causal.

Temporal Markers (TM): The explicit temporal markers (*when, while, before, after, for a year* etc.) are identified from the prepositional dependency relations [*prep()*].

Causal Markers (CM): The lists for *causal* verbs are prepared by processing the XML files of English VerbNet (Kipper-Schuler, 2005). If a class contains any frame with semantic type as *Cause,* we collect the member verbs from that XML class file. The list contains a total of 250 *causal* verbs (e.g., *cause, happen, occur* etc.).

Different unigram and bi-gram context features (word, POS tag, Intensifier, negation) and their combinations were generated from the training corpus. We have included some strategies and features as considered in (Das and Bandyopadhyay, 2010) to improve the performance of the supervised system. The strategies and features include the application of Information Gain Based Pruning (IGBP), Admissible Tag Sequence (ATS), Class Splitting technique and Emotional Composition features.

5 Evaluation

The ISEAR dataset contains the emotional statements that in turn contain the emotional sentences. Thus, all the sentential emotion tags are considered as the potential candidates for their corresponding emotional statement. The standard metrics, *Precision* (Prec.), *Recall* (Rec.) and *F-Score* (FS) have been considered for evaluation of the statement level emotion tagging.

The evaluation of the baseline model is straightforward. The baseline system assigns each of the statements with multiple emotion tags. Therefore, an error analysis has been conducted with the help of confusion matrix as shown in Table 1. A close investigation of the evaluation results suggests that the errors are mostly due to the uneven distribution between *joy* and other emotion tags. The crucial feature of the lexicon based baseline system is that it achieves an average 50.6% *F-Score* with respect to the five emotion classes. But, the system suffers due to the coverage of some affect lists (e.g., *disgust, anger*).

Class	***anger***	***disgust***	***fear***	***joy***	***sadness***
anger	246	5	16	133	65
disgust	35	229	21	141	55
fear	23	25	315	124	101
joy	8	3	6	422	18
sadness	14	8	10	213	212

Table 1. Confusion matrix for Baseline Model for five emotion classes

The supervised system assigns a single emotion tag to each statement. Thus, the similarity measures are considered for evaluating the statements contained in each of the clusters. The results with respect to five emotion classes for the baseline and supervised systems are shown in Table 2. It has been observed that supervised system outperforms the baseline system significantly.

Emotion	***Baseline***			***Supervised***		
Class	***Prec.***	***Rec.***	***FS***	***Prec.***	***Rec.***	***FS***
anger	.52	.45	.48	.65	.52	.59
disgust	.47	.46	.46	.60	.55	.57
fear	.53	.57	.55	.71	.80	.76
joy	.92	.44	.59	.94	.62	.74
sadness	.46	.45	.45	.55	.60	.57

Table 2. Precision (Prec.), Recall (Rec.) and F-score (FS) of the Baseline and Supervised Models for five emotion classes

Therefore, the supervised system has been employed to identify the emotions from the emotional statements of the clusters. The results are shown in Table 3 for each of the clusters that are either based on an individual variable or the combinations of variables.

Cluster	***Supervised***		
(#5120 sentences each)	***Prec.***	***Rec.***	***FS***
INTS	0.87	0.75	0.81
INTS ~ WHEN	0.76	0.63	0.70
INTS ~ LONG	0.72	0.69	0.71
ERGO	0.67	0.62	0.64
TROPHO	0.65	0.58	0.61
TEMPER	0.68	0.55	0.60
ERGO ~ TRPHO	0.64	0.65	0.64
ERGO ~ TEMPER	0.59	0.53	0.56
TROPHO ~ TEMPER	0.61	0.57	0.59

Table 3. Average Precision (Prec.), Recall (Rec.) and F-Score (FS) of the Supervised Model with respect to five emotion classes for different clusters

It is found that the incorporation of *intensity* and *discourse* level textual clues into the supervised system improves the performance in identifying the potential emotion tags. But, like general *intensity*, the clues for the physiological variables (e.g., *Temperature, Arousals*) do not appear explicitly in text. A close investigation elicits the fact that the absence of textual hints related to general variables fails to capture the emotions from the statements that contain high values of physiological variables. But, it can be concluded that, in absence of the physiological variables, the supervised system identifies the emotions by only capturing the textual clues related to general variables.

6 Conclusion

The work reported in the paper has presented different frequency statistics and observations with respect to emotions that are based on the three general variables such as *intensity, timing* and *longevity* as well as three physiological *arousals*. The present work also describes two different frameworks for emotion tagging, a lexicon based baseline model followed by a SVM based supervised model. The incorporation of *intensity* and discourse level *temporal* and *causal* textual clues yields higher performance than the baseline system using single words alone. Future work will focus on devising a method for similarity pattern acquisition from the statements of each emotion cluster. The similarity measures will thus help to recognize other implicit symptoms of emotions from textual contents.

Acknowledgments

The work reported in this paper is supported by a grant from the India-Japan Cooperative Programme (DST-JST) 2009 Research project entitled “Sentiment Analysis where AI meets Psychology” funded by Department of Science and Technology (DST), Government of India.

References

Alm, C. O., Roth, D. and Sproat, R. 2005. Emotions from text: machine learning for text-based emotion prediction. *HLT-EMNLP*, pp. 579 - 586

Baccianella Stefano, Esuli Andrea and Sebastiani Fabrizio. 2010. SentiWordNet 3.0: An Enhanced Lexical Re-source for Sentiment Analysis and Opinion Mining. *Language Resources and Evaluation*, pp. 2200-2204.

Chattopadhyay S., 2006. Psyconsultant I: A DSM-IV-Based Screening Tool For Adult Psychiatric Disorders In Indian Rural Health Center. *The Internet Journal of Medical Informatics*, 3(1).

Cortes C. and V. Vapnik. 1995. Support-Vector Network. *Machine Learning*, 20, pp. 273–297.

Das, D. and Bandyopadhyay, S. 2010. Identifying Emotional Expressions, Intensities and Sentential Emotion Tags using A Supervised Framework. *24th PACLIC*, Japan.

Ekman, P.1993. Facial expression and emotion. *American Psychologist*, 48(4):384–392.

Gellhorn E. 1970. The emotions and the ergotropic and trophotropic systems. *Psychological Research*, 34(1):67-94, DOI: 10.1007/BF00422863

Grefenstette Gregory, Yan Qu, James G. Shanahan, and David A. Evans. 2004. Coupling niche browsers and affect analysis for an opinion mining application. *RIAO-04*, pp. 186–194

Kipper-Schuler, K. 2005. *VerbNet: A broad-coverage, comprehensive verb lexicon*. Ph.D. thesis, Computer and Information Science Dept., University of Pennsylvania, Philadelphia, PA.

Ku, L. W., Liang, Y. T. and Chen, H. H. 2006. Opinion extraction, summarization and tracking in news and blog corpora. *AAAI-2006 Spring Symposium on Computational Approaches to Analyzing Weblogs, AAAI Technical Report*, pp. 100-107.

Mishne, G. and Rijke, M. de. 2006. MoodViews: Tools for Blog Mood Analysis. *AAAI-2006 Spring Symposium on Computational Approaches to Analyzing Weblogs, AAAI Technical Report.*

Myers, David G. 2004. Theories of Emotion. *Psychology*: Seventh Edition, New York, NY: Worth Publishers, pp. 500.

Neviarouskaya, A., Prendinger, H., and Ishizuka, M. 2007. Narrowing the Social Gap among People Involved in Global Dialog: Automatic Emotion Detection in Blog Posts. *International Conference on Weblogs and Social Media.*

Quirk, R., Greenbaum, S. Leech, G. and Svartvik, J. 1985. A Comprehensive Grammar of the English Language. *Longman.*

Read Jonathon and Caroll John. 2010. Annotating expressions of Appraisal in English. *Language Resource and Evaluation.*

Scherer K. R. 2005. What are emotions? And how canthey be measured? *Social Science Information*, 44(4):693–727.

Strapparava, C. and Valitutti, A. 2004. Wordnet-affect: an affective extension of wordnet. *Language Resource and Evaluation.*

Strapparava, C. and Mihalcea, R. 2007. SemEval-2007 Task 14: Affective Text. *Association for Computational Linguistics.*

Turney, P.D. 2002. Thumbs Up or Thumbs Down? Semantic Orientation Applied to Unsupervised

Classification of Reviews. *Association for Computational Linguistics*, pp.417- 424.

Wiebe, J., Wilson, T. and Cardie, C. 2005. Annotating expressions of opinions and emotions in language. *Language Resource and Evaluation*, 39(2-3):165-210.

Yang, C., Lin, K. H. Y., and Chen, H. H. 2009. Writer Meets Reader: Emotion Analysis of Social Media from both the Writer's and Reader's Perspectives. *009 IEEE/WIC/ACM*, pp. 287-290.

Yeh Jui-Feng, Chung-Hsien Wu, Liang-Chih Yu, Yu-Sheng Lai. 2008. Extended probabilistic HAL with close temporal association for psychiatric query document retrieval. *ACM Trans on Information System, 27*(1).

Yu Liang-Chih, Chung-Hsien Wu, Chin-Yew Lin, Eduard Hovy and Chia-Ling Lin. 2007. Topic Analysis for Psychiatric Document Retrieval. *Association for Computational Linguistics*, pp. 1024-1031.

Enriching Social Communication Through Semantics and Sentics

Praphul Chandra
Hewlett Packard Labs,
India
praphul.chandra@hp.com

Erik Cambria
National University of Singapore,
Singapore
cambria@nus.edu.sg

Alvin Pradeep
Hewlett Packard,
India
alvin.pradeep@hp.com

Abstract

Online communication is one of the key value propositions of mobile devices. While a variety of instant messaging clients offer users the ability to communicate with other users in real-time, the user experience remains dominated by a basic exchange of textual content. When compared to face-to-face communication, this experience is significantly poorer. In our proposed solution, we seek to enhance the chat experience by using an intelligent adaptive user interface that exploits semantics and sentics, that is the cognitive and affective information, associated with the ongoing communication. In particular, our approach leverages sentiment analysis techniques to process communication content and context and, hence, enable the interface to be adaptive in order to offer users a richer and more immersive chat experience.

1 Introduction

Online communication is an extremely popular form of social interaction. Unlike face-to-face communication, online instant messaging (IM) tools are extremely limited in conveying emotions or the context associated with a communication. Users have adapted to this environment by inventing their own vocabulary, e.g., by putting actions within asterisks ('I just came from a shower *shivering*'), by using emoticons (☺), by addressing a particular user in a group communication (@Ravi).

Such evolving workarounds clearly indicate a latent need for a richer, more immersive user experience in social communication. We address this problem by exploiting the semantics and sentics, that is the cognitive and affective information, associated with the ongoing communication to develop an adaptive user interface (UI) capable to change according to content and context of the online chat.

2 Related Work

Popular approaches to enhance and personalize computer mediated communication (CMC) include emoticons, skins, avatars, customizable status messages, etc. However, all these approaches require explicit user configuration or action: the user needs to select the emoticon, status-message or avatar, which best represents her. Furthermore, most of these enhancements are static – once selected by the user, they do not adapt themselves automatically. There is some related work on automatically updating the status of the user by analyzing various sensor data available on mobile devices (Milewski and Smith, 2000). However, most of these personalization approaches are static and do not automatically adapt.

Our approach is unique in that it is: *intelligent*, as it analyzes content and does not require explicit user configuration; *adaptive*, as the UI changes according to communication content and context; *inclusive,* as the emotions of one or more participants in the chat session are analyzed to let the UI adapt dynamically.

The underlying technique in our approach is based on sentiment analysis of natural language text. Text analysis for understanding the underlying semantics is a large and well-established field of work (Fellbaum, 1998). Sentiment analysis is also an active research field and has been applied previously for a variety of applications including customer reviews (Hu and Liu, 2004) and news content (Subasic and Huettner, 2001).

Proceedings of the Workshop on Sentiment Analysis where AI meets Psychology (SAAIP), IJCNLP 2011, pages 68–72,
Chiang Mai, Thailand, November 13, 2011.

Uniquely, our approach applies sentiment analysis techniques to social communication in order to create an adaptive UI. Our module architecture can be deployed either on the cloud (if the client has low processing capabilities) or on the client (if privacy is a concern). Another advantage of our solution is that, even when the interface is used by only one participant in the communication session, it enhances the experience of that user.

3 The Weather Metaphor

Most IM clients offer a very basic UI for text communication. In this work we focus on extracting the semantics and sentics embedded in the text of the chat session to provide a UI, which adapts itself to the mood of the communication. For our prototype applicationwe worked with the weather metaphor, as it is scalable and has previously been used effectively to reflect the subject's mood (Chang, 2009) or content's 'flavor' (Pampalk et al., 2002).

In our UI, if the detected mood of the conversation is 'happy', the UI will reflect a clear sunny day. Similarly a gloomy weather reflects a melancholy tone in the conversation. Of course, this is a subjective metaphor – one that we think scales well with conversation analysis. We can think of other scalable metaphors that are relevant, e.g., colors (Havasi et al., 2010).

Our adaptive UI primarily consists of three features: the stage, the actors and the story. For any mapping these elements pay a crucial role in conveying the feel and richness of the conversation mood, e.g., in the 'happy' conversation the weather 'clear sunny day' will be the stage, the actors will be lush green valley, the rainbow and the cloud which may appear or disappear as per the current conversation tone of the story. The idea is similar to a visual narrative of the mood the conversation is in; as the conversation goes on the actors may come in or go off as per the tone of the thread.

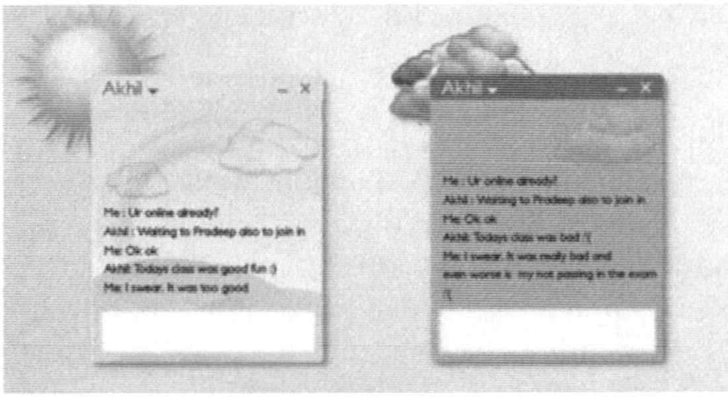

"Figure 1. Happy and Sad adaptive UI"

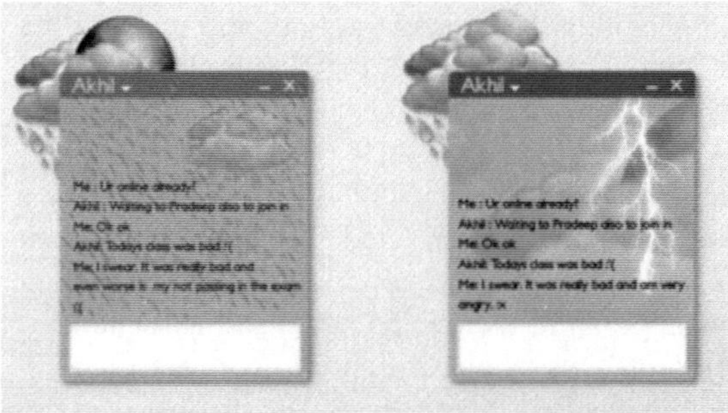

"Figure 2. Cry and Anger adaptive UI"

By analyzing the semantics and sentics associated with communication content (data) and context (metadata), the UI may adapt to include images of landmarks from remote-user's location (e.g., Times Square), images about concepts in the conversation (pets, education, etc.) or time of day of remote user (e.g., sunrise or dusk).

4 Social Communication Analysis

For the extraction of semantics and sentics, we leverage sentic computing (Cambria et al., 2010a), a multi-disciplinary approach to opinion mining and sentiment analysis that exploits both computer and social sciences to better recognize, interpret and process emotions over the Web. In sentic computing, the analysis of natural language is based on common sense reasoning tools and domain-specific ontologies.

Unlike statistical classification, which generally requires large inputs and thus cannot appraise texts with satisfactory granularity, sentic computing enables the analysis of documents not only at page- or paragraph-level but also at sentence and clause-level.

In particular, we exploit the following four modules (re-adapted for real-time analysis): a natural language processing (NLP) module, which performs a first skim of chat text, a Semantic Parser, whose aim is to extract concepts from the lemmatized text, the ConceptNet module, for the inference of semantics, and the AffectiveSpace module, for the extraction of sentics.

4.1 Preprocessing Modules

The NLP module parses the textual metadata associated with media to output lemmatized text. It recognizes and interprets the affective valence indicators usually contained in text such as special punctuation (e.g., '!!!!'), complete uppercase words ('I DID NOT SAY THAT'), exclamations ('as if!'), degree adverbs, emoticons (☹) etc. This makes the NLP module suitable for short emotive texts used in chat.

The Semantic Parser extracts concepts from the lemmatized text and deconstructs it into concepts using a lexicon based on n-grams. The lexicon we use is ConceptNet (Havasi et al., 2007), a semantic graph built from a corpus of common sense knowledge collected and rated by volunteers on the Web. The nodes of this graph are 'concepts' and its labeled edges are assertions of common sense that connect two concepts. Therefore, ConceptNet expresses assertions as relations between concepts, selected from a limited set of relations such as IsA, UsedFor and HasA.

4.2 Extracting Semantics

ConceptNet is an extremely large lexicon with several thousand concepts. In order to adapt our messaging UI on concept-based themes, we need to cluster the social communication around some core concepts. First, we find a set of 'core concepts' for some a-priori categories extracted from Picasa's popular tags. These categories are meant to cover common topics found in personal communication, e.g., friends, travel, wedding, holiday, movies etc.

We assume that these are the set of concepts we are likely to find in online communication, i.e., we use social media as representative of social communication in terms of the concepts they entail. To find these core concepts, we use a technique called CF-IOF (Cambria et al., 2010b) (similar to TF-IDF). Using the popular tags in Picasa as common social categories, CF-IOF is used to find a set of concepts from ConceptNet which are most related to these categories.

We define n_{ij} := number of occurrences of concept-i (c_i) in the comments, description, tags etc. of j-tagged photos and |M| := total number of photos divided by the number of photos containing the concept-i (c_i). Then,

$$(CF-IOF)_i = \sum_j \frac{n_{ij}}{\sum_k n_{kj}} log \frac{|M|}{|\{m: c_i \varepsilon\, m\}|}$$

"Figure 3. A subnet from ConceptNet"

Second, we expand this set of 'core concepts' with semantically related concepts using an approach called spectral association (Havasi et al., 2010), similar to spreading activation. In this technique, we represent the ConceptNet as a square symmetric concept-concept matrix with each entry in the matrix containing the weight of the assertion in ConceptNet. The normalized form of this matrix, C, when applied to a vector containing a single concept (derived from the text content of an online chat session), spreads that concept's value to other concepts connected to this concept in the ConceptNet.

Applying C^2 spreads the concept's value to neighboring concepts two hops away and so on. To spread the activation with diminishing number of links, we use the operator:

$$1 + C + \frac{C^2}{2!} + \frac{C^3}{3!} + \cdots = e^C = Ve^AV^T$$

The right hand equation holds true because C is a symmetric square matrix and can therefore be decomposed as VAV^T where V is an orthogonal real matrix of the eigenvectors of C and A is a diagonal matrix of its eigenvalues (spectral decomposition). Raising this decomposed form, to any power cancels everything but the power of A. This approach is especially suitable for sparse matrices like our matrix C, derived from ConceptNet since we can easily truncate the decomposition by considering only the top-k eigenvectors and thus save space while generalizing from similar concepts.

The role of the ConceptNet module is to map the concepts extracted by the Semantic Parser to this 'expanded core set' of concepts. By focusing the conversation around a limited set of concepts, we aim to provide a manageable yet powerful set of UIs to adapt according to the conversation.

4.3 Extracting Sentics

The aim of the AffectiveSpace module is to derive the affective valence of the concepts output by the ConceptNet module. To achieve this, the AffectiveSpace module projects the retrieved concepts into a multi-dimensional vector space (Cambria et al., 2009).

Since ConceptNet does not have any information regarding the affective information related to these concepts, we use WordNet-Affect (Valitutti and Strapparava, 2004), a linguistic resource for the lexical representation of affective knowledge. We combine the ConceptNet and WordNet-Affect matrices linearly into a single large matrix. In this matrix, the rows are concepts (from ConceptNet, e.g., dog) and columns are either common-sense assertion relations (from ConceptNet, e.g., isA-pet) or affective features (from WordNet-Affect, e.g., hasEmotion-joy). We then apply truncated singular value decomposition (TSVD) (Wall et. al. 2003) on this large matrix. The resulting matrix has the form $A_k = U_k S_k V_k^T$ and is a low-rank approximation of A, the original data. This approximation is based on minimizing the Frobenius norm of the difference between A and A_k under the constraint rank(A) = k. Thus, A_k is the best approximation of A in the Frobenius norm sense when $\sigma_i = s_i$ (i = 1, 2.... k) and the corresponding singular vectors are the same as those of A. If we choose to discard all but the first-k principal components, common sense concepts and emotions are represented by vectors of k coordinates: these coordinates can be seen as describing concepts in terms of eigenmoods that form the axes of AffectiveSpace, that is, the basis $e_0,...,e_{k-1}$ of the vector space. By selecting the top-k eigenvalues, we are in effect, clustering the concepts.

The clustering of this multi-dimensional space, with respect to emotion-categories can therefore help us derive sentics in the chat text. In particular, we use the Hourglass of Emotions (Cambria et al., 2010c) to infer the affective valence of the retrieved concepts according to the relative position they occupy in the multi-dimensional vector space.

In the hourglass model, emotions are classified into four concomitant but independent dimensions in order to understand the Pleasantness, Attention, Sensitivity and Aptitude. Each of these dimensions is characterized by six levels of activation, called sentic levels, which determine the intensity of the expressed/perceived emotion as a float between [-3, 3]. Thus, we specify the affective information as a four dimensional sentic vector, that can potentially express any human emotion in terms of Pleasantness, Attention, Sensitivity and Aptitude.

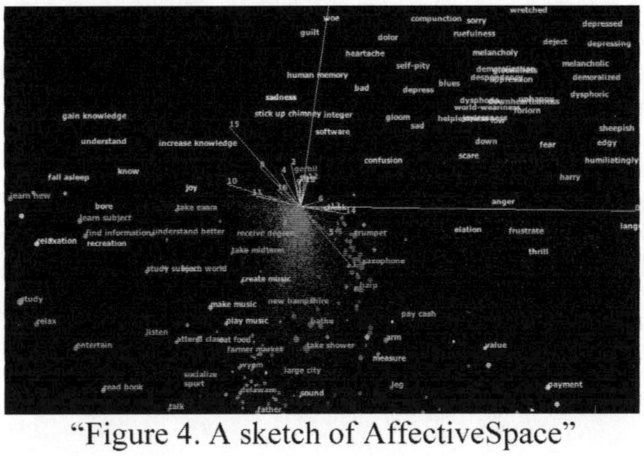

"Figure 4. A sketch of AffectiveSpace"

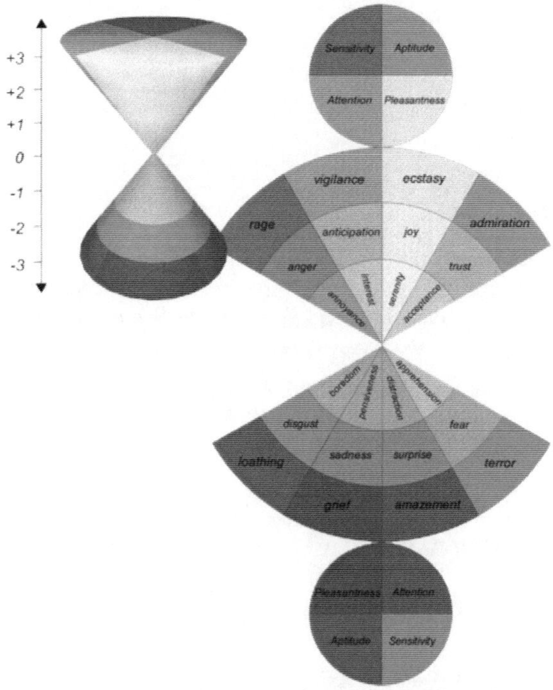

"Figure 5. The Hourglass of Emotions"

Thus, by exploiting the information sharing property of TSVD, concepts with the same affective valence are likely to have similar features, that is, concepts conveying the same emotion tend to fall near each other in AffectiveSpace, e.g., we can find concepts such as 'beautiful day', 'birthday party', 'laugh' and 'make person happy' very close in direction in the vector space, while concepts like 'sick', 'feel guilty', 'be laid off' and 'shed tear' are found in a completely different direction (nearly opposite with respect to the center of the space).

5 Discussion and Future Work

Popular approaches to enhance CMC include emoticons, skins, avatars, customizable status messages, etc. Sharing photos or combining video streams with text is also supported in popular IM clients. However, our approach of adaptive UI for chat is a novel concept. Text analysis for understanding the underlying semantics is a large and well-established field of work as well as sentiment analysis is an active research field.

Uniquely, our approach applies sentic computing techniques to social communication in order to create an adaptive UI. Our module architecture can be deployed either on the cloud (if the client has low processing capabilities) or on the client (if privacy is a concern). In the next future, we also plan to explore other metaphors of adaptive UIs, both sentic and semantic based.

Acknowledgments

We would like to thank Vimal Sharma for his guidance on the design of the user interface.

References

Allen Milewski and Thomas Smith. 2000. Providing Presence Cues to Telephone Users. In *Proceedings of the 2000 ACM Conference on Computer Supported Cooperative Work.*

Christiane Fellbaum. 1998, WordNet: An Electronic Lexical Database, *The MIT Press* ISBN-13: 978-0262061971.

Minqing Hu and Bing Liu. 2004. Mining and Summarizing Customer Reviews. In *Proceedings of the tenth ACM SIGKDD.*

Pero Subasic and Alison Huettner. 2001 Affect Analysis of Text Using Fuzzy Semantic Typing. *IEEE Transactions on Fuzzy Systems*, volume 9, issue 4, pages 483-496.

Hsia Chang. 2009. Emotion Barometer of Reading: User Interface Design of a Social Cataloging Website. In *Proceedings of the 27th International Conference Extended Abstracts on Human Factors in Computing Systems.*

Elias Pampalk, Andreas Rauber, and Dieter Merkl. 2002. Content-based Organization and Visualization of Music Archives. In *Proceedings of the tenth ACM International Conference on Multimedia.*

Catherine Havasi, Robert Speer, and Justin Holmgren. 2007. Automated Color Selection Using Semantic Knowledge. In *Commonsense Knowledge: Papers from the AAAI Fall Symposium.*

Erik Cambria, Amir Hussain, Catherine Havasi, and Chris Eckl. 2010a. Sentic Computing: Exploitation of Common Sense for the Development of Emotion-Sensitive Systems. volume 5967 of *Lecture Notes in Computer Science*, pages 148–156. Springer, Berlin Heidelberg.

Catherine Havasi, Robert Speer, and Jason Alonso. 2007. ConceptNet 3: a Flexible, Multilingual Semantic Network for Common Sense Knowledge. In *Proceedings of RANLP.*

Erik Cambria, Amir Hussain, Tariq Durrani, Catherine Havasi, Chris Eckl, and James Munro. 2010b. Sentic Computing for Patient Centered Applications. In *IEEE ICSP10.*

Erik Cambria, Amir Hussain, Catherine Havasi, and Chris Eckl. 2009. AffectiveSpace: Blending Common Sense and Affective Knowledge to Perform Emotive Reasoning. In *WOMSA* at *CAEPIA.*

Alessandro Valitutti and Carlo Strapparava. 2004. WordNet-Affect: An Affective Extension of WordNet. In *Proceedings of the 4th International Conference on Language Resources and Evaluation.*

Michael Wall, Andreas Rechtsteiner, and Luis Rocha. 2003. Singular Value Decomposition and Principal Component Analysis. In Berrar, D. et al. (eds.) *A Practical Approach to Microarray Data Analysis.* pages 91-109. Kluwer, Norwell.

Erik Cambria, Amir Hussain, Catherine Havasi, and Chris Eckl. 2010c. SenticSpace: Visualizing Opinions and Sentiments in a Multi-Dimensional Vector Space. volume 6279 of *Lecture Notes in Computer Science*, pages 385–393. Springer, Berlin Heidelberg.

User Profile Construction in the TWIN Personality-based Recommender System

Alexandra Roshchina
Social Media Research Group,
ITT Dublin / Ireland
sasharo@itnet.ie

John Cardiff
Social Media Research Group,
ITT Dublin / Ireland
John.Cardiff@ittdublin.ie

Paolo Rosso
NLE Lab-ELiRF, Universidad Politécnica de Valencia / Spain
prosso@dsic.upv.es

Abstract

The information overload experienced by people who use online services and read user-generated content (e.g. product reviews and ratings) to make their decisions has led to the development of the so-called recommender systems. We address the problem of the large increase in the user-generated reviews, which are added to each day and consequently make it difficult for the user to obtain a clear picture of the quality of the facility in which they are interested.

In this paper, we describe the TWIN ("Tell me What I Need") personality-based recommender system, the aim of which is to select for the user reviews which have been written by like-minded individuals. We focus in particular on the task of User Profile construction. We apply the system in the travelling domain, to suggest hotels from the TripAdvisor[1] site by filtering out reviews produced by people with similar, or like-minded views, to those of the user. In order to establish the similarity between people we construct a user profile by modelling the user's personality (according to the Big Five model) based on linguistic cues collected from the user-generated text.

1 Introduction

With the transformation of the Web from a static data source into an interactive environment that allows users to actively communicate with each other and produce shared content, the amount of the information available online has grown tremendously. As a result the task of automatic data analysis has emerged to help people make better choices of the ever increasing number of products and services. In situations where the number of alternatives is very large, people tend to rely on the opinions of experts. Regarding the Web, so-called "recommender systems" (Ricci et al., 2010) have been constructed to serve this expert function following the user-oriented approach in the online world. There are many existing recommenders on the Internet nowadays serving different purposes such as recommending films (Movies2Go [2]), music and TV programs (Last.fm[3]), etc.

One of the domains in which the necessity of making a good choice is very important is travelling. People are faced with a high degree of uncertainty when choosing a place (hotel, restaurant) they have never been to, consequently they must rely on other travellers' reviews which sites such as TripAdvisor provide. However, when the number of such reviews becomes large, it is critical to provide a filtration system, whereby the reviews most likely to be valued by the reader are highlighted. In Viney (2008), it has been shown that people normally do not go further than the second or third page in search results.

In this paper, we propose the "Tell me What I Need" (TWIN) recommender system, the goal of which is to select reviews written by people with like-minded views to those of the reader to get

[1] http://www.tripadvisor.com

[2] http://www.movies2go.net
[3] http://www.last.fm

Proceedings of the Workshop on Sentiment Analysis where AI meets Psychology (SAAIP), IJCNLP 2011, pages 73–79, *Chiang Mai, Thailand, November 13, 2011.*

the list of hotels that could be of interest for him. A critical component of this task is to accurately construct the profile of the user. Traditionally, this has been constructed from the person's preferences or their explicit or implicit ratings (Ricci et al., 2010), however in our case we follow the emerging approach of personality-based user profile construction (Nunes, 2008) from linguistic cues retrieved from the text of the user reviews (Mairesse et al., 2007).

The paper is organized as follows. In Section 2 we provide an overview of online recommender systems and proceed to discuss the modelling of personality with the emphasis on the identification of a writer's personality from the text they write. We give an overview of the importance of the social sites in the online travelling domain. In Section 3 we present the prototype of the TWIN recommender system. In Section 4 we discuss the preliminary work on the evaluation of the TWIN system in regard to the User Profile construction. Finally, the conclusions are presented in Section 5.

2 Background

2.1 Recommender systems

The function of a recommender system is to assist a person to make the right decision about choosing a particular product or service, from the vast number that is available. This functionality is beneficial not only for customers but also for business providing the product or service, as positive recommendations will increase the volume of sales. Some of these systems are being built for commercial reasons (to sell more diverse goods, etc.), while others are purely for research needs (to improve recommendation algorithms, study users' needs more precisely, etc.) (Ricci et al., 2010).

Types of recommender systems

The main two types of recommender systems are *content-based* and *collaborative filtering* (Marmanis and Babenko, 2009). Content-based systems rely on the attributes of items and require users to provide their initial preferences in order to recommend items which match those preferences. One of the main advantages of this type of recommender system is that a user's unique taste is not smoothed by the preferences of others (Nageswara and Talwar, 2008) and people with extreme likes will still receive appropriate recommendations.

Collaborative filtering algorithms are the most popular nowadays (Ricci et al., 2010). They use various similarity measures to estimate the distance between items (item-item approach) or between people (user-based neighborhood construction methods). The widely used similarity measures are: *cosine similarity* (each item's attributes are seen as a multidimensional vector and to assess the similarity between two such vectors the cosine of the angle between them is considered). The *Pearson correlation similarity* is based on the correlation between two items, and *probability-based similarity,* where if the user purchased one item after another then the probability of the similarity of those items increases.

Other types of recommender systems which include *demographic* recommender systems (based on the age, country or language of the user), *knowledge-based* recommenders (specialize in recommending data from a particular domain of knowledge through estimating person's needs in that field), *community-based* (recommendations are based on the items that are favorable for user's friends) and *hybrid* recommender systems (utilize a combination of the above mentioned approaches) (Ricci et al., 2010).

2.2 Personality traits

One of the most the widely addressed philosophical questions (having its roots in works of Aristotle) has been the variance of personality traits between people, and how this variance influences people's behavior. The appearance of the scientific trait theory has become possible at the beginning of the 20th century through systematic data collection and the development of statistical methods like data correlation techniques and factor analysis (Matthews et al., 2009). A number of statistical approaches are used to find correlations between various traits and then factor analysis techniques are subsequently applied to group positively correlated traits into larger groups. Each dimension consists of a number of traits that are related to each other and thus if the person has one of the traits in a particular dimension he is likely to have other traits from the same group.

Big Five model

The Big Five personality trait classification is one of the most widely used and recognized models (Matthews et al., 2009) utilized for the research as well as for the staff recruitment purposes. It consists of the five major trait categories: *Extraversion* (the desire of active and energetic participation in the world around), *Agreeableness* (the tendency to eagerly cooperate with others and generally be more helpful and generous), *Conscientiousness* (the ability to control the impulses and to hold to the long-term plans as well as being able to foresee the consequences of one's behavior), *Neuroticism* (which is positively correlated with the susceptibility to experiencing negative feelings such as anxiety, anger and depression) and *Openness to experience* (the tendency of the person to be sensitive to new ideas, non-conventional thinking and to being intellectually curious).

2.3 Personality from the text

Research has shown that there is a correlation between the "The Big Five" dimensions and linguistic features found in texts. In particular, Tausczik and Pennebaker (2009) have discovered that the use of first-person singular pronouns correlates with depression levels while the amount of positive emotions words reveals extraversion. Mairesse et al. (2007) has shown that emotional stability (as an opposite of neuroticism) is correlated with the amount of swearing and anger words used by the person while agreeableness is associated with back-channelling (personality types were estimated form self-reports and observers' reports). Some of the traits were studied more thoroughly (for example, extraversion) which could be caused by a higher level of representativeness of the particular trait-related linguistic cues (Mairesse et al., 2007).

In our research we utilize the Personality Recognizer which is one of the available tools that allow estimating Big Five personality scores (Mairesse et al., 2007).

2.4 Travelling and social media sites

One of the fast developing online domains is the travelling sector. Travellers trying to find a suitable accommodation tend to rely on a number of factors. In particular their choice depends on the hotel awareness (the place is somehow more familiar to the person, for example as a result of advertising) and hotel attitude based on the attributes of the hotel that are pivotal to the person (for example location, cleanliness, service, etc.) (Vermeulen and Seegers, 2008). Thus the choice the traveller makes can become highly influenced by the market games, advertising, popularity of some locations, etc. For this reason many people tend to trust more the opinions of other travellers when making a decision about a particular place to go (O'Connor, 2010).

Research shows that the role of social sites in online travelling domain that allows experience sharing is significant and a high percent of search engine results are links to the social media sites belonging to a number of major categories like virtual community sites, review sites, personal blog sites and social networking tools (Xiang and Gretzel, 2010).

Recently social sites such as TripAdvisor have started to emerge to allow their users to publish reviews of the places they travelled to. TripAdvisor provides the interface to search through the travel facilities (hotels, restaurants, etc.), check their availability for a specific date and read the reviews associated with them. Most of the users of TripAdvisor (97%) return to the site and utilize its content to plan their next trip (O'Connor, 2010). But as the volume of the available reviews is growing in size every day, it is impractical for users to manually retrieve and consider each review.

In our approach, we propose a recommender system based on the hypothesis that users are more likely to be interested in the views of others who have the same personality traits as themselves. Accordingly, in the TWIN System we aim to identify key personality characteristics of users (both readers and writers) based on their writings in order to identify texts written by reviewers who are similar to the reader.

3 The TWIN system

The proposed personality-based recommender system follows a user-based collaborative filtering approach. We make an assumption that the "similarity" between people can be established by analyzing the context of the words they are using. Accordingly, the occurrence of the particular words in the particular text reflects the personality of the author. This suggestion leads to the possibility of the text-based detection of a circle of "twin-minded" authors whose choices of particular places to stay (hotels reviewed in TripAdvisor, in our case) could be quite similar and thus could be recommended to each other. This approach provides recommendations that rely on the factors independent in many ways from the user's preexisting attitudes in the hotels' market and also avoids the subjective step of specifying explicit preferences.

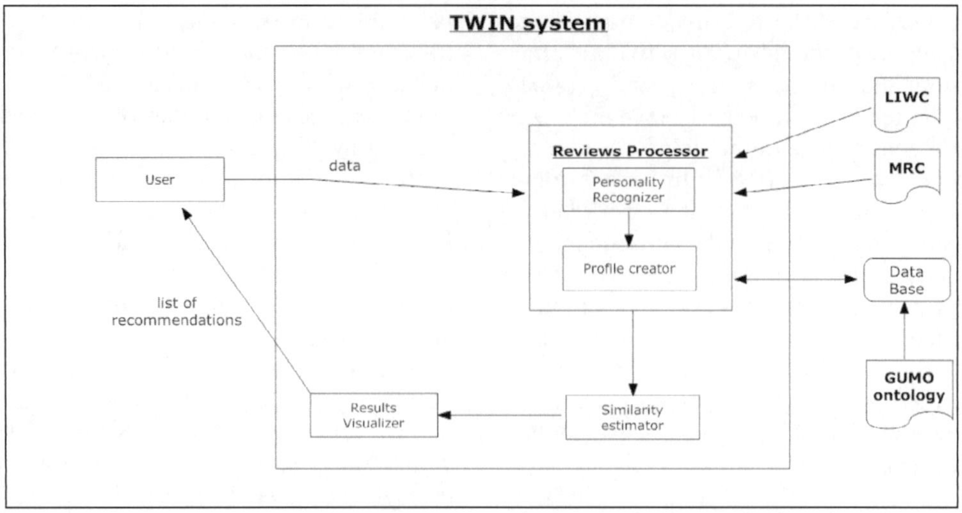

Figure 1. TWIN system architecture

3.1 Architecture

The diagram in Figure 1 represents the main components of the proposed TWIN recommender system described below.

Reviews Processor

The Reviews Processor component retrieves the textual data from the user (plain text written by person) and does the text preprocessing step (dealing with special characters, etc.).

Personality Recognizer

The Personality Recognizer tool is utilized for the estimation of personality scores (ranging from 1 to 7). It maps words found in the text to LIWC [1] (Linguistic Inquiry and Word Count) (Tausczik and Pennebaker, 2009) and MRC (Medical Research Council) Psycholinguistic database[2] (Coltheart, 1981) categories and calculates the number of words in each one. Then it applies the pre-constructed WEKA[3] (data analysis tool) (Hall et al., 2009) models of each of the Big Five dimensions to calculate the corresponding scores based on the found correlations between above the mentioned categories and each of the traits. There are 4 different models that are currently supported by the Personality Recognizer: Linear Regression, M5' Model Tree, M5' Regression Tree and SVM with Linear Kernel.

Profile creator

The Profile Creator stores the general information about the user (login, age group, etc.) as well as personality scores in the user profile that follows the GUMO ontology (General User Model Ontology) (Heckmann, 2005). This model provides a way of extensive description of the user and is a part of the framework that realizes the concept of ubiquitous user modelling. It includes demographic information, psychological state and a lot of other aspects. It has appropriate classes to represent the Big Five model personality parameters as well as general user data (age, gender, etc.).

Similarity Estimator

The Similarity Estimator component utilizes the Weka clustering model built using the K-Means algorithm (Witten and Frank, 2005). During the recommendation process the above-mentioned model is assigning the person to the appropriate cluster based on his profile information. Recommendations are calculated considering the items liked by people in this estimated cluster.

Results Visualizer

The Results Visualizer is constructed as a web-based Flash application to represent the results of the recommendation for the user, i.e. the list of hotels.

---

[1] http://www.liwc.net

[2] http://www.psy.uwa.edu.au/mrcdatabase/uwa_mrc.htm

[3] http://www.cs.waikato.ac.nz/ml/weka/

4 Evaluation

This section provides an overview of the work undertaken to date on the TWIN system construction. In particular we focus here on the structure of the personality-based user profile. For the purposes of the experiments we describe, a dataset of hotel reviews was constructed, as described in the following section.

4.1 Dataset description

We built a Java crawler and constructed a dataset based on reviews submitted to the TripAdvisor website. The dataset consists of hotels reviews (texts and numerical ratings of the particular hotel) and the information about their authors (username, age group and gender) crawled from the TripAdvisor user profiles. For evaluation purposes, we have considered only authors who have more than 5 reviews. The description of key characteristics of the dataset is shown in Table 1.

Dataset parameter	Value
Num of reviews	14 000
Num of people	1030
Total amount of words	1.9 million
Avg num of reviews per person	13.8
Min reviews per person	5
Max reviews per person	40
Num of all words	2.9 million
Avg num of words per review	210.8
Avg num per sentence	16.6
Min words per sentence	3
Max words per sentence	39.7

Table 1. TripAdvisor dataset description

4.2 User profile

The common way to store information about people and model their identity within the recommender system is to create User Profiles. These profiles can be knowledge-based (if person's details are acquired through the questionnaire) or behavior-based (extracted by means of various natural language processing techniques) (Nunes, 2008). Here we follow the behavior-based approach, retrieving the profile data implicitly through the analysis of the reviews written by the particular person.

To model the personality we store the mean score of each of the Big Five parameters calculated from the text of each of the reviews written by the particular person. We selected 15 people from our dataset who have contributed more than 35 reviews. Using the Personality Recognizer (with a linear regression algorithm) we have obtained personality scores for each of the texts written by each individual. As each score is calculated from the text of the review independently we have analyzed them separately. The visualized scores per each of the Big Five dimensions are presented in Figures 2 – 6.

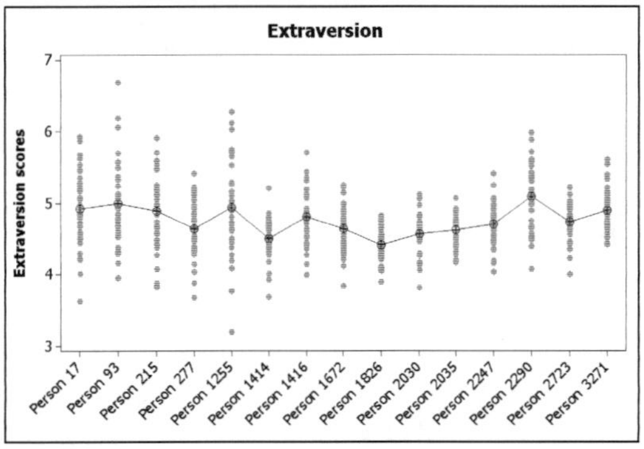

Figure 2. Extraversion scores distribution with means per each set of 15 people's reviews

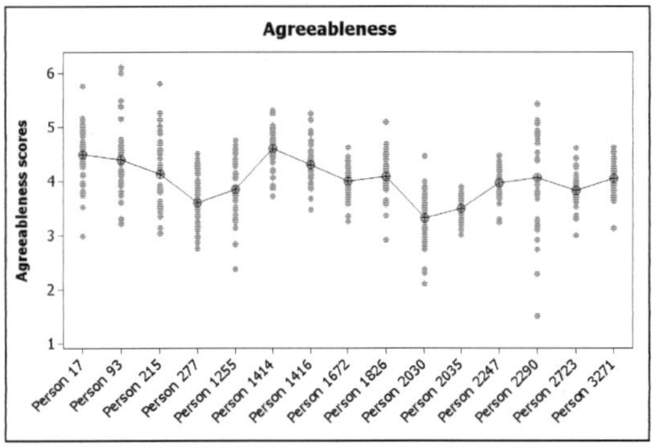

Figure 3. Agreeableness scores distribution with means per each set of 15 people's reviews

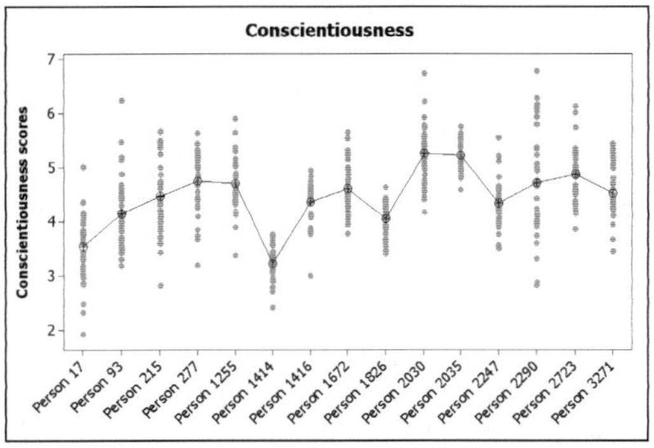

Figure 4. Conscientiousness scores distribution with means per each set of 15 people's reviews

The ANOVA test (Meloun and Militky, 2011) has shown significant differences ($p < 0.001$) between persons in each of the Big Five categories. Thus it could be concluded that the mean scores vary sufficiently from one person to another which enables us to use the mean score as the estimation of the personality in each of the 5 dimensions.

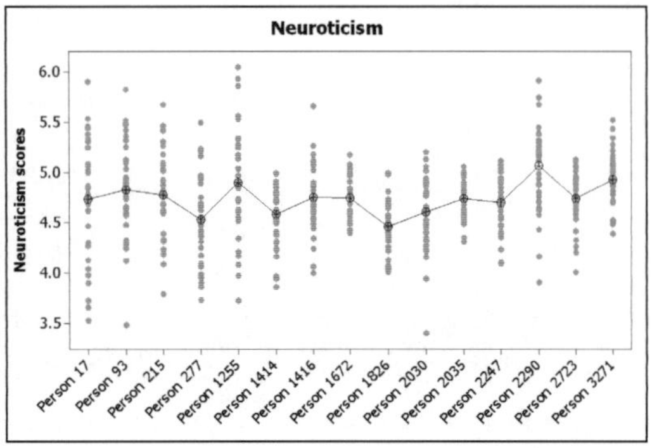

Figure 5. Neuroticism scores distribution with means per each set of 15 people's reviews

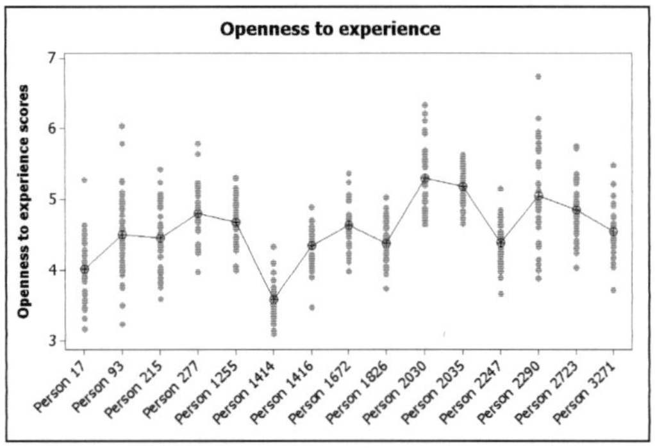

Figure 6. Openness to experience scores distribution with mean scores per each set of 15 people's reviews

It can be seen that openness to experience scores have the highest variability in means which suggests that this trait may be the easiest to detect. This result is in agreement with Mairesse et al. (2007) who had found that openness to experience is the easiest trait to model.

5 Conclusion and future work

In this paper, we have described the architecture of the TWIN Personality-based Recommender System. A fundamental tenet of our approach is that users will value reviews of like-minded people more highly. A critical factor in the success of our approach is the ability to determine personality characteristics (i.e. User Profiles) of reviewers using only the texts they write.

In this paper, we have determined that using a set of texts written by individuals who have contributed a large number of reviews, it is possible to differentiate personality types, and consequently to match a user with reviews written by like-minded people.

In the future work we are going to compare the performance of the other 3 algorithms available in the Personality Recognizer to choose the one that will provide better results. In order to evaluate the TWIN system we are planning the experiment that involves clustering (K-Means algorithm) of reviews in the collected dataset to estimate the percentage of rightly grouped ones.

Acknowledgments

We would like to thank James Reilly for his helpful comments on this paper. This work has been done in the framework of the VLC/CAMPUS Microcluster on Multimodal Interaction in Intelligent Systems and it has been partially funded by the European Commission as part of the WIQEI IRSES project (grant no. 269180) within the FP 7 Marie Curie People Framework, by MICINN as part of the Text-Enterprise 2.0 project (TIN2009-13391-C04-03) within the Plan I+D+i.

References

Coltheart, M. 1981. *The MRC Psycholinguistic Database.* Quarterly Journal of Experimental Psychology, 33A(4):497-505.

Hall M., Frank E., Holmes G., Pfahringer B., Reutemann P., Witten I. H. 2009. *The WEKA Data Mining Software: An Update.* SIGKDD Explorations, 11(1).

Heckmann D. 2005. *Ubiquitous User Modeling.* IOS Press.

Mairesse F., Walker M. A., Mehl M., Moore R. 2007. *Using Linguistic Cues for the Automatic Recognition of Personality in Conversation and Text.* Journal of Artificial Intelligence Research, 457-500.

Marmanis H., Babenko D. 2009. *Algorithms of the intelligent web.* Manning Publications. USA.

Matthews G., Deary I. J., Whiteman M. C. 2009. *Personality Traits*. Cambridge University Press, Cambridge, UK.

Meloun M., Militky J. 2011. *Statistical data analysis: A practical guide.* Woodhead Publishing India.

Nageswara Rao K., Talwar V. G. 2008. *Application Domain and Functional Classification of Recommender Systems – A Servey*. DESIDOC Journal of Library & Information Technology, 28(3):17-35.

Nunes M. A. S. N. 2008. *Recommender Systems based on Personality Traits*, PhD thesis. Université Montpellier 2.

O'Connor P. 2010. *Managing a Hotel's Image on TripAdvisor*. Journal of Hospitality Marketing & Management, *19*:754-772.

Ricci F., Rikach L., Shapira B., Kantor P. 2010. *Recommender Systems Handbook*. Springer, US.

Tausczik Y. R., Pennebaker J. W. 2009. *The Psychological Meaning of Words: LIWC and Computerized Text Analysis Methods*. Journal of Language and Social Psychology, *29*(1):24-54.

Vermeulen I. E., Seegers D. 2008. *Tried and tested: The impact of online hotel reviews on consumer consideration*. Tourism Management, 30(1):123-127.

Viney D. 2008. *Get to the Top on Google: Tips and Techniques to Get Your Site to the Top of the Search Engine Rankings -- and Stay There*. Nicholas Brealey Publishing.

Witten I. H., Frank E. 2005. *Data Mining: Practical Machine Learning Tools and Techniques. Machine Learning*. Morgan Kaufmann.

Xiang Z., Gretzel U. 2010. *Role of social media in online travel information search.* Tourism Management, 31(2):179-188.

What is new? News media, General Elections, Sentiment, and named entities

Khurshid Ahmad
Computer Science
Trinity College
Dublin Ireland
kahmad@scss.tcd.ie

Nicholas Daly
Computer Science
Trinity College
Dublin Ireland
dalyni@scss.tcd.ie

Vanessa Liston
Political Science
Trinity College
Dublin Ireland
vliston@tcd.ie

Abstract

The repetition of names of persons, places, ideas and events, is used sometimes for emphasis. The same is true of the repetition of affect words - repeated preferentially to show negative/positive sentiment. During an election campaign, this repetition may have a bearing on the electability of politicians and on the reputation of political parties. News media covering an election may be involved in endorsing political parties, attempting to set aspects of election agenda, and may have gender bias. Using Rocksteady, an affect analysis system, we have analyzed samples of news published nationally and regionally by Irish media between 21st December 2010 and 20th Feb. 2011 - in the run up to the Irish General Election on 25th February 2011. Our results show that a diachronic study of the coverage, based on named-entity dictionary crafted from electoral lists and with key financial and economic terms added, supplemented by a General Inquirer type dictionary of affect, helped us to distinguish between the winners (two opposition parties that have subsequently formed a coalition government) from the loser (the incumbent party).

1 Introduction

Literature on sentiment analysis is boldly going where others will fear to tread: sentiment of large populations within a community is being extracted and aggregated by 'review mining, product reputation analysis, multi-document summarization, and multi-perspective question answering'(Riloff et al., 2006). The fields covered are wide ranging and include sentiment/opinion extraction from film reviews (Namenwirth et al., 2002), from letters to the Editors in major newspapers(Asher et al, 2009), and from politically sensitive documents in multiple languages (Ahmad, 2011).

There is burgeoning literature on the impact of sentiment on financial markets(Daly et al., 2009), where it has been shown that negative sentiment reflects at one time has an impact on prices in the markets subsequently(Tetlock, 2007). The extraction of sentiment in particular and affect in general is a multi-faceted issue; aspects of affect-bearing writing is based on the use of metaphors(Ahmad, 2011).

However, evaluation frameworks on the choice of data, especially who wrote or spoke sentiment bearing documents, are still evolving(Pang & Lee, 2008). As a result, studies on the impact of the articulated affect in general, and sentiment in particular, are limited in the sentiment analysis literature.

The question of data source is important because of the multiple sources of bias that can be introduced at the data production stage: particularly when print/TV/digital news media is changing rapidly with considerable reliance on social media and 'active news gathering' in decline partly because of commercial pressures(Krause, 2011).

Sentiment can be deliberately generated by a news publisher who is keen on focussing a discourse on charismatic personalities or certain topics that will benefit those supported by the publisher(Curtice, 1999;Druckman, 2005). It is equally possible that a news publisher may be pandering to the political, social and economic views of a community to maximise financial gain from selling advertisements in their print/offline publication(Gentzkow, Shapiro, 2010). The affect articulated by an opinionated person or organisation may be rooted in their racial and/or gender bias -both articulated vividly in the 2008 US Presidential Elections(Parks et al., 2008). Such bias has been defined by authors as "a deviation from the informative media function, which may result in

Proceedings of the Workshop on Sentiment Analysis where AI meets Psychology (SAAIP), IJCNLP 2011, pages 80–88,
Chiang Mai, Thailand, November 13, 2011.

a distorting effect on political attitudes and outcome" (Brandenburg, 2005).

A large political science literature is dedicated to such influence of the media on electoral outcomes. One branch focuses on the possible impact of newspapers endorsing a candidate or a political party; this practice is common in the USA, the UK and Canada.

Some scholars have argued that endorsements have a weak impact on electoral outcomes. In an influential study Erikson(1976) studied the impact of 223 newspapers that were defined as *local* to a given community voting patterns in 200 northern US counties found that while there was a substantial change in endorsements patterns, this did not translate into a significant change in votes cast. Erikson has argued that the estimated effect of 'presidential endorsements treatments' is about 5% or so (Erikson, 1976, pp.215).

Curtice (1999) reports an experience similar to that of Erikson's when there was a 'break from homogenous media treatment' in the United Kingdom. Curtice looked at 1,976 voters and asked these voters to name the newspapers out of a sample of 10 papers they read, The author's analysis suggests that the change or otherwise in the voting intentions of his subjects suggests that whilst 'partisan press does have some influence on the way in which their readers vote', it is not clear that the imbalance between readership of pro-party newspapers (Conservative vs Labour) 'over any period of time tends to be small if evident at all' Curtice, 1999:28).

Contrary to Erikson and Curtis, some recent studies that account for credibility of the source of an endorsement, suggest that newspaper endorsements may have a direct effect on voter choice. Voters are more likely to endorse the candidate of publication but only where the endorsement is credible. For example, endorsements for Democratic candidates from left-leaning newspapers exert less influence that those from neutral or right-leaning newspapers(Chiang & Knight, 2011).

In order to account for the various biases of the various humans and organisations involved in the supply of data used in sentiment analysis, and in the subsequent evaluation of such systems, we draw upon studies in political science, and political and media communications, specifically, the techniques used in the study of general elections where media affect and sentiment and its impact on the outcome of the elections, is the focus. We examine newspaper content for word frequencies that can generate 'bias' in coverage of parties, gender and party agendas in the run-up to the Irish general election 2011. While our study does not draw a causal relationship between bias and electoral outcome, it clearly demonstrates that sentiment analysis must factor in context and bias analysis in order to support a broad field of impact studies.

2 Media Bias and Perceptions

In this section we present the various types of bias which are the focus of empirical investigation in the literature of political science and political communications. We specifically look at endorsement, coverage, agenda and gender.

2.1 Types of Bias and Perceptions

Endorsement: There are different levels of political description when we attempt to discern the impact of media on the outcomes of elections. First, a meta-level political description where we might look at the attitude of publishers towards a political party or party leader as articulated directly in an endorsement during the course of an election campaign. The most common empirical finding is that the impact to be minimal except when a major change on the political scene also takes place - especially the vote against a government that has been in power for a long period.

This is suggested by frequency data on endorsements during the electoral campaigns in the USA (2004, 2008), the UK (2005, 2010) and Canada (2006, 2008, 2011). In the USA and the UK, there was a change in the government after the elections in 2008 and 2010 respectively; in both cases the incumbent parties were in power for over 8 years. The switch over by newspapers supporting the incumbent over to the opposition that goes on to win the election: In the USA, during the 2008 Democratic Party was endorsed by 70% of the newspapers and won the same percentage of votes: the 'swing' in endorsement was 18% and in votes cast it was 16%. The situation in the UK is similar but differs in a crucial detail: The endorsements for the ruling Labour Party dropped by over 40% in 2010 when compared with the 60% endorsements in the previous elections held in 2005: the drop in Labour's vote was 6% and the opposition Conservative gained 4% in the 2010 elections. The Canadian election cycle shows no discernible effect of newspaper endorsement over the last 3 elections: the Conservatives have had an average of 70% endorsement but their share of the vote of the seats in parliament is still just above 50%. The overall message of our observations of the elections in the three countries is that endorsements may have an impact and this is perhaps more pronounced when a change in government is imminent (see Table 1 for details).

It appears that newspapers have a greater impact than TV news broadcast in some cases. This may be due to a number of reasons and here are some reasons that have been reported recently: (a) Panel studies suggest that only 2 in 100 news viewers pay much attention to the news about presidential elections and, in any case, news about elections makes up less than 10% of TV news output(Gentzkow, Shapiro, 2010); but there is some evidence that political advertising on the TV can persuade parts of a populace in exceptional circumstances(Beltrn, 2007). (b) Voters typically follow trusted news sources - so the modality of the medium, visual or linguistic, may not be an issue(Miller & Krosnick, 2000). (c) Partisan coverage, as in Fox News, has an impact in that this coverage tends to nudge the voter away from their original choice of party/candidate; contrarily, some scholars have suggested that 'opinionated news is no more likely to contribute to partisan polarisation than non-opinionated news' (Feldman, 2011:pp178). (d) Politicians on the periphery of the mainstream political systems, depend as much on TV news and interviews as on coverage in the newspapers (Bos et al. , 2011). (e) The coverage of a candidate is usually positive if the candidate discusses issues that relate to his or her party(Hayes, 2008). (f) Both the committed voters and the undecided voters can be influenced by the positive coverage of a party in the media, and the undecideds are influenced more(Hopmann et al., 2010).

Gender: In an experimental study, neuropsychologists(Chiao, et al., 2008) confirmed that gender affects how people perceive and evaluate facial appearance(Keating, 1985) in the context of an election(Little et al., 2006). Gender bias in the media can also perversely serve as an advantage for incumbent female politicians especially in the US House of Representatives(Milyo & Schosberg, 2000). Female incumbents have been shown to be of higher average quality than their male counterparts and this quality is perhaps underestimated by male opponents in an election. The higher quality of the female incumbent, however, may be due to the 'barriers to entry' that women face in joining political institutions. Some early analysis of the 2008 US Presidential election, where race (President Obama's ethnicity) and gender (Senator Clinton's female persona), there is good news to be had in that it appears that US voters are moving away from their stereotypical images of both women and people of colour(Miller & Krosnick, 2000).

2.2 Bias in the Irish Context

Returning to the Irish context with which this study is concerned, Brandenburg(2005) has looked at the media coverage Irish General Election of 2002. He studied three biases in the coverage by 4 newspapers and two TV stations namely: first, coverage of political parties; second, the bias shown by the coverage of a given party's actual or contrived expertise in a policy area; and third, the judgemental or evaluative tone of the coverage expressed in terms of positive or negative statements made by a newspaper about individual political parties. Brandenburg analysed 220,180 lines of text and the lines were coded along 12 policy dimensions and five campaign dimensions. He also included the location of the text - whether the text appeared in the editorial columns, on the front page, as a photo caption or in a cartoon. Brandenburg's analysis shows that coverage was higher for incumbent parties and lower for the opposition. Coverage was proportional to the election results of 2002 and very similar to the campaign poll average of the parties involved. Of the 5 major parties in the election, the agenda of only three parties (*Fianna Fáil, Fine Gael and Labour*) 'find a certain degree of reflection in the media coverage' (Brandenburg, 2005 pp310). The author concludes by noting that whilst the Irish papers were not as openly partisan about a political party yet the papers were 'prone to various forms of bias'(Brandenburg, 2005 pp 318). Specifically, he finds a homogenous anti-politics bias.

Gender bias in the media and its impact on electoral outcome has not been extensively studied in the Irish context. An initial study demonstrates that in the 2002 general election, candidate gender was not a factor affecting voter choice(McElroy & Marsh, 2010). However, by 2011 gender had

USA Year	Democrats Endors.	Votes	Republicans Endors.	Votes	Votes Cast (Millions)
2004	52%(206)	54%	48%(191)	46%	59.46
2008	70%(497)	70%	30%(213)	30%	69.45
Canada	**Conservative** Endors.	Seats	**All Others** Endors.	Seats	**Seats in Parliament**
2006	88% (22)	40.30%	12%(3)	59.70%	308
2008	62% (21)	46.40%	38%(13)	53.60%	308
2011	82% (28)	53.90%	18%(6)	46.10%	308
UK	**Conservative** Endors.	Popular Votes	**Labour** Endors.	Popular Votes	**Votes Cast (Millions)**
2005	41%(7)	32%	59%(10)	35%	27.15
2010	71%(12)	36%	18%(3)	29%	29.36

Table 1: Endorsements and Election outcomes: The proportion of endorsements in US, Canadian and British Press in the recent elections. The two parties that have governed the UK up until 2010 have less than 70% of the popular votes but their votes translate into a higher proportion of the seats in the UK parliament; hence the numbers in the UK columns do not add up-to 100%. The numbers in parentheses give the actual number of newspapers supporting a party.

become a salient political issue with a discourse emerging on quotas for women candidates, particularly by such civil society organisations as 50:50 (50:50 civil society group,). Most parties in large constituencies aimed to increase their percentage of female candidates. We are then concerned with gender balanced coverage to the extent that it was a popular discourse during the election campaign. Specifically, we ask, to what extent was this new discourse on gender reflected in the frequency by which women candidates were referenced in the newspaper medium.

3 Method and Data

Our data for this study is derived from newspaper content.

We focus on samples of news published nationally and regionally by Irish newspapers between 21st December 2010 and 20th February 2011 - in the run up of the 2011 Irish General Election on 21st February 2011. We set out to investigate the presence of three biases: gender; agenda; and party coverage. We also run an analysis of general affect specifically focused on well-being and power.

The data was extracted using the news aggregator *LexisNexis* which allows access to news media across Ireland: this data, part of *LexisNexis* data deluge, has to be *curated*(Witt et al., 2009). The news is organised in a time series and the content analysed automatically by an affect analysis system *Rocksteady* developed at Trinity College, Dublin, Ireland.

3.1 Data Curation

Criteria A strict search criterion for news data was implemented whereby only articles from Irish publications would be selected and must contain the terms Ireland and Politics, or Ireland and Elections(s) within the headline or opening paragraph.

Media concentration There are 59 titles that are published in Ireland including 6 published in Northern Ireland with total circulation of 1.56 million copies. There are 29 publishers in total and one publisher (Independent Publishing) owns 17 titles with a total audited circulation of 652,000 copies including the highest circulation *Irish Independent* (138,00 copies). There are 23 publisher with only one title including the 2nd highest circulation *Irish Times* (102,000 copies) and the *Irish Examiner* (46,000 copies). Sunday newspapers account for 1/3 of all copies in circulation.

Collection Data was retrieved using the *LexisNexis* online repository which allows for searches for a wide number of sources based on the criteria laid out above. An initial corpus of 3,024 articles was created covering the time period of 55 days between 21 Dec 2010 and 20 Feb 2011 with a total of 41 sources: 11 nationwide, including the Irish state TV network *RTE*, and 30 regional newspapers . *LexisNexis* provides the ability to batch download articles into a single file comprising 500 of the returned news items. Once collected data may be sanitised and organised in a consistent manner.

Sanitisation Once data has been collected it is important that any meta data included within the text be removed as it would alter the total word count within the article and provide erroneous results. When dealing with news data a key issue is that of reprints; reprints may occur whereby a regional newspaper re-releases the same item from a national paper or may be due to minor modifications of corrections of the news item, news items may also be expanded over the course of the day. We have developed a system for the identification and possible deletion of duplicate items within a news collection.

The Levenshtein distance algorithm provides a metric of the differences between two texts representing the number of alterations required to change one to the other. While intended for small strings the method may be scaled to examine larger texts. We have found there is as much as 35% of the texts may be duplicated leaving a balance of 65% texts that do not substantially overlap.

3.2 Data Analysis

The *Rocksteady* system uses a combination of general purpose affect dictionaries, like Stone's General Inquirer Dictionary, and an optional domain specific dictionary. The Irish general election dictionary contained candidate names as terms with party affiliation, constituency, party role, qualifications and gender as categories. This resulted in a dictionary with 517 terms and 39 categories. The names of the candidates, party affiliation and constituency where retrieved from www.electionsireland.org.

For general affect analysis we focussed on evaluation (positive/negative), a deference category, words related to power, and one welfare category, well-being. (See Table 2):

We have used a frequency count approach and we have not used special purpose algorithms for identifying variants of a proper noun or attempted to resolve pronominal references. Our frequency count focuses on single and compound words and a dictionary look-up informs which of the many categories the words belong to. The categories include: affect (negative/positive, strong/weak); domain specific-categories (election vocabulary, Irish place names that are used as labels for constituencies); personal attributes including gender and official status. The results are then aggregated over a chosen time period, weekly in our case for instance .

Category	Instances
Evaluation	Positive (1915) /Negative (2291) : So-called sentiment words.
Deference	Power (1266): words indicating the influence to affect the policies of others
Welfare	Well-being (486): words describing the health and safety of organism:

Table 2: General Inquirer categories used in our study

4 Results

4.1 Coverage: Leaders and Parties

The citations for all leaders shows an increase between week beginning December 27th 2010 through to the week beginning February 14th 2011, with some notable changes in the trend. The citations to the leaders (and parties) is partially inflated for Micheál Martin and his party. During the period of study the ruling FF had leadership election which unseated the party leader (Mr Brian Cowen) and Mr Martin was elected after a three-week contest ending on 26th January 2011 - after which his citations and that of his party declined and his party lost the elections to the two opposition leaders (Kenny and Gilmore) (See Figure 1)

Our analysis of citation parties for the parties and leaders shows a good correlation with the results of the 2011 General Election as measured in terms of the *first preference votes*. The citation patterns in our newspaper corpus shows a progressive better correlation with the first preference votes (FPV) cast over a 7 week period (see Table 3). The FPV appear to be a good measure of real public opinion. There are a number of changes in the correlation between citations to the political parties, including the citations to the independents and minor parties, and the FPV. These changes relate to the leadership challenge within the party of the government (*Fianna Fáil*) and its outcome - reducing the correlation well below 50%. However, once the 'honeymoon' period of the new leader is over three weeks before the election , we see that

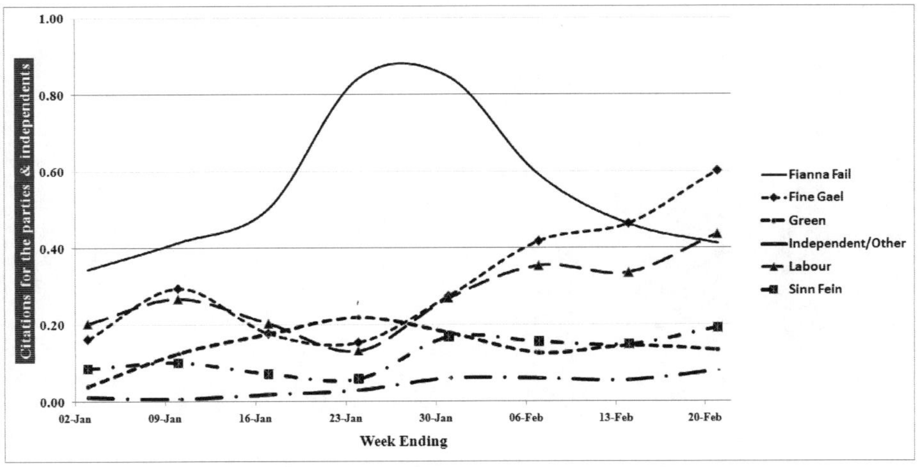

Figure 1: Time variation of the citations of the 5 main political parties and independents in the Irish General Elections 2011 in our corpus. The fortunes of the respective party leaders show similar trends

Week Starting	FPV vs Party	FPV vs Leader	Comments
27-Dec	40%	54%	
03-Jan	50%	82%	
10-Jan	13%	-1%	FF leadership challenge
17-Jan	2%	3%	
24-Jan	18%	39%	Election on 26/01/2011; New FF leader
31-Jan	56%	69%	Election rescheduled for 25/02/2011
07-Feb	70%	82%	
14-Feb	84%	96%	

Table 3: Correlation of the first preference votes casted in the Genereal Election (22/02/2010) with weekly citations of parties and leaders

the correlation between our findings and the FPV rise from 69% to around 96%.

4.2 Even handed Coverage?

The discussion in section 2 suggests that news media shows preference for one particular party - indeed Brandenburg(2005) noted that this was the case in the Irish elections in 2002. The party of government, *Fianna Fáil* (FF), is given greater coverage by all the news papers, the main opposition parties (*Fine Gael* and *Labour*) are collectively given greater coverage than is the case for FF, but individually the two parties receive less than 2/3rd of the citations for FF (Figure 2).

4.3 Agenda Coverage

The 2011 election was followed by a high level visit from the International Monetary Fund and the European Central Bank (ECB) for restructuring the Irish government debt. The severest economic downturn meant that economic terms dominated the discussion in the newspaper. The ECB organised the so-called *bail out* and can be seen to dominate the discussion (Figure 3)

4.4 Gender

There where 517 candidates contesting the election, 448 male candidates and 69 female candidates. The ratio of male to female contestants (6.45), does not generally correspond to the amount of coverage given to male or female candidates - on average male candidates are referred to 8 times more than the women; the best ratio for women-to-men citations is 6.3 and the worst is 10.7 (See Figure 4) These results are not surprising. Due to the high-stakes nature of the election, new female candidates were unlikely to achieve much press in comparison with issue coverage. As dominant players in the parties are male and these dominate issue coverage, a future study will test whether male and female new candidates were allocated equal coverage.

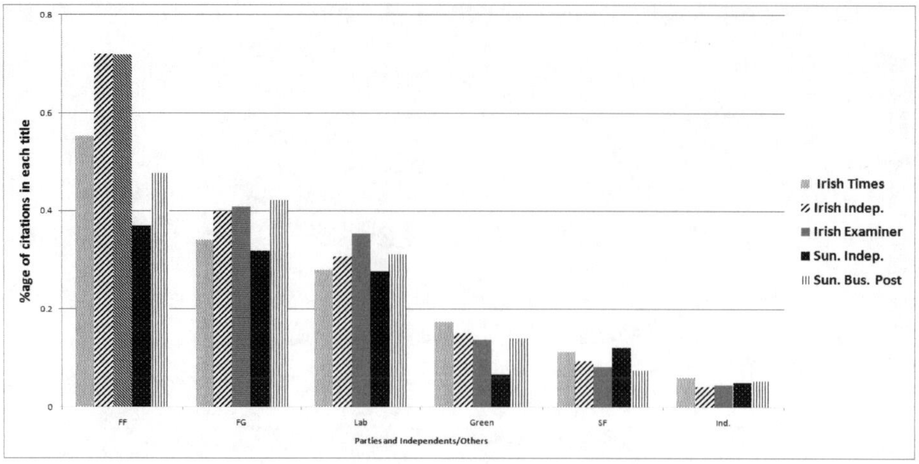

Figure 2: Coverage by major Irish newspapers of the 5 main parties and independents.

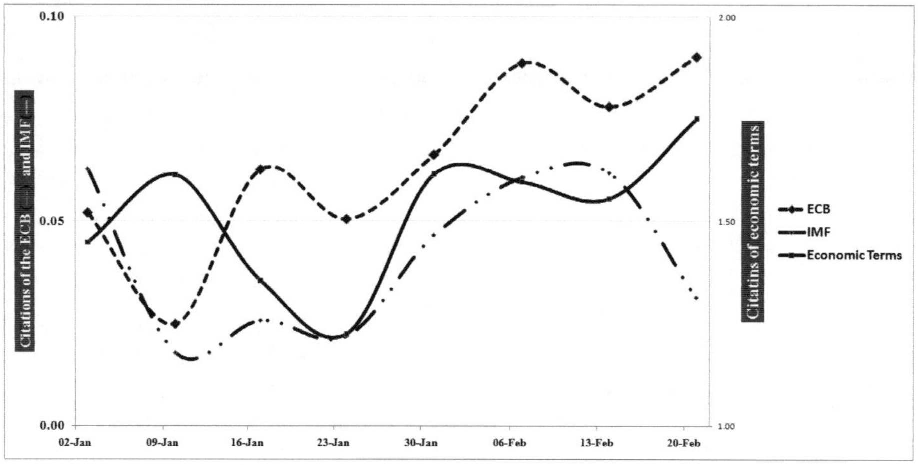

Figure 3: Variation of economic terms and named entities in our diachronic corpus

4.5 Sentiment, Power and Well being change

Finally, the 2011 election in Ireland was held in the backdrop of the worst economic crisis in the Republic's history and the incumbent parties' economic wherewithal was under serious criticism. The atmosphere was quite gloomy and the news-media carried substantial amount of negative sentiment. We noted a higher positive sentiment which remained constant throughout the campaign - however, positive sentiment has usually little impact as the analysis of financial markets suggests (Daly et al., 2009;Tetlock, 2007). The variation of power words is mild and shows a slight rise in the period when the Fianna Fáil party had its internal election. The distribution of well being words also remained static with a small decline towards the end of the campaign.

5 Afterword

We have described the work undertaken in political science, political and media communication to show how sentiment analysis is conducted in real world. The impact of sentiment can be seen in the results of political processes such as elections.

That affect of certain sentiment, activity and orientation can be deliberately introduced has been noted especially in the context of the concentration of media ownership. Media does tend to set up or influence political agenda and this can distort the reporting of the mood and attitude of the populace in the elections.

We have described how a large sample of newspaper output (43 of the 59 publications within Ireland) collated over two months of an election can be analysed using well known methods used in po-

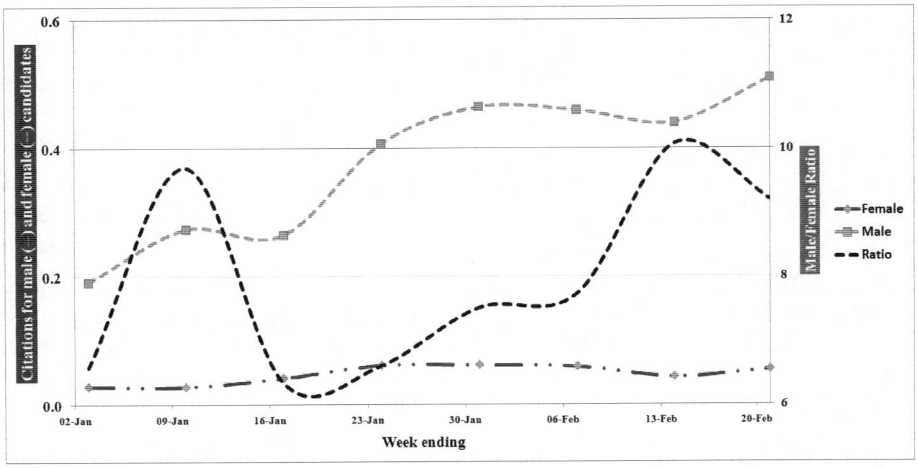

Figure 4: The gender chasm is magnified during the Irish General Election

litical opinion analysis. This sample has captured key issues -economic downturn- and has shown that a diachronic generated by the *Rocksteady* systems was closer to the final observed reality that is the election of *Fine Gael* and the *Labour Party*. The gender chasm was there for anybody to see: not only did fewer women contested the election they did not even receive the coverage proportionate to their numbers contesting the election.

We are in the process of analysing sentiment expressed about individual parties and their leaders and conducting a multivariate analysis to validate the descriptive analysis we have presented in this paper. We also intend to look at the results of sanitisation and measure what the impact of deleting duplicate items will be.

References

Ahmad, Khurshid. 2011. Affective Computing and Sentiment Analysis: Metaphors, Emotions and Terminology. *Springer Verlag*, 200 pp.

Asher, Nicholas, Farah Benamara & Yvette Yannick Mathieu. 2009. Appraisal of Opinion Expressions in Discourse. *Lingvistical Investigationes* . Volume 32 (No. 2) pp 279-292.

Beltrn, Ulises. 2007. The Combined Effect of Advertising and News Coverage in the Mexican Presidential Campaign of 2000. *Political Communication*, Vol 24 (1), pp 37-63.

Bos, Linda., van der Brug, Wouter., and de Vreese, Claes. 2011. How the Media Shape Perceptions of Right-Wing Populist Leaders. *Political Communication*, Vol 28, pp 182-206.

Brandenburg, Heinz. 2005. Political Bias in the Irish Media: A Quantitative Study of Campaign Coverage during the 2002 General Election. *Irish Political Studies.*, Vol. 20, (No. 3), pp 297-322.

Chiang, Chun-Fang., and Brian Knight. 2011. Media Bias and Influence: Evidence from Newspaper Endorsements. *Review of Economic Studies. (forthcoming).*, (http://www.restud.com/paper/media-bias-and-influence-evidence-from-newspaper-endorsements/)

Chiao JY, Bowman NE, Gill H . 2008. The Political Gender Gap: Gender Bias in Facial Inferences that Predict Voting Behavior *PLoS ONE*, Vol. 3(No. 10): e3666

Curtice, John. 1999. Was it the Sun wot won it again: The influence of newspapers in the 1997 election campaign. *CREST Working Paper*, No. 75, pp 31. http://www.crest.ox.ac.uk/papers/p75.pdf on 16 June 2011).

Daly,Nicholas., Colm Kearney and Khurshid Ahmad 2009. Correlating Market movements with consumer confidence and sentiments: A longitudinal study *Text Mining Services 2009, Leipzig, Germany, 23 March 2009, edited by Gerhard Heyer* Leipzeiger Beitrage zur Informatik, 2009, pp169 - 180.

Druckman, James. 2005. 'Media Matter: How Newspapers and Television News Cover Campaigns and Influence Voters'. *Political Communication*, Vol 22 (4), pp 463-481

Erikson, Robert, S. 1976. The Influence of Newspaper Endorsements in Presidential Elections: The Case of 1964. *American Journal of Political Science*, Vol. 20, No. 2 (May, 1976), pp. 207-233.

Feldman, Lauren. 2011. The Opinion Factor: The Effects of Opinionated News on Information Processing and Attitude Change. *Political Communication.*, Vol 28 (No. 2), pp 163-181.

Gentzkow, Matthew., and Jesse M. Shapiro 2010. What drives media slant? Evidence from the U.S. daily newspapers. *Econometrica*, Vol. 78 (No. 1, January, 2010), pp 35-71.

Hayes, Danny 2008. 'Party Reputations, Journalistic Expectations: How Issue Ownership Influences Election News'. *Political Communication*, Vol 25 (No. 4), pp 377-400

Hopmann, David Nicolas., Rens Vliegenthart, Claes De Vreese, and Erik Albk. 2010. Effects of Election News Coverage: How Visibility and Tone Influence Party Choice. *Political Communication*, Vol. 27 (No. 4), pp 389-405.

Krause, Monika. 2011. Reporting and the transformation of the journalistic field: US news media, 1890-2000. *Media, Culture Society*, Vol 33 (No.1), pp 89-104.

Keating, Caroline F. 1985. Gender and the physiognomy of dominance and attractiveness. *Social Psychology Quarterly*, Vol. 48, pp 61-70

Little Anthony C., Burris Robert P., Jones B.C., and Roberts S.C. 2006. Facial appearance affects voting decisions. *Evolution and Human Behavior*, Vol. 28, pp 18-27

McElroy, Gail., and Michael Marsh. 2010. Candidate Gender and Voter Choice: Analysis from a Multimember Preferential Voting System. *Political Research Quarterly*, Vol. 63: 822-833.

Miller, Joanne, M., and Jon A. Krosnick. 2000. News media Impact on the Ingredients of Presidential Evaluations: Politically knowledgeable citizens are guided by a trusted source. *American Journal of Political Science*, Vol 44 (No.2, April 2000), pp 301-315.

Milyo, Jeffrey., and Schosberg, Samantha. 2000. Gender Bias and Selection Bias in House Elections. *Public Chioce*, Vol 105, pp 41-59.

Namenwirth, Zhi and Lasswell, Harrold 1970. The changing language of American values : a computer study of selected party platforms. *Beverly Hills (Calif.) :Sage Publications.*

Pang, Bo., Lillian Lee, and S. Vaithyanathan 2002. Thumbs up? Sentiment classification using machine learning techniques. *Proc. of the Conf. on Empirical Methods in Natural Language Processing (EMNLP)* pp. 79-86.

Pang, Bo., and Lillian Lee. 2008. Opinion Mining and Sentiment Analysis. *Foundations and Trends in Information Retrieval* Vol. 2 (Nos1-2) pp 1-135

Parks, Gregory Scott and Rachlinski , Jeffrey J. 2008. A Better Metric: The Role of Unconscious Race and Gender Bias in the 2008 Presidential Race. *Cornell Legal Studies Research Paper* Paper No. 08-007. (Available at SSRN: http://ssrn.com/abstract=1102704).

Riloff, Ellen., Siddharth Patwardhan, and Janyce Wiebe. 2006. Feature Subsumption for Opinion Analysis. *Proc. of the 2006 Conf. on Empirical Methods in Natural Language Processing (EMNLP 2006)* pp 440-448. Sydney, July 2006.

Tetlock, Paul C. 2007. Giving Content to Investor Sentiment: The Role of Media in the StockMarket. *Journal of Finance* Vol. 62 (No. 3), pp 1139-1168

Vliegenthart, Rens & Walgrave, Stefaan 2011 When the media matter for politics: Partisan moderators of the mass media's agenda-setting influence on parliament in Belgium *Party Politics*. Volume 17 (No. 3) pp 321-342.

Witt, Michael., Jacob Carlson, D. Scott Brandt, Melissa H. Cragin 2009. Constructing Data Curation Profiles *Int. Journal of Digital Curation.* Volume 4 (No. 3) pp 93-103.

50:50 civil society group Available at http://5050-group.com/blog/

Chinese Sentiment Analysis Using Maximum Entropy

Huey Yee Lee
ePulze Sdn Bhd, C-41-2, Block C,
Jaya One, No 72a, Jalan Universiti,
46200, Petaling Jaya, Selangor Darul
Ehsan, Malaysia.
leehueyyee@hotmail.com

Hemnaath Renganathan
ePulze Sdn Bhd, C-41-2, Block C,
Jaya One, No 72a, Jalan Universiti,
46200, Petaling Jaya, Selangor Darul
Ehsan, Malaysia.
hemnaath@live.com

Abstract

This paper presents the use of Maximum Entropy technique for Chinese sentiment analysis. Berger, Vincent and Stephen (1996) prove that Maximum Entropy is a technique that is effective in a number of natural language processing applications. In this paper, Maximum Entropy classification is used to estimating the polarity of given comments of from electronic product. These messages are classified into either positive or negative. Apart from presenting the results obtained via Maximum Entropy technique, we also analyze the feature selection and pre-processing of the comments for training and testing purpose.

1 Introduction

Nowadays, there are lots of comments about products, movies, hotels, or restaurants available in on-line documents such as blogs, Facebook, Twitter and Amazon. As part of the effort to better classify information for users, researchers have actively investigated sentiment analysis. Sentiment analysis, attempts to gather the overall opinion towards the comments – for example, whether a product feedback is positive or negative.

This system is useful for consumers who want to research the sentiment of products before making a purchase, and companies that want to monitor the public opinion of their products. Labeling these comments correspondently, their sentiment would provide succinct summaries to both readers and organizations.

Research in sentiment analysis has been done mainly using the English language. In this paper however, we examine the effectiveness of applying machine learning techniques which is Maximum Entropy classification to the Chinese sentiment analysis. Maximum Entropy is a technique that uses probability distribution estimation and widely used for a variety of natural language tasks. The challenging aspect that is different from ordinary sentiment analysis is that the comments to be analysis are in Chinese language.

Section 2 presents the related work and Section 3 describes the idea of using Maximum Entropy classification. Meanwhile Section 4 discusses the pre-processing methods and feature selection techniques for constructing Maximum Entropy model which include segmentation, conjunction rules, stop words and punctuation elimination, negation, and lastly is keyword-based. The experimental result will be present on Section 5 and finally the conclusion and future work in Section 6.

2 Related Work

There has been a wide research effort on analyzing sentiment in languages other than English by applying bilingual resources and machine translation techniques to employ the sentiment analysis approach existing for English. For an example, Yao *et al.* (2006) had proposed a method of determining sentiment orientation of Chinese words using a bilingual lexicon and achieve precision and recall of 92%.

So far, many researchers have conducted on sentiment classification. These researches have fallen into two categories which is machine learning techniques and semantic orientation. Machine learning technique attempt to train a sentiment classifier based on occurrence frequencies of the various words in the documents. There are several Machine learning

Proceedings of the Workshop on Sentiment Analysis where AI meets Psychology (SAAIP), IJCNLP 2011, pages 89–93,
Chiang Mai, Thailand, November 13, 2011.

methods, such as Naïve Bayes (NB), Maximum Entropy (ME), Support Vector Machine (SVM), unsupervised learning and etc. Hemnaath and Low (2010) propose sentiment analysis using Maximum Entropy and Support Vector Machine.

Meanwhile, semantic orientation is to classify words into two classes, such as 'positive' or 'negative', and then count in the overall score of the text. Yuen *et al.* (2004) presents a method for inferring the semantic orientation of a Chinese word from their association with strongly-polarized Chinese morphemes.

Among several machine learning algorithms, Maximum Entropy is the convenient for natural language processing, since it allows the unrestricted use of contextual features, and combines them in a principled way. Besides, Wang and Acero (2007) also mentioned that the Maximum Entropy model has a convex objective function and consequently they converge to a global optimum with respect to a training set. Because of these advantages, Maximum Entropy Classification is selected to develop Chinese sentiment analysis.

3 Maximum Entropy Classification

Maximum Entropy is a machine learning method based on empirical data and provides the probabilities for which sentence belongs to a particular class. Kamal *et al.* (1999) found that Maximum Entropy works better than Naïve Bayes for their experiment. The fundamental principle of Maximum Entropy is that the distribution should be uniform. Besides, constraints for the model that characterize the class-specific expectations for the distribution are derived from labeled training data.

When using maximum Entropy, the first step is to identify a set of feature functions which define a category. For an example, in case of documents features could be the words that belong to the documents in that category; for each feature, measure its expected value over the training data and treat this as constraint for the model distribution. Maximum Entropy models are feature-based models. In a two-class scenario, it is the same as using logistic regression which corresponds to the Maximum Entropy classifier for independent observations.

Like any learning technique, the outputs generated from the process are relied on the given dataset of input. The dataset is analyzed, and from it, a model is generated, encapsulating all the rules about the process that could be inferred from the dataset. This model is then used to predict the output of the process, when supplied with sets of input that is not found in the sample dataset.

Each of these rows of dataset represents a training event. Each training event has an outcome which consists of the predicates and lead to the outcome of the event. Each time it runs, the model is built from the training dataset. In order to train a classifier, it's usually requires several stage of pre-processing to hand-label the training data.

4 Pre-processing

4.1 Stage 1: Segmentation

Unlike western languages, normally sentences in Chinese text are represented by strings of Chinese characters without spaces between words. Therefore, Chinese sentences are ongoing problems in information retrieval (IR) and computational linguistics. Each Chinese character represents a meaning, while two or more characters combined to form a word that has different meanings. Therefore, segmentation needed to retrieve the meaning of the sentence. For an example,

今天的天气很好 (Today's weather is very nice)

If the sentence is separated by characters, each character has their own meaning.

今	This
天	Day
的	The
天	Sky
气	Gas
很	Very
好	Nice

Meanwhile, by using segmentation, it can identify which character should be combined to form the word and carry the actual meaning of the sentences.

After segmentation: 今天 的 天气 很 好

今天	Today
的	The
天气	Weather
很	Very
好	Nice

Thus, to process any word-based or token-based linguistic processing on Chinese, segmentation plays an important role in determining word boundaries. Wang and Christopher (2007) previously mentioned indexing of Chinese document is impossible without a proper segmentation algorithm. Before either task can take place, the sentence must be broken into tokens; it must be segmented and it is the necessary stage in pre-processing of Chinese sentiment analysis.

4.2 Stage 2: Conjunction Rules

The main purpose of applying conjunction rules is to extract the accurate meaning or expression from a given sentence using grammar rules. Generally, a sentence only expresses one opinion orientation unless there is some certain conjunction such as BUT, ALTHOUGH, HOWEVER, WHILE and etc word which changes the direction of the sentence. Conjunction rules explanations are shown as below.

1. Although (虽然，尽管，虽，虽说)

   Although __(Phrase A)__, __(Phrase B)__.

   E.g. 虽然这相机很好，可惜电池寿命很短。
   (Although this camera is nice, too bad has short battery life.)

   In this case, phrase A will be cut off, and phrase B will be remain as sentence sentiment.

2. But (但，但是，而，不过，却，可是，然而，只是，可是，可，只，然)

   __(Phrase A)__, but __(Phrase B)__.

   E.g. 这相机的外观不美，但很耐用。
   (The camera appearance is not beautiful, but very durable.)

   In this case, phrase A also will be cut off, and phrase B will be remain as sentence sentiment.

3. Although..., but.... (虽然…但是，虽然…可是，尽管…却，……)

   Although __(Phrase A)__, __(Phrase B)__,but __(Phrase C)__.

   E.g. 虽然这相机很好，可惜电池寿命很短，但我还是喜欢用它。
   (Although this camera is nice, too bad has short battery life, but I still like it.)

   For this example, phrase A and phrase B will be cut off, while phrase C is remain as new sentence for sentiment.

By applying conjunction rules, the sentences become more understandable and straightforward; it is because having two polarities in a sentence which can affect the result of sentiment analysis. Hemnaath and Low (2010) proved that with conjunction rules, accuracy of sentiment analysis can be increased by approximately 5%.

4.3 Stage 3: Stop words and Punctuation Elimination

The next important stage in pre-processing of sentiment analysis is to simplify the text. Zou *et al.* (2006) claimed that in modern information retrieval system, effective indexing can be achieved by removal of stop words. Stop words are very common words that appear in the text that carry little meaning; they serve as a syntactic function but do not indicate subject matter.

For an example, words "and", "of", and "the" are appearing frequently in the document. They can affect the retrieval effectiveness because they have a very high frequency and tend to diminish the impact of frequency differences among less common words, thus affecting the training process in sentiment. Also, these stop words may result in a large amount of unproductive processing. The removal of the stop words and punctuation also changes the document length, subsequently affect the learning algorithm.

Those stop words and punctuation that having minor help in determining polarity of text can be removed. Ibrahim (2006) previously also showed that identifying a stop words list or a stoplist and eliminate them from text processing is essential to an information retrieval system.

4.4 Stage 4: Negation

One issue of accurate sentiment analysis identified in recent of research is negation detection. The treatment is very relevant for all NLP applications that involve deep text understanding. Li *et al.* (2010) showed that the negation word feature is an important feature for sentiment analysis. Negation needed to discriminate between factual and non-factual information in information extraction for sentiment analysis which process the actual meaning of the texts.

This is the process by which a negation word, such as 'not' inverts the evaluative value of as affective word. For an example, 'not good' is similar to saying 'bad'. By adapting a technique proposed by Das and Chen (2001), a tag 'NOT_' was added to every word between a negation word and the first punctuation mark following the negation word. Applying this, a new corpus variation was obtained.

我 不 喜欢 这 电影 (I do not like this movie)
我 不_喜欢 这 电影 (I do NOT_like this movie)

In unigrams, the value of 'like' is positive, but there is a negation word 'not', therefore a 'NOT_' is replaced and joint with the consequent word. As a result, 'NOT_like' can indirectly affect the value of the word; subsequently affect the polarity of entire sentence. In Chinese, instead of 'NOT_' , '不_' was applied, and the list of supported negation includes '不', '不是', '没', '没有', '无', '别' and etc.

4.5 Stage 5: Keyword-based

Comparison of keywords is an extra feature for sentiment analysis. Kaji and Kitsuregawa (2007) mentioned recognizing polarity requires a list of polar words and phrases such as 'good', 'bad' and 'high performance' etc. At first, lists of positive and negative polarities keywords are obtained by using the NTU Sentiment Dictionary. Consequently, the numbers of positive keywords and negative keywords that appear in the input sentence are counted. The polarity with the higher count returns as an extra feature for sentiment analysis.

5 Experiment

5.1 The analysis data

Our test-corpus is derived from product reviews harvested from the website IT168, which can be downloaded from http://product.it168.com. All the reviews have been tagged by their authors as either positive or negative. The corpus consists of 10 sub-corpora containing a total of 7818 reviews, distributed between 10 product types which are monitor, mobile phone, digital camera, MP3 player, computer part, video camera, networking, office equipment, printer and computer peripheral.

From these reviews, 2909 of both positive and negative comments are used as training data, while 1000 comments for both polarities are used for testing purpose. In addition, the Entropy model is manually set to discriminate >=0.5 as positive and <0.5 as negative.

5.2 Experiment 1

Segmentation is an initial and compulsory stage in Chinese sentiment analysis, without applying any other pre-processing stage for training and testing data, the overall accuracy for sentiment analysis is 81.65%. Table 1 shows that by apply each pre-processing, the overall accuracy is increased compared to the one without any pre-processing. It proves that the pre-processing stages discussed are functional in sentiment analysis.

Pre-processing	Accuracy		
	positive	**negative**	**overall**
Segmentation	77.2%	86.1%	81.65%
Conjunction rules	73.0%	90.8%	81.90%
Stopwords & punctuation elimination	80.9%	85.5%	83.20%
Negation	81.4%	86.1%	83.75%
Keyword - based	78.9%	87.6%	83.25%

Table 1: Result of sentiment analysis by applying pre-processing steps separately.

5.3 Experiment 2

In this experiment, each review for both training and testing datasets is going through 5 stages of pre-processing according the sequences as shown in Table 2. Table 2 shows the result that the overall accuracy of sentiment analysis is increased stage by stage which is increased from 81.65% to 87.05%.

Pre-processing	Accuracy		
	positive	**negative**	**overall**
Segmentation	77.2%	86.1%	81.65%
Conjunction rules	73.0%	90.8%	81.90%

Stopwords & punctuation elimination	80.2%	86.3%	83.25%
Negation	85.1%	86.8%	85.95%
Keyword - based	87.3%	86.8%	87.05%

Table 2: Result of sentiment analysis by applying pre-processing steps in stages.

6 Conclusion and Future Work

In this paper, we explore the steps of pre-processing that can reduce the features and extract the polarity of the Chinese texts. It is proved Maximum Entropy classification can achieve high accuracy for classifying sentiment when using these steps. Empirical results from the experiments demonstrate the feasibility of our approach. Besides classifying positive and negative sentences, entropy model results that lie between 0.48 – 0.52 can be pronounced as neutral sentences.

In our future work, we plan to future improve the feature selection techniques for constructing Maximum Entropy model, which is Word Sense Disambiguation. We believe that identify the actual meaning of the words can help to increase the accuracy of Chinese sentiment analysis. In addition, our next work will draw on more heavily Chinese Natural Language Processing technique, such as Chinese parsing and semantic annotation. We look forward to addressing these challenges in future work.

References

Berger, A. L., Vincent, J. D., and Stephen, A. D. 1996. A Maximum Entropy Approach to Natural Language Processing. *Computational Linguistics, 22(1)*: 39-71.

Das, S., and Chen, M. 2001. Yahoo! for Amazon: Extracting market sentiment from stock message boards. *8th Asia Pacific Finance Association Annual Conference (APFA).*

Hemnaath, R., and Low, B. W. 2010. Sentiment Analysis Using Maximum Entropy and Support Vector Machine. *Semantic Technology and Knowledge Engineering in 2010.* Kuching,Sarawak.

Ibrahim, A. E.-K. 2006. Effect of Stop Wprds Eliminationfor Arabic Information Retrievel: A Comparative Study. *International Journal of Computing & Information Sciences*, 119-133.

Kaji, N., and Kitsuregawa, M. 2007. Building Lexicon for Sentiment Analysis from Massive Collection of HTML Documents. *Proceedings of the 2007 Joint Conference on Empirical Methods in Natural Language Processing and Computational*, 1075–1083. Prague.

Kamal, N., John, L., and Andrew, M. 1999. Using Maximum Entropy for Text Classification. *IJCAI-99 Workshop on Machine Learning for Information Filtering.*

Li, S., Zhang, H., Xu, W., Chen, G., and Guo, J. 2010. Exploiting Combined Multi-level Model for Document Sentiment Analysis. *2010 International Conference on Pattern Recognition*, 4141-4144.

Wang, F. L., and Christopher, C. Y. 2007. Mining Web Data for Chinese Segmentation. *Journal of The American Society For Information Science and Technology*, 58(12): 1820–1837.

Wang, Y. Y., and Acero, A. 2007. Maximum Entropy Model Parameterization with TF*IDF Weighted Vector Space Model. *IEEE Automatic Speech Recognition and Understanding Workshop*, 213-218. Kyoto, Japan: Institute of Electrical and Electronics Engineers, Inc.

Yao, J., Wu, G., Liu, J., and Zheng, Y. 2006. Using bilingual lexicon to judge sentiment orientation of Chinese words. *Computer and Information Technology, 2006. CIT '06. The Sixth IEEE International Conference.*

Yuen, R. W., Chan, T. Y., Lai, T. B., Kwong, O., and T'sou, B. K. 2004. Morpheme-based Derivation of Bipolar Semantic Orientation of Chinese Words. *Proceedings of the 20th international conference on Computational Linguistics,* 1008-1014. USA.

Incorporating Lexicon Knowledge into SVM Learning to Improve Sentiment Classification

Ji Fang
Intelligent Systems Laboratory
Palo Alto Research Center
Palo Alto, California 94304, USA
fang@parc.com

Bi Chen
College of Information Sciences and Technology
Pennsylvania State University
Pennsylvania, USA
cb.chenbi@gmail.com

Abstract

Two typical approaches to sentiment analysis are lexicon look up and machine learning. Even though recent studies have shown that machine learning approaches in general outperform the lexicon look up approaches, completely ignoring the knowledge encoded in sentiment lexicons may not be optimal. We present an alternative method that incorporates sentiment lexicons as prior knowledge with machine learning approaches such as SVM to improve the accuracy of sentiment analysis. This paper also describes a method to automatically generate domain specific sentiment lexicons for this learning purpose. Our experiment results show that the domain specific lexicons we constructed lead to a significant accuracy improvement for our sentiment analysis task.

1 Introduction

Two typical approaches to sentiment analysis are lexicon look up and machine learning. A lexicon look up approach normally starts with a lexicon of positive and negative words. The overall sentiment of a text is determined by the sentiments of a group of words and expressions appearing in the text (Liu, 2007; Zhou and Chaovalit, 2008). However, a significant challenge to this approach is that the polarity of many words is domain and context dependent. For example, *long* is positive in *long battery life* and negative in *long shutter lag*. Such words are associated with sentiment in a particular domain, but are not subjective in nature. Nevertheless, current sentiment lexicons do not capture such domain and context sensitivities of sentiment expressions. They either exclude such expressions or tag them with an overall polarity tendency based on statistics gathered from certain corpus. While excluding such expressions leads to poor coverage, simply tagging them with a polarity tendency leads to poor precision.

Because of these limitations, machine learning approaches have been gaining increasing popularity in the area of sentiment analysis (Pang et al., 2002; Gamon, 2004). A machine learning approach such as Support Vector Machine (SVM) does not rely on a sentiment lexicon to determine the polarity of words and expressions, and can automatically learn some of the context dependencies illustrated in the training data.

Although recent studies have shown that machine learning approaches in general outperform the lexicon look up approaches for the task of sentiment analysis (Pang et al., 2002), completely ignoring the advantages and knowledge provided by sentiment lexicons may not be optimal. We present an alternative method that incorporates sentiment lexicons as prior knowledge with machine learning approaches such as SVM to improve the accuracy of sentiment analysis. This paper also describes a method to automatically generate domain specific sentiment lexicons for this learning purpose. Our experiments show that compared to general purpose domain independent sentiment lexicons, the domain specific lexicons lead to more significant accuracy improvement.

The sentiment analysis task performed in this paper is a fine grained product aspect level sentiment classification task for camera reviews. Namely, for each sentence in the camera reviews, we need to predict whether this sentence discusses any camera aspects, and if so, what is the associated sentiment.

2 Related Work

Given the task and the approaches of this study, we review the related works from three areas: 1. product aspect level sentiment analysis; 2. combining lexicon-based and machine learning approaches

Proceedings of the Workshop on Sentiment Analysis where AI meets Psychology (SAAIP), IJCNLP 2011, pages 94–100,
Chiang Mai, Thailand, November 13, 2011.

for sentiment analysis; 3. sentiment lexicon generation.

Product aspect level sentiment analysis aims to determine both the product aspects/features and their associated opinion at the sentence level. Earlier works include Hu and Liu (2004) and Popescu and Etzioni (2005). Both of these works extract frequent noun phrases as product aspects. Therefore, they do not identify implicitly expressed product aspects, and they do not further categorize the extracted noun phrases.

In our study, we extract both the explicitly and implicitly expressed product aspects, and we further categorize the semantically related aspects. Zhao et al. (2010)'s work is close to ours in this sense. However, in terms of opinion extraction, they only extract opinion words associated with product aspects, and they do not further identify the polarities of the opinion words. By contrast, we aim to identify the polarities associated with the product aspects. Our approach features incorporating lexicon information into machine learning. Thus we review studies that combine lexicon-based and machine learning approaches for sentiment analysis next.

In previous studies, the lexicon-based and machine learning approaches have been incorporated in two ways. The first way is to develop two weighted classifiers using these two approaches and then integrate them into one system. Andreevskaia and Bergler (2008)'s work falls into this category. The second way is to incorporate lexicon knowledge directly into learning algorithms. Our work falls into this category.

In the second category, Wilson et al. (2005), melville et al. (2009), Dang et al. (2010) and Sindhwani and Melville (2008) all use a general purpose sentiment dictionary to improve polarity classification. Our work differs from these previous studies in that we incorporate not only a general purpose sentiment lexicon but also *Domain Specific Sentiment Lexicons* into SVM learning, and we use this method for identifying both product aspects and their associated polarities. More importantly, our experiment results show that while a general purpose sentiment lexicon provides only minor accuracy improvement, incorporating domain specific dictionaries leads to more significant improvement.

Regarding the construction of sentiment lexicon, earlier studies have focused on generating general purpose dictionaries. These methods range from manual approaches (Wiebe et al., 2005) to semi-automated (Hu and Liu, 2004; Kim and Hovy, 2004; Zhuang and Jing, 2006) and automated approaches (Mohammad et al., 2009). More attention has been devoted to domain specific lexicon construction recently. For example, Fahrni and Klenner (2008) present a method to identify polarity adjectives specific to food targets extracted from wikipedia. Jijkoun et al. (2010) generate a topic-specific lexicon from a general purpose polarity lexicon. In this paper, we present a method to build domain specific sentiment lexicons from scratch using a combination of corpus filtering, web searching using linguistic patterns and dictionary expansion techniques. Among these techniques, web searching using linguistic patterns was first introduced by Hatzivassiloglou and Sebastiani (1997) to generate domain independent sentiment adjectives. Kobayashi et al. (2004) designed patterns to extract co-occurring aspect nouns and opinion adjectives. Fahrni and Klenner (2008) also used this technique and their lexicon is also limited to adjectives . By contrast, we use this technique to generate domain specific lexicon not limited to adjectives and nouns. Our method is described in detail below.

3 Generating Domain Specific Lexicons

As discussed above, the sentiments of many words or phrases are context or domain dependent. For example, *long* is positive if it is associated with the camera aspect of 'Battery Life'. However, the same word carries negative sentiment when it is associated with the camera aspect of 'Shutter Lag'. Therefore, it is critical to know the topic/domain being discussed when we try to determine the associated sentiment.

Based on this observation, we aim to build domain/topic specific lexicons covering both expressions indicating a specific domain and expressions indicating different sentiments associated with that particular domain. For example, our lexicon regarding 'Camera Picture Quality' would consist of two sub-lexicons. One includes words and phrases such as *picture, image, photo, close up* etc, which are good indicators for the topic of 'Picture Quality' in the area of digital cameras. The other one includes words and expressions that carry positive or negative sentiments if the associated topic is camera picture quality. For example, this second sub-lexicon would indicate that while *sharp* and *clear* are positive, *blurry* is negative when they are associated with camera picture quality. We achieved our goal by using a combination of corpus filtering, web search with linguistic patterns and dictionary expansion. Each of these techniques is described in detail in the following subsections.

3.1 Corpus Filtering

We first use a training corpus, in which each camera review sentence is annotated with a camera aspect as well as the associated sentiment, to build a foundation for our domain specific lexicons. Our approach is as follows.

First, for each camera aspect such as *Durability*, we extract all of the content words and phrases that occur in the training sentences labelled as expressing that aspect. The content words and phrases we extracted include nouns, verbs, adjectives, adverbs as well as their negated forms. This step produces an initial list of lexicon for each camera aspect.

Second, for each word and phrase in the list for each of the camera aspects, we check to see if that word or phrase also occurs in any other camera aspect lexicon. If yes, we remove it from the lexicon. After this step of filtering, we obtained a list of lexicon for each camera aspect, which contains only words and phrases unique to that camera aspect.

The quality of the lexicons produced using this approach is in general very high. For example, the following lexicon regarding the camera *Durability* was generated based on our relatively small training corpus with 2131 sentences covering 23 categories (22 camera aspects and a category of 'none', meaning that none of the 22 camera aspects was discussed).

Durability Lexicon: *[scratch, construct, build, rock, repair, damage, flimsy, not flimsy, junk, sturdy, sturdier, solid, durable, tough, bent, hard, not worth, firm, rug, broke, bulletproof]*

However, the drawback of this approach is that the coverage of the lexicons would completely rely on the coverage of the corpus, and annotating a broad coverage training corpus is time consuming, expensive and sometimes very difficult for a task such as sentiment analysis because of the richness of natural language.

We overcome this drawback by augmenting the initial domain specific lexicons we obtained from the training corpus through web search and filtering using linguistic patterns as well as dictionary expansion. These two approaches are illustrated in the next two subsections.

3.2 Web Search and Filtering Using Linguistic Patterns

To improve the coverage of the domain specific lexicons we obtained from our training corpus, we designed two linguistic patterns and used them as searching queries to find more words and phrases conceptually associated with the camera aspects. The two linguistic patterns we used are as follows.

Pattern 1: "Camera Aspect include(s) *"

Pattern 2: Camera Aspect + "Seed Word and *"

In these two patterns, 'Camera Aspect' refers to expressions such as *camera accessories* and *camera price*. 'Seed Word' refers to seed words for a particular camera aspect. For example, *cheap* and *expensive* can serve as seed words for camera aspect *price*. Note that in Pattern 1, the camera aspect name is included as part of an exact search query, whereas in Pattern 2, the camera aspect name serves as the context for the search query.

Depending on the semantic nature of a camera aspect, we choose one of these two patterns to find expressions conceptually related to that aspect. For example, while "camera accessories include *" is very effective for finding accessory expressions, 'camera picture + "clear and *"' is better for finding expressions related to camera pictures.

When we use Pattern 1, we send it as a query to a search engine such as Bing[1]. We then extract words following 'include' or 'includes' in the top 50 results returned by the search engine. In each returned result, we extract words that follow 'include' or 'includes' until we hit the sentence boundary. The final step is to remove common stop words such as *the* and function words such as *with* and *of* from the extracted words. As an example, the following lexicon for camera accessory is generated using this method.

Accessory Lexicon: *[chip, chips, case, bag, card, software, tripod, strap, cable, adapt, charger, port, storage, hood, connector, kit, accessory, glove, belt, usb, mic, beltloop, flash, program, leather, pack, connect, not belt, not strap, zipper]*

[1] In our experiments, we used Bing for convenience. However, our approach is applicable using other search engines such as Google as well.

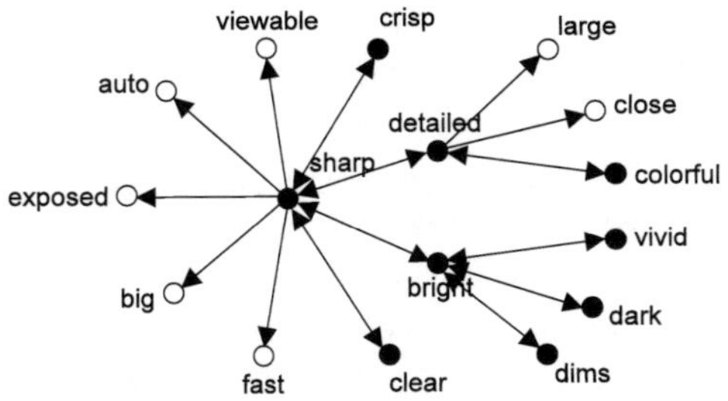

Figure 1: Noisy Words v.s. Non-noisy Words for Camera Picture Quality

When we use Pattern 2, we also extract words in the top 50 returned results. However, we adopt a different algorithm for filtering out noise in the returned results. For example, for finding expressions conceptually related to camera's picture quality, we use 'camera picture' as context words and 'clear' as a seed word. This pattern would match both 'clear and sharp' and 'clear and normal'. However, while 'sharp' is commonly used to describe picture quality, 'normal' is not. To filter noisy words such as 'normal', we use each of the candidate words as a new seed word in Pattern 2, and if the top 50 results returned by the new query include the original seed word 'clear', the candidate word is retained. Otherwise, it is discarded. For example, in our experiments, while 'camera picture + "sharp and *"' would return results matching 'sharp and clear', 'camera picture + "normal and *"' would not return results matching 'normal and clear'. Through this approach, we can distinguish 'sharp' from 'normal', and identify 'normal' as a noisy word. Figure 1 shows some of the noisy words identified by this approach when we extract expressions conceptually related to camera pictures. In this figure, words represented by hollow circles are identified as noise and removed from the camera picture quality lexicon. By contrast, words represented by solid circles are retained in our lexicon.

3.3 Dictionary Expansion

Although expansion through looking up synonyms and antonyms recorded in dictionaries is a commonly used approach when a general purpose sentiment lexicon is built (Hu and Liu, 2004), we found this approach to be not always suitable for building domain specific lexicons. The reason is that building domain specific lexicons requires finding expressions that are conceptually related; however expressions that are conceptually related are not necessarily synonyms or antonyms. For example, 'sharp' and 'clear' are conceptually related to camera picture qualities, but they are not true synonyms from a linguistic perspective.

However, in some cases, using dictionaries can still be very effective. For example, we built the following lexicon for camera price through web searching and filtering using Pattern 2.

Price Lexicon: *[cheap, lowest, discount, promo, coupon, promote, expensive, worthy, value]*

By including the synonyms of 'cheap' and 'expensive' in WordNet (Fellbaum, 1998), we are able to further expand the Price Lexicon.

3.4 Domain Specific Polarity Lexicon

So far we have described how we build domain specific lexicons for different camera aspects. The next step is to separate expressions that carry positive sentiment from those that carry negative sentiment in each domain lexicon.

For example, we want to be able to build the following sub-lexicons for 'Picture Quality'.

PictureQuality Positive Lexicon: *[clear, sharp, bright, sober, stable, tidy, vivid, sunny, crisp]*

PictureQuality Negative Lexicon: *[dark, dim, humid, fuzzy, gray, blurry, blur, indistinct, grainy, hazy, blurred]*

Our approach is as follows. For each expression in the Picture Quality Lexicon that we constructed through the combination of corpus filtering, web search and dictionary expansion, we check to see if it only appears in the training data labelled as expressing a positive opinion or a negative opinion about the camera's picture quality. If it is the former case, we include that expression into the PictureQuality Positive Lexicon, while if it is the latter case, we include that expression into the PictureQuality Negative Lexicon.

Having illustrated our approach for constructing domain specific sentiment lexicons, we next describe how we incorporate lexicon knowledge into SVM learning to improve sentiment classification.

4 Incorporating Lexicon Knowledge into SVM Learning to Improve Sentiment Classification

Our sentiment classification task is as follows. For each review sentence about cameras, we need to predict both the camera aspect discussed in that sentence as well as the associated sentiment regarding that camera aspect. We achieve this goal by performing a two step classification. In step 1, we train a classifier to predict the camera aspect being discussed. In step 2, we train a classifier to predict the sentiment associated with that camera aspect. Finally, we aggregate the two step prediction results together to produce the final prediction.

In both steps, we incorporate the lexicon knowledge into conventional SVM learning. To illustrate our approach, we use sentence (1) as an example.

(1) *The case is rigid so it gives the camera extra nice protection.*

Using nouns, verbs, adjectives and adverbs as unigram feature words in a conventional SVM learning, this sentence can be represented as the following vector of words.

[case, rigid, give, camera, extra, nice, protection]

By incorporating the knowledge encoded in the lexicons, we automatically generate and insert additional features into the above representation.

For example, when we perform the step 1 aspect classification, because the feature word 'case' in the above representation is listed in our domain specific lexicon about camera accessories, we would insert an additional feature word 'accessory', and produce the following new representation.

[case, rigid, give, camera, extra, nice, protection, accessory]

By doing this, we promote the possibility of the camera aspect being 'accessory' if expressions of camera aspects occur in the sentence.

In the next step of polarity prediction, we incorporate both our domain specific sentiment lexicon and a general purpose domain independent sentiment lexicon extracted from the MPQA opinion corpus (Wiebe et al., 2005) [2].

For example, because 'nice' is indicated as a positive word in the MPQA lexicon, we would insert a feature word 'positive'. In addition, if the first step prediction result for sentence (1) is 'accessory', and 'rigid' is also a positive word in our domain specific lexicon regarding camera accessories, we would generate an extra feature word 'positive' in our final representation for sentence (1) for the second step polarity prediction as shown below.

[case, rigid, give, camera, extra, nice, protection, positive, positive]

We thus promote a 'positive' prediction regarding the aspect of 'accessory'.

Our experiments show that incorporating lexicon knowledge into SVM learning significantly improves the accuracy for our classification task; compared to the general purpose MPQA sentiment lexicon, the domain specific lexicon we constructed is more effective. Our experiment setting and results are reported in the next section.

5 Experiment Setting and Results

The sentiment analysis task we performed is a combined 45-way sentiment classification task. These 45 classes are derived from 22 aspects related to camera purchases such as *picture quality, LCD screen, battery life and customer support* and their associated polarity values *positive* and *negative*, as well as a class of *no opinion* about any of the 22 aspects. An example of such a class is *picture quality: positive*. The goal is to map each input sentence into one of the 45 classes.

As mentioned in the previous section, we performed a two step classification for our task. Namely, our final combined classifier consists of two classifiers. The first is an 'Aspect Classifier', which performs a 23-way camera aspect classification. The second is a 'Polarity Classifier', which performs a 3-way (*positive*, *negative* and *none*) classification. The final predictions are aggregated from the predictions produced by these two classifiers.

The classification accuracy is defined as follows.

$$Accuracy = \frac{NumberofSentencesCorrectlyClassified}{TotalNumberofSentences}. \quad (1)$$

In our experiment we labeled 2718 sentences randomly chosen from the Multi-Domain Sentiment Dataset created by Blitzer et al. (Blitzer et al., 2007); therefore, the classes in this data set are not balanced, and the majority class has 13% of the sentences.

As mentioned in the Related Work section, our task is different from those of the early studies on product aspect level sentiment analysis. Earlier works such as Hu and Liu (2004) and Popescu and Etzioni (2005) only extract explicitly expressed product aspects, and they do not identify implicitly

[2]We only extracted the words that are indicated as strongly subjective out of context from the MPQA opinion corpus

expressed product aspects. In addition, they do not further categorize the extracted noun phrases. By contrast, we need to extract both the explicitly and implicitly expressed product aspects and further categorize the semantically related expressions regarding product aspects. Zhao et al. (2010)'s work did extract both explicitly and implicitly mentioned product aspects, and they also further categorized the product aspects. However, in terms of opinion extraction, they only extracted opinion words associated with product aspects, and did not further identify the polarities of the opinion words. By contrast, we need to identify the polarities associated with the product aspects. Therefore, we cannot compare our results directly with those presented in the earlier works. Instead, we used the majority class (13%) as our baseline, and we compared our approach to incorporating lexicon knowledge with SVM learning mainly with a conventional SVM learning, because the latter is the state-of-the-art algorithm reported in the literature for sentiment analysis. Our results show that both the conventional SVM learning and our approach significantly outperform the majority class baseline.

We selected the Nouns, Verbs, Adjectives and Adverbs as our unigram word features. All of them are stemmed using the Porter Stemmer (Rijsbergen et al., 1980). Negators are attached to the next selected feature word. We also use a small set of stop words[3] to exclude copulas and words such as *take*. The reason that we choose these words as stop words is because they are both frequent and ambiguous and thus tend to have a negative impact on the classifier. The SVM algorithm we adopted is implemented by Chang and Lin (2001). We use linear kernel type and use the default setting for all other parameters.

We conducted 4 experiments. In experiment 1, we used the conventional SVM algorithm, in which no lexicon knowledge was incorporated; we refer to this experiment as SVM. In experiment 2, we incorporated only the knowledge encoded in the domain independent MPQA opinion dictionary into SVM learning; we refer to this experiment as 'MPQA + SVM'. In experiment 3, we incorporated only the knowledge encoded in the domain specific lexicons we constructed into SVM learning; we refer to this experiment as 'DomainLexicons + SVM'. In experiment 4, we incorporated both the knowledge encoded in the MPQA and the domain specific lexicons we constructed into SVM learning; we refer to this experiment as 'DomainLexicons + MPQA + SVM'. All of our results are based on 10-fold cross-validation, and they are summarized in Table 1.

The results in Table 1 show that incorporating both the domain independent MPQA lexicon and the domain specific lexicons that we built achieves the best overall performance. Of these two types of lexicon, incorporating the domain specific lexicons is more effective, as they contributed the most to the improvement of the classification accuracy. The improvement achieved by our approach is statistically significant with $p < 0.000001$ according to paired t-test.

Learning Method	Accuracy
SVM	41.7%
MPQA + SVM	44.3%
DomainLexicons + SVM	46.2%
DomainLexicons + MPQA + SVM	**47.4%**

Table 1: Overall Performance Comparison

Our results reported in Table 2 further illustrate that incorporating lexicon knowledge with SVM learning significantly improves both the accuracy for camera aspect classification and the accuracy for polarity classification. Both improvements are statistically significant with $p < 0.000001$ and $p < 0.05$ respectively according to paired t-test.

Learning Method	Aspect Accuracy	Polarity Accuracy
SVM	47.1%	65.6%
DomainLexicons + MPQA + SVM	**56.2%**	**66.8%**

Table 2: Breakdown Performance Comparison

6 Conclusions

To summarize, we have shown that incorporating the knowledge encoded in sentiment lexicons, especially domain specific lexicons, can significantly improve the accuracy for fine-grained sentiment analysis tasks. We have also described how we constructed our domain specific sentiment lexicons for the domain of camera reviews through a combination of corpus filtering, web searching and filtering and dictionary expansion. In addition, we have developed a method to incorporate the lexicon knowledge into machine learning algorithms such as SVM to improve sentiment learning.

[3]The stop words we use include copulas and the following words: *take, takes, make, makes, just, still, even, too, much, enough, back, again, far, same*

References

A. Andreevskaia and S. Bergler. 2008. When specialists and generalists work together: overcoming domian dependence in sentiment tagging. In *Proceedings of ACL*.

John Blitzer, Mark Dredze, Fernando Pereira. Biographies, Bollywood, Boom-boxes, and Blenders. 2007. Domain adaptation for sentiment classification. In *Proceedings of the Association for Computational Linguistics (ACL)*.

Chih-Chung Chang and Chih-Jen Lin, 2001. *LIBSVM: A Library for Support Vector Machines*. Software available at http://www.csie.ntu.edu.tw/ cjlin/libsvm.

Yan Dang, Yulei Zhang, and Hsinchun Chen. 2010. A lexicon enhanced method for sentiment classification: An experiment on online product reviews. *IEEE Intelligent Systems*, 25.

A. Fahrni and M. Klenner. 2008. Old wine or warm beer: target-specific sentiment analysis adjectives. In *Symposion on Affective Language in Human and Machine, AISB Convention*.

Christiane Fellbaum, editor. 1998. *Wordnet: An Electronic Lexical Database*. MIT Press, Cambridge, MA.

Michael Gamon. 2004. Sentiment classification on customer feedback data: noisy data, large feature vectors, and the role of linguistic analysis. In *Proceedings of the COLING*.

V. Hatzivassiloglou and F. Sebastiani. 1997. Predicting the semantic orientation of adjectives. In *Proceedings of ACL*.

M. Hu and B. Liu. 2004. Mining and summarizing customer reviews. In *Proceedings of the KDD*.

V. Jijkoun, M.d. Rijke, and W. Weerkamp. 2010. Generating focused topic-specific sentiment lexicon. In *Proceedings of ACL*.

S.-M. Kim and E. Hovy. 2004. Determining the sentiment of opinions. In *Proceedings of the COLING*.

N. Kobayashi, K. Inui, Y. Matsumoto, K. Tateishi, and T. Fukushima. 2004. Collecting evaluative expressions for opinion extraction. In *Proceedings of IJC-NLP*.

Bing Liu. 2007. *Web Data Mining*. Springer, New York.

Prem melville, Wojciech Gryc, and Richard D. Lawrence. 2009. Sentiment analysis of blogs by combining lexical knowledge with text classification. In *Proceedings of the KDD*.

Saif Mohammad, Cody Dunne, and Bonnie Dorr. 2009. Generating high-coverage semantic orientation lexicons from overtly marked words and a theasaurus. In *Proceedings of the EMNLP*.

Bo Pang, Lillian lee, and shivakumar Vaithyanathan. 2002. Thumbs up? sentiment classification using machine learning techniques. In *Proceedings of the EMNLP*.

A.M. Popescu and O. Etzioni. 2005. Extracting product features and opinions from reviews. In *Proceedings of HLT/EMNLP*.

C.J. Van Rijsbergen, S.E. Robertson, and M.F. Porter. 1980. New models in probabilistic information retrieval. Technical report, British Library Research and Development Report, no. 5587.

Vikas Sindhwani and Prem Melville. 2008. Document-word co-regularization for semi-supervised sentiment analysis. In *Proceedings of the ICDM*.

Janyce Wiebe, Theresa Wilson, and Claire Cardie. 2005. Annotating expressions of opinions and emotions in language. *Language Resources and Evaluation*, 39.

Theresa Wilson, Janyce Wiebe, and Paul Hoffmann. 2005. Recognizing contextual polarity in phrase-level sentiment analysis. In *Proceedings of the HLT-EMNLP*.

W.X. Zhao, J. Jiang, H. Yan, and X. Li. 2010. Jointly modeling aspects and opinions with a maxent-lda hybrid. In *Proceedings of EMNLP*.

L. Zhou and P. Chaovalit. 2008. Ontology-supported polarity mining. *Journal of the American Society for Information Science and technology*, 59.

L. Zhuang and F. Jing. 2006. Movie review mining and summarization. In *Proceedings of the CIKM*.

Towards Enhanced Opinion Classification using NLP Techniques

Akshat Bakliwal
SIEL, IIIT-Hyderabad
akshat.bakliwal@research.iiit.ac.in

Piyush Arora
SIEL, IIIT-Hyderabad
piyush.arora@research.iiit.ac.in

Ankit Patil
SIEL, IIIT-Hyderabad
ankit.patil@research.iiit.ac.in

Vasudeva Varma
SIEL, IIIT-Hyderabad
vv@iiit.ac.in

Abstract

Sentiment mining and classification plays an important role in predicting what people think about products, places, etc. In this piece of work, using basic NLP Techniques like NGram, POS-Tagged NGram we classify movie and product reviews broadly into two polarities: Positive and Negative. We propose a model to address the problem of determining whether a review is positive or negative, we experiment and use several machine learning algorithms Naive Bayes (NB), Multi-Layer Perceptron (MLP), Support Vector Machine (SVM) to have a comparative study of the performance of the method we devised in this work. Along with this we also did negation handling and observed improvements in classification. The algorithm we proposed achieved an average accuracy of 78.32% on movie and 70.06% on multi-category dataset. In this paper we focus on the collective study of Ngram and POS tagged information available in the reviews .

1 Introduction

"What people think and feel" is the most important information for a business to promote and improve their product or for a production house to hit the blockbuster. Reviews are increasing with a rapid speed and are available over internet in natural language. This proves to be of utmost use for consumers and also for the manufacturers to improve the performance of their product. Sentiment analysis tries to classify reviews on the basis of their polarity either positive or negative, which can be used in various ways and in many applications for example, marketing and contextual advertising, suggestion systems based on the user likes and ratings, recommendation systems etc. The ratings and the reviews of the products helps the user to have a better overview of the product and make a choice based on overall rating of multiple reviews of the same product. In this paper, we propose a method to classify reviews as positive or negative. We devised a new scoring function and test on two different approaches which are

- Simple NGram (N=1/2/3) matching: Unigrams, bigrams and trigrams of a review are been used to assign score to a review and thus classify it as positive or negative.
- Pos-Tagged NGram matching: NGrams in this case are formed using the POS-Tagged information of a review, Trigrams, Bigrams and Unigrams combination of only Adjectives (JJ) and Adverbs (RB) are used for scoring a review.

In another variant we used a combination of simple Ngram and POS-Tagged Ngram approaches. Based on the final score of a review it is classified as positive or negative. We also applied machine learning algorithms Naive Bayes(NB), Multi-Layer Perceptron (MLP) and Support Vector Machine (SVM) to study the performance of our method. The method was applied on two datasets movie review and product review.

In section 2, we describe the related work done in the past. Section 3, describes the algorithm proposed by us in this work. Section 4, describes tools, techniques and data used here. Section 5, focus on the experiments done and results of same. In section 6, small discussion over the results is done. Section 7, gives a conclusion of the present work.

2 Related Work

Identifying the sentiment polarity is a complex task, to address the problem of sentiment classi-

Proceedings of the Workshop on Sentiment Analysis where AI meets Psychology (SAAIP), IJCNLP 2011, pages 101–107, *Chiang Mai, Thailand, November 13, 2011.*

fication various methodologies have been applied earlier. Following are Unsupervised approaches.

1. Syntactic approach towards sentiment classification using Ngrams. This approach was used by Pang et al.(Pang et al., 2002) in their work.

2. Semantic approach using part of speech information. Thumbs Up or Thumbs Down? Semantic Orientation Applied to Unsupervised Classification of Reviews (Turney, 2002) and Sentiment Analysis: Adjectives and Adverbs are better than Adjectives Alone (Benamara et al., 2007) used this approach for binary classification.

3. Extracting sentiment expressions using various NLP techniques. Sentiment Analysis: Capturing Favorability Using Natural Language Processing (Nasukawa and Yi , 2003) and Extracting Appraisal expressions (Bloom et al., 2007) used techniques like word sense disambiguation, chunking, n-gram and others to perform binary polarity classification.

Supervised approach uses machine learning supervised algorithms. Sentiment Classification for Chinese Reviews Using Machine Learning Methods Based on String Kernel (Zhang et al., 2008), Pang et al.(Pang et al., 2002), Twitter Sentiment Classification using Distant Supervision (Go et al., 2009) deduced some features to perform supervised machine learning.

Pang et al.(Pang et al., 2002) used the traditional n-gram approach along with POS information as a feature to perform machine learning for determining the polarity. They used Naive Bayes Classification, Maximum Entropy and Support Vector Machines on a three fold cross validation. In their experiment, they tried different variations of n-gram approach like unigams presence, unigrams with frequency, unigrams+bigrams, bigrams, unigrams + POS, adjectives, most frequent unigrams, unigrams + positions. They concluded from their work that incorporating the frequency of matched n-gram might be a feature which could decay the accuracy. Maximum accuracy achieved by them among all the experiments they performed was 82.9% which was obtained in unigrams presence approach on SVM.

Turney (Turney, 2002) also worked on POS information. He used some tag patterns with a window of maximum three words (i.e) till trigrams. In his experiments, he considered JJ, RB, NN, NNS POS-tags with some set of rules for classification. His work is extension to the work done on adjectives alone (Hatzivassiloglou and McKeown, 2004) because he considers RB, NN/NNS. Given a phrase he calculates the PMI (Point-wise Mutual Information) from the strong positive word "excellent" and also from the strong negative word "poor", and the difference will give you the semantic orientation of the phrase.

Dave et al.(Dave et al., 2003) devised their own scoring function which was probability based. They performed some lexical substitutions to negation handling and used rainbow classifiers to decide the class of the review.

Our work is motivated from each of these works. Pang et al.(Pang et al., 2002) used POS information with unigram, we extended this work using POS information with bigrams and trigrams. Turney (Turney, 2002) also used POS[1] information with trigrams but he restricted trigram formation with some rules. He used PMI to evaluate the classification and here in this research we propose a new scoring function to classify. Dave et al.(Dave et al., 2003) devised some rules for negation handling and thus motivated us to work on negation handling.

3 Algorithm

To perform polarity classification we devised our own algorithm. This algorithm was applied on all our approaches. In our experiments we performed 5-fold cross-validation and we divided the pre-annotated data into two parts namely training set and testing set to check the correctness. After dividing the data we form trigrams, bigrams and unigrams on the training data and store them in individual n-gram dictionary. We create two separate models each for positive and negative polarity. For every testing review we create trigrams in the similar manner. Then we check if this trigram exists in our positive and negative trigram dictionary. If it exist then, we increase the count of trigram matched else we break this trigram into two bigrams. These bigrams thus formed are cross checked in the bigram dictionary, If found then the bigram match count is increased otherwise each bigram is further split into two unigrams. These unigrams are then checked against the unigram

[1]http://nlp.stanford.edu/software/tagger.shtml

dictionary. Refer *Figure 1* for diagrammatic representation of algorithm.

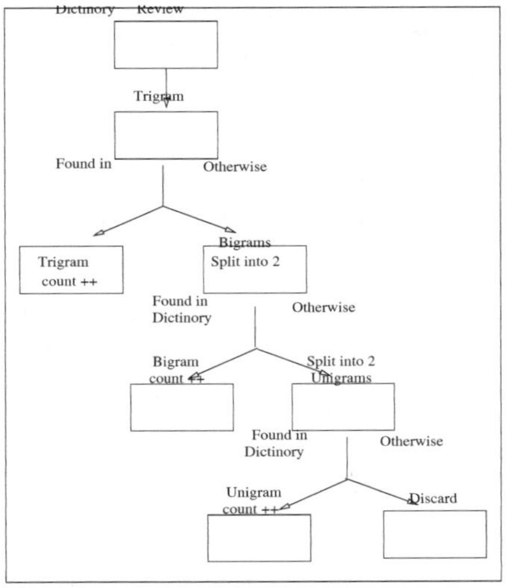

Figure 1: Algorithm Flow

We also propose a scoring function which gives priority to trigram matching followed by bigrams and unigrams.

$$\begin{aligned} Score = \ & x * Count\_Tri - gram + \\ & y * Count\_Bi - gram \ + \\ & z * Count\_Uni - gram \end{aligned}$$

here x = 7/11, y = 3/11, z = 1/11, Count_N-gram = Number of N-grams matched (N = Uni/Bi/Tri). The values 7,3,1 are chosen to ensure that (1) score for matching a trigram > score for matching 2 bigrams. (2) score for matching a bigram > score for matching 2 unigrams. In the scoring function we have given the least possible integer value to unigram, bigram and trigram keeping the above constraints in mind. The rationale behind having these constrains while deciding the values of x, y, z was that higher n-gram carries more weight then a lower n-gram and also matching of a higher n-gram should be weighed more than matching of two lower n-grams. Then we have normalized these values on a scale of 0 to 1. So the final x, y, z parameters are x=7/11, y=3/11 and z=1/11.

4 Framework

This section describes various tools, techniques and data used by us in this work. We are using two different datasets in this work. One is Product Review dataset (*Refer Section 4.2.1*) which has reviews on multiple products belonging to different categories like apparels, books, software, etc. This dataset is a multi category dataset in contrast to the other dataset which has only one category i.e. movies. Movie review dataset (*Refer Section 4.2.2*) contains reviews on various movies by critiques.

4.1 Tools and Algorithms

This section provides a brief details of the machine learning algorithms used in the experiments.

4.1.1 Naive Bayes (NB)

Naive Bayes Classifier uses Bayes Theorem, which finds the probability of an event given the probability of another event that has already occurred. Naive Bayes classifier performs extremely well for problems which are linearly separable and even for problems which are non-linearly separable it performs reasonably well. We used the already implemented Naive Bayes implementation in Weka[2] toolkit.

4.1.2 Multi-Layer Perceptron (MLP)

Multi Layer perceptron (MLP) is a feed-forward neural network with one or more layers between input and output layer. Feed-forward means that data flows in one direction from input to output layer (forward). We used the already implemented MLP in Weka toolkit.

4.1.3 Support Vector Machine (SVM)

This classifier constructs N-dimensional hyperplane which separates data into two categories. SVM models are closely related to a Neural Network. SVM takes the input data and for each input data row it predicts the class to which this input row belongs. SVM works for two class problems and is a non probabilistic binary linear classifier. We used libSVM[3] classifier which is available as a add on to Weka toolkit.

4.2 Datasets

This section provides a brief details of the datasets used by us in our experiments.

4.2.1 Product Review Dataset

Multi-Domain Sentiment Dataset (Version 2.0)[4] (Blitzer et al., 2007) contains product reviews taken from Amazon.com belonging to different (total 25) categories like apparels, books, toys and

[2]http://www.cs.waikato.ac.nz/ml/weka/
[3]http://weka.wikispaces.com/LibSVM
[4]http://www.cs.jhu.edu/~mdredze/datasets/sentiment/

games, videos, etc. We considered 4000 positive and 4000 negative reviews randomly sampled from 5 domains. Domains were chosen with utmost care so that they can represent non intersecting domains and 800 reviews of each polarity i.e. positive and negative are taken from each domain.

4.2.2 Movie Review Dataset

Polarity Dataset (Version 2.0)[5] (Pang and Lee , 2004) contains 1000 positive and 1000 negative processed movie reviews on various movies. Reviews are pre-processed and divided into two categories positive and negative.

5 Experiments

We performed various experiments on the review data which were based on NLP techniques like n-gram, POS-Tagged n-grams, etc. We divided our work in two approaches.

5.1 Simple NGram Approach

While classifying the review the lexical information plays a very important role. The lower order n-grams i.e. unigrams and bigrams does not carry much information as compared to the higher order n-grams like trigrams or beyond. For example consider the phrase "not good product", here unigrams formed are 'not','good' and 'product' but they does not carry sufficient information for polarity classification. When we move to bi-grams "not-good" and "good product", "good-product" has a sentiment towards positive polarity and "not-good" is negating the positivity of good but the trigram "not good product" gives enough information to classify the trigram in negative class.

We experimented with different N-grams variation (unigram, bigram and trigrams) and its combinations (unigram + bigram and unigram + bigram + trigram). The results *(Refer Table 1)* shows that the presence of trigrams with bigrams and unigrams has a favourable effect on classification of the reviews as positive and negative.

5.2 POS-Tagged NGram Approach

In this approach we used the part of speech information to deduce the opinion and subjective information in a given text. Adjective and Adverbs play an important role in deducing the subjective information since they reflect the qualitative judgment about a text. In this approach we create

[5]http://www.cs.cornell.edu/People/pabo/movie-review-data/

	Movie Reviews	**Product Reviews**
Unigram only	64.1	42.91
Bigram only	76.15	69.62
Trigram only	76.1	71.37
(Uni + Bi) gram	77.15	72.94
(Uni + Bi + Tri) gram	**80.15**	**78.67**

Table 1: Results of Simple NGram

	Movie Reviews	**Product Reviews**
POS-(U + B + T)-JJ	75.00	50.425
POS-(U + B + T)-RB	65.50	36.76
POS-(U + B + T)-(JJ + RB)	**76.50**	**62.06**

Table 2: Results of POS-Tagged NGram. U = Unigram, B = Bigram, T = Trigram

trigrams, bigrams, unigrams of only those words whose part-of-speech tag is either Adjective (JJ) or Adverb (RB). For trigram we have *-JJ/RB-*, Bigrams *-JJ/RB or JJ/RB-* and unigrams are JJ/RB. here * signifies any other pos-tag. Consider this review "This is a good product", POS-tagged output of this review is "this_DT is_VBZ a_DT good_JJ product_NN". For this review we have 1 trigram "a-good-product", 2 bigrams "a-good" "good-product" and 1 unigram "good".

Similarly we find possible n-grams for RB Tag. After forming these NGrams we apply our algorithm and based on the score we get from both the positive and negative model we deduce the nature of the opinion. *Table 2* reports the accuracy of our scoring function on the two datasets after considering different variation of POS-tags such as only adjectives (JJ), only adverbs (RB) and both combined together.

In a variation to the above approach, we also incorporated negation handling and observed an increment in the overall performance. For negation handling our approach was: first we identified all the words with pos-tag JJ/RB. Then for negation handling we took a sliding window of 1-3 words in left from that word. If any of the words in this window were string 'not' then we modified the original word by appending a # sign in front of it. This # sign signified that the word was preceded by a negative word. Consider this review "This is not a good product", POS-Tagged

	Movie Reviews	Product Reviews
POS-(U + B + T)-JJ	75.80	51.50
POS-(U + B + T)-RB	65.9	37.55
POS-(U + B + T)-(JJ + RB)	**77.35**	**62.75**

Table 3: Results of POS-Tagged NGram with Negation Handling. U = Unigram, B = Bigram, T = Trigram

output of this review is "this_DT is_VBZ not_RB a_DT good_JJ product_NN". Now for this review if we make trigrams, bigrams and unigrams without negation handling, they will be 2 trigrams "is-not-a" "a-good-product", 4 bigrams "is-not" "not-a" "a-good" "good-product" and 2 unigram "not" "good".

None of these n-grams show the effect of not on good but if we do negation handling then the n-grams formed will be 2 trigrams "is-not-a" "a-#good-product", 4 bigrams "is-not" "not-a" "a-#good" "#good-product" and 2 unigram "not" "#good".

After negation handling n-grams formed clearly indicates that the information of a negative word "not" preceded by good is incorporated. *Table 3* reports the accuracy of our scoring function on the two datasets after applying negation handling.

To assert the performance of our scoring function, we formed a feature vector with features very closely similar to our scoring function. In our scoring function we considered the count of n-grams matched and the feature vector is also formed with the same information. Features are selected in a way that they only differ in terms of weighted parameters(x, y, z) from the scoring function. Our feature vector composed of 6 features + class which are calculated from the annotated data. Our features were $<$ **PUM, PBM, PTM, NUM, NBM, NTM, class** $>$ where PUM = Positive Unigram Matched, PBM = Positive Bigram Matched, PTM = Positive Trigram Matched, NUM = Negative Unigram Matched, NBM = Negative Bigram Matched, NTM = Negative Trigram Matched and class = Actual class of the review. We formed this feature vector for both the above mentioned approaches.

5.3 Feature Vector Approach

In the above two approaches (N-gram and POS tagged approach) we devised our own scoring function and calculated the polarity of an opinion but it might be the case that the function we used are biased, so in this approach we divided the dataset into training and testing set and extracted the features for the training set and formed feature vector for each of the opinion, we used machine learning algorithms for classification. We used WEKA toolkit for classification of the testing set (opinions). The feature vector was devised for both approaches.

For NGram and POS-tagged feature vector was the same as mentioned above. *Table 4* reports the accuracy of machine learning approach on Simple NGram and POS-Tagged NGram approaches.

We also combined Approach 1 (Simple NGram) and Approach 2 (POS-Tagged NGram) and the results were as shown in *Table 5*. Feature Vector for the combined training was $<$ **PUM, PBM, PTM, NUM, NBM, NTM, pt-PUM, pt-PBM, pt-PTM, pt-NUM, pt-NBM, pt-NTM, class** $>$ where where PUM = Positive Unigram Matched, PBM = Positive Bigram Matched, PTM = Positive Trigram Matched, NUM = Negative Unigram Matched, NBM = Negative Bigram Matched, NTM = Negative Trigram Matched, pt-PUM = POS-Tagged Positive Unigram Matched, pt-PBM = POS-Tagged Positive Bigram Matched, pt-PTM = POS-Tagged Positive Trigram Matched, pt-NUM = POS-Tagged Negative Unigram Matched, pt-NBM = POS-Tagged Negative Bigram Matched, pt-NTM = POS-Tagged Negative Trigram Matched and class = Actual class of the review

6 Result Analysis

In this section we compare the performance of our algorithm with the machine learning algorithm. Our algorithm reported accuracy well in consistence with machine learning algorithms. Among the various experiments done in approach 1 (Simple NGram) for movie review dataset, our algorithm reports maximum accuracy for (unigram + bigram + trigram) which is 80.15 and close equivalent to machine learning algorithm. SVM reports 81.15 and MLP reports 81.05 accuracy for (unigram + bigram + trigram) combination. For product review dataset also, results are closely related. Our algorithm reports accuracy of 78.76

	Movie Reviews			Product Reviews		
	NB	**MLP**	**SVM**	**NB**	**MLP**	**SVM**
NGram Feature	75.50	81.05	**81.15**	62.50	79.27	**79.40**
POS-Tagged Feature	72.35	**76.35**	75.45	68.81	**70.87**	67.88
POS-Taged Feature with Negation Handling	72.80	**76.65**	75.00	68.83	**70.95**	67.95

Table 4: Results of Approach 1 and Approach 2 on Machine Learning Algorithms

	Movie Reviews			Product Reviews		
	NB	**MLP**	**SVM**	**NB**	**MLP**	**SVM**
Simple + POS-Tagged NGram Feature	78.05	**81.60**	78.45	69.25	**79.47**	78.86
Simple + POS-Tagged NGram with Negation Handling Feature	79.35	**81.60**	78.50	69.17	**79.39**	79.03

Table 5: Results of Approach 1 Approach 2 Combined on Machine Learning Algorithms

while SVM reports 79.4 and MLP reports 79.27. This shows that our algorithm performs as good as supervised learning approach and the selection of the parameters x, y, z in our algorithm are close to accurate.

For approach 2 (POS-Tagged NGram), we observed a similar adjacency between our algorithm and machine learning. For movie review dataset our algorithm performed best for (JJ + RB + Negation Handling) and accuracy attained was 77.35 which is higher than that achieved using SVM (75) and MLP (76.65). In case of product review dataset accuracy attained by our approach was 62.75 while the machine learning algorithms SVM (67.95) and MLP (70.95) dominated.

An observation we made while experimenting was that our model performs well when the reviews are domain specific (i.e. movie review) but when it comes to a larger or multiple domains (multi category product reviews) our performance drops down. Possible reason behind this could be that when we train on multiple categories together there may be cases that a specific category performes poorly and thus it pulls the over all performance down.

Main problem while dealing with sentiment analysis on reviews is that reviews span over multiple sentences. There are cases when a review contains multiple sentences and among them few sentences have opposite sentiment. For ex. "This movie was superb, good dialogs and action. The plot was awful". In this review the first sentence shows positive polarity and the second sentence show negative polarity. It may be the case that though the review was rated positive by the reviewer but the negative scored dominated and hence our system classified this as negative. This problem sometimes also occur within the sentence. Consider this review "This mobile phone has awesome features but the camera really sucks". In this sentence, the part before 'but' is positive and the part after but is negative. This review is neither positive nor negative and fails while classifying.

7 Conclusion

Based on these basic experiments which are simple to understand and perform one can get a approximate idea of the sentiments carried by reviews. We have presented simple techniques which are not restricted to review domain. With small simple modifications one can extend this work to various spheres like blogs, news (though we have not tested for the same and thus we make no claims). We obtained a general increment of 2-5% from the work done previously. This work will provide enough help to business industry to analyze what consumers think about their company and products.

Acknowledgments

We would like to thank Manisha Verma and Karan Jindal for extending their help, support and guidance during this work. We also extend our heartiest thanks to Prasad Pingalli of SETU Softwares for his guidance.

References

Farah Benamara, Carmine Cesarano, Antonio Picariello, Diego Reforgiato, and V. S. Subrahmanian. Sentiment analysis: Adjectives and adverbs are better than adjectives alone. In *Proceedings of the International Conference on Weblogs and Social Media (ICWSM)*, 2007. Short paper.

John Blitzer, Mark Dredze, and Fernando Pereira. Biographies, bollywood, boomboxes and blenders: Domain adaptation for sentiment classification. In *In ACL*, pages 187–205, 2007.

Kenneth Bloom, Navendu Garg, and Shlomo Argamon. Extracting appraisal expressions. In *Proceedings of Human Language Technologies/North American Association of Computational Linguists*, 2007.

Kushal Dave, Steve Lawrence, and David M. Pennock. Mining the peanut gallery: Opinion extraction and semantic classification of product reviews. pages 519–528, 2003.

Alec Go, Richa Bhayani, and Lei Huang. Twitter sentiment classification using distant supervision. pages 1–6, 2009.

Vasileios Hatzivassiloglou and Kathleen R. McKeown. Predicting the semantic orientation of adjectives. pages 174–181, 1997.

Tetsuya Nasukawa and Jeonghee Yi. Sentiment analysis: capturing favorability using natural language processing. In *Proceedings of the 2nd international conference on Knowledge capture*, K-CAP '03, pages 70–77, New York, NY, USA, 2003. ACM.

Bo Pang, Lillian Lee, and Shivakumar Vaithyanathan. Thumbs up? Sentiment classification using machine learning techniques. In *Proceedings of the 2002 Conference on Empirical Methods in Natural Language Processing (EMNLP)*, pages 79–86, 2002.

Bo Pang and Lillian Lee. A sentimental education: Sentiment analysis using subjectivity summarization based on minimum cuts. In *Proceedings of the ACL*, pages 271–278, 2004.

Peter Turney. Thumbs up or thumbs down? semantic orientation applied to unsupervised classification of reviews. pages 417–424, 2002.

Changli Zhang, Wanli Zuo, Tao Peng, and Fengling He. Sentiment classification for chinese reviews using machine learning methods based on string kernel. In *Proceedings of the 2008 Third International Conference on Convergence and Hybrid Information Technology - Volume 02*, pages 909–914, Washington, DC, USA, 2008. IEEE Computer Society.

Author Index

Association for Computational Linguistics
209 N. Eighth Street
Stroudsburg, Pennsylvania 18360

CURRAN ASSOCIATES INC
proceedings.com